THE DEVIL
IN MASSACHUSETTS

MARION L. STARKEY was born in Worcester, Massachusetts. Hers is an old New England family, dating back to Peregrine White, born on the *Mayflower*. Miss Starkey is a graduate of Boston University, receiving her B.S. in 1922 and her M.A. in 1935. She also attended the Harvard Graduate School of Education. A free-lance writer, her articles have appeared in many of the Boston papers, and from 1923–27 she was Editor of the *Saugus Herald*. She is also the author of *Land Where Our Fathers Died* (1962), *Striving to Make It My Home* (1964), and *Congregational Way* (1966). Her background includes extensive foreign travel, both as a WAC and a civilian, and six months at Macy's in New York. Miss Starkey has taught at the Woodhull, New York, High School, Hampton Institute, and the University of Connecticut at New London. She lives in Saugus, Massachusetts.

THE DEVIL
IN MASSACHUSETTS

A MODERN ENQUIRY INTO
THE SALEM WITCH TRIALS

MARION L. STARKEY

Anchor Books
Doubleday & Company, Inc.
Garden City, New York

The Devil in Massachusetts was originally published by Alfred A. Knopf, Inc. in 1949. This edition is published by arrangement with Marion L. Starkey.

Anchor Books edition: 1969

ACKNOWLEDGMENTS

My thanks to all those who gave me a hand at the Widener Library at Harvard, the Massachusetts Historical Society, the Massachusetts Archives at the State House in Boston, and the public libraries in Saugus, Salem, Lynn, Boston, and New London. Nearly everyone at the Essex Institute in Salem has helped me at one time or another, in particular Miss Florence Osburne, reference librarian, and her assistant, Miss Esther Usher. At the Suffolk County Court House in Boston, Mr Joseph B. Aigen, chief clerk of the Suffolk Superior Court, and Mr George Collins, principal clerk, once spent the better part of an afternoon helping me run down a miscellany of witch documents. Nor can I forget the courtesy of Mr Archie N. Frost, clerk of courts, and his staff in the Clerk's Office of the Superior Court in the Essex County Court House in Salem, Massachusetts.

Mrs William L. Tisdel assisted me in some of my tours of the witch country in Danvers. Mrs Robert S. Randall of that town hospitably showed us the delightful home she and her husband have made of the house that once belonged to poor Sarah Osburne. I enjoyed similar courtesies at the homestead of Rebecca Nurse and the Holton house in Danvers, and at Jonathan Corwin's home and the witch prison in Salem.

I had sound psychological counsel from Dr Hermann O. Schmidt and Dr Ferruccio DiCori at the Norwich State Hospital in Connecticut, and from Dr O. H. Mowrer, now of the University of Illinois. Since these have not seen the completed manuscript, however, I must absolve them from blame if anyone disagrees with my own diagnosis of the afflicted girls.

Dr Robert E. Moody of Boston University, College of Liberal Arts, encouraged me with this project and guided me during early phases of the research. I profited much from critical readings of the completed manuscript by Mr Laurence L. Winship of the *Boston Globe,* Dr Odell Shepard, Dr Kenneth Murdock, Dr Gerald Warner Brace, Mr Louis Bromfield, and Mr Arthur Schlesinger, Jun. Mr Henry Harris of the *Boston Globe* advised me on several legal technicalities involved in the witchcraft prosecution. In the grind of preparing the manuscript for the press, I am indebted to my father, Mrs Edward Beyer, Miss Barbarann Read, Mrs Albert S. Daddario, Miss Julia Imbriaco, and Mrs Elsie M. Bueter.

CONTENTS

PREFACE

The Salem witchcraft of 1692, of which this is a record, did not start in Salem. It started in what has since become Danvers, at a point from which the Danvers State Hospital (for mental cases) is now visible, and which serves as an unintended but highly appropriate monument to the whole sorry business.

There is still something of the feeling of old "Salem Village" about that corner of Danvers. Even the First Church is there, and its doors open. You may of a Sunday worship with the parish that nearly three centuries ago, cowering under the impact of the prophecies of crazed little girls, caused the hanging of both communicant and minister.

The actual physical structure of the original meeting-house has, to be sure, long since been replaced, but else-where, up the road a piece and roundabout, authentic landmarks of the witchcraft still remain. Benjamin Holton's fine white house, for instance—that same Holton whose hogs once got into Rebecca Nurse's garden patch. "Witch" Osburne's house, removed from its original site to Route 62, but piously preserved by its present owner. And much closer to the church, though it has to be hunted down in a stretch of open country that remains much as it must have been in 1692, that most touching memorial of all, the lovely, weather-beaten house where Rebecca Nurse thought to end her days in peace and the little family burying-ground whither her body was brought from the gallows.

2

The tragedy which was once enacted in this pleasant neighbourhood originated in the childish fantasies of some very little girls and was carried on to its deadly climax by what one might now call a pack of "bobby-soxers," were not the term pictorially incongruous. It was largely these older girls, who, inflamed by the terrors of Calvinism as their immature minds understood it, depressed by the lack of any legitimate outlet for their natural high spirits, found relief for their tensions in an emotional orgy which eventually engulfed not only their village but the Massachusetts Bay Colony.

The result was by no means the most sensational example of witch hysteria on record. Only twenty witches were executed, a microscopic number compared to the tens of thousands who had been put to death in Europe and England in the course of similar outbreaks in the late Middle Ages, and compared to the millions who have died in the species of witch-hunts peculiar to our own rational, scientific times.

Yet the Massachusetts affair is possibly the most celebrated of all witch-hunts, and people will never be done studying and writing about it. Its numerical modesty is indeed one of its attractions. It is a manageable episode in a way that catastrophes involving astronomical figures are not. The human reality of what happens to millions is only for God to grasp; but what happens to individuals is another matter and within the range of mortal understanding. This Salem story has the virtue of being a highly individualized affair. Witches in the abstract were not hanged in Salem; but one by one were brought to the gallows such diverse personalities as a decent grandmother grown too hard of hearing to understand a crucial question from the jurors, a rakish, pipe-smoking female tramp, a plain farmer who thought only to save his wife from molestation, a lame old man whose toothless gums did not deny expression to a very salty vocabulary.

These people emerge from the records as real as the people who live next-door. And after you have studied their lives faithfully, a remarkable thing happens; you discover that if you really know the few, you are on your way to understanding the millions. By grasping the local, the parochial even, it is possible to make a beginning at understanding the universal.

Thus, though this narrative of what happened in Essex County, Massachusetts, is local history, it also has intimations of history on the grander scale. For Salem Village of 1692, for all its apparent remoteness, was not "an island to itself," but a throbbing part of the great world. Its flareup of irrationality was to some extent a product of the ideological intensities which rent its age no less than they do ours; its swing to sanity through the stubborn refusal of the few to give way to the hysteria and mad logic of the many marked the turn of a moral season in New England. During the witchcraft, and to some extent through the witchcraft, thinking people in Massachusetts passed over the watershed that divides the mystery and magic of late medieval thinking from the more rational climate of opinion referred to as "the Enlightenment."

Yet although this particular delusion, at least in the form of a large-scale public enterprise, has vanished from the western world, the urge to hunt "witches" has done nothing of the kind. It has been revived on a colossal scale by replacing the medieval idea of malefic witchcraft by pseudo-scientific concepts like "race," "nationality," and by substituting for theological dissension a whole complex of warring ideologies. Accordingly the story of 1692 is of far more than antiquarian interest; it is an allegory of our times. One would like to believe that leaders of the modern world can in the end deal with delusion as sanely and courageously as the men of old Massachusetts dealt with theirs.

3

No definitive history of the Salem witchcraft has ever been written or is likely to be, for it would take a lifetime and would be encyclopedic in dimension. The nearest approach—unpublished—is the typescript compiled by the Works Progress Administration in three enormous volumes from the court records scattered in the courthouses in Essex, Middlesex, and Suffolk counties, in the Massachusetts State House, the Essex Institute, the Massachusetts Historical Society, and other private collections. Even this document, invaluable as it is, is not definitive, for to uncover the complete story one must supplement the court records with study of other contemporary sources, the writings of Cotton and Increase Mather, Robert Calef, Deodat Lawson, Thomas Brattle, Samuel Willard, Samuel Sewall, John Hale—to mention only a few. Also the WPA volumes do not pretend to be history; they contain only the raw material of history.

Of the more formal writings on the witchcraft, the two most comprehensive histories are Charles W. Upham's *Salem Witchcraft,* published in 1867, and Winfield S. Nevins's *Witchcraft in Salem Village,* first published in 1892, though I am best acquainted with the fifth edition, which appeared in 1916.

Of these two, Upham's is the more exhaustive. No one is likely to duplicate the years of research he put into investigating the minutiæ of life in Salem Village, or to challenge the general results. Nevins's is to some extent a rewrite of Upham's work; indeed he has been more interested in writing a series of essays on various aspects of the episode than in telling the story. The soundest of these essays, one that I have by no means improved on, is his analysis of the legal aspects of the case.

What have I added to the work of these authorities? For one thing, I have uncovered a number of vital primary sources of which they seem to have been ignorant. For another, I have tried to uncover the classic dramatic form of the story itself, for here is real "Greek tragedy," with a beginning, a middle, and an end. I have tried to present it impersonally, letting the characters speak for themselves, have made an effort not to blur their portraits with the sentimentality and flares of moral indignation to which Upham was prone. (Who in my day has a right to be indignant with people in Salem of 1692?)

Most important of all, I have tried to review the records in the light of the findings of modern psychology, particularly of the Freudian school. Indeed I came to my decision to undertake this research after completing two graduate courses in psychology with Dr O. H. Mowrer at Harvard in 1946. No thorough psychological study has ever been written of the Salem affair. Nevins made a beginning in his preface to his fifth edition, and there is also a *Psychology of the Salem Village Excitement of 1692* by George M. Beard; but this is a slight, superficial account, and the date of publication—1882—invalidates its claim to modernity.

The psychological side of my research has included exploration of the works of Janet, Freud, and studies in hypnotism, spiritualism. Once I made a visit to the Norwich State Hospital in Connecticut to talk over my diagnosis of the witchcraft not only with members of the staff but with a gifted patient whose mania lay along cognate lines.

In spite of these exertions, however, I have by no means written anything like a psychological monograph. The nearest I have come to doing so is in the chapters describing the children, where I have, as I trust the text makes clear, tried to fill in some of the *lacunæ* in the historical records by falling back on the psychological probabilities, and even here the narrative pattern takes precedence over formal analysis. I have in general avoided analysis in the technical sense, and have eschewed the jargon which goes with it. My emphasis has been on telling the story, making psychological interpretation implicit in the course of narrative rather than a thing by itself.

4

One thing I want to make plain. This is history, not fiction. Certain chapters are as rich in dialogue as any novel, but this dialogue is not of my invention; it is copied out of the records, for which I refer you to the documentation in the back of the book.

Here and there, but rarely, I have taken slight liberties with the records. In reporting the examination of John Alden, for instance, I occasionally transposed indirect to direct quotation. In the account of Betty Parris's breakdown, I put words into the child's mouth for which I have no real authority. (This is part of my "psychological reconstruction.") In presenting the examination of Martha Cory I have blended two separate eyewitness accounts (Deodat Lawson's and the court reporter's) so that a historian acquainted with only one source might suppose I had let my imagination run wild. In fact, when I first rechecked that scene with my own notes I thought so myself. I had not, however.

There is one other detail in which the careful reader may notice deviation from other sources—the spelling of names. Here was one subject on which Massachusetts Puritans were splendidly uninhibited; most of them spelled their names as variously as did Shakespeare. Mary Esty, for instance, is also down on the records as Easty, Eastey, and even Eastich. Even so simple a name as Nurse has the variant Nourse, which her descendants seem to have adopted. In this dilemma I have tried less for the "authoritative"—if there is such a thing—than for simplicity, and, I hope, consistency.

If there are other deviations from the records they come under the heading of error, not invention. I have striven mightily to be without flaw, but eyestrain and lapses of judgment may have sometimes defeated my intention. If there be error yet, tell me about it, and I'll try to make amends.

One other comment, this one wholly gratuitous. It's bad business meddling with the devil; it makes you superstitious.

I find myself impelled to report that the very hour I began my formal research (in Kittredge's *Witchcraft in Old and New England*) a small hurricane came through my open window, wrecked the room, brought every tree in the yard crashing against the house, and toppled the steeple of the East Saugus Community Church, visible in the lightning beyond my window. Then again, the evening of the day I finally shipped off this manuscript, there came a plague of lightning, continuous and directly overhead, striking neighbours' houses but missing mine.

My excuse for setting down these observations is that Cotton Mather, my colleague in the field of New England history, would value them and know exactly what to make of them.

THE DEVIL
IN MASSACHUSETTS

CHAPTER I

THE EASIEST ROOM IN HELL

One does not commonly shape destiny at the age of nine or eleven, and until the middle of January 1692, Betty and Abigail had given no indication that they were about to do so. Before that time it was possible for visitors to the parsonage in Salem Village to ignore the little girls they found there.

The children in question were the Reverend Samuel Parris's nine-year-old daughter Betty, and her cousin and senior by two years, Abigail Williams. In this early phase they were quite ordinary children, and not prodigies at all. The pair of them, got up like small prim matrons in longgown, apron and kerchief, absorbed in knitting or some other small household duty, presented a pretty picture of carefree innocence.

The appearance of children, however, may be deceiving, as even adults should know, especially in this time and place where nearly everyone had once endured the rigours of a Calvinist childhood. Though Betty was a really sweet, biddable little girl, ready to obey anyone who spoke with conviction, including, to her misfortune, her playmate Abigail, she was not carefree. She had been exposed too long to the hell-fire in her father's composition. And Abigail, exposed too, but somehow responding differently, was not innocent; from the eyes of this child an authentic hellion looked out on a world it would make over if it got a chance.

The little girls were indeed already somewhat gravely ill. It wasn't a physical thing. They had successfully passed through the illnesses of their babyhood, had come through a recent smallpox epidemic unscathed. The freshness of their complexions attested to their essential physical well-being. But spiritually it was another story. Each in her different way was sickening from the inhuman strain of coping with an adult world which had been arranged without understanding of the needs and capacities of children.

Betty and Abigail had been born in a bitter era, in a century which throughout the western world had brought not peace but a sword. Although they were probably as ignorant as sparrows of its historical details, of its revolutions and ideological conflicts, they could not escape its impact. The very spirit of the times had bred in their elders a creed high and severe, a knowledge that strait is the way and few there be that find it; and under that creed they were being brought up. What were they making of it?

The little girls doubtless responded to their catechism in one dutiful singsong, but they took it with a difference. Betty was the sort of Puritan child who really shared her parents' attempt to look on the terrors of life unflinching. But such an enterprise demands adult grasp and resolution. Poor Betty quailed before such terrible realities as predestination and damnation. Ever since she had had the latter explained to her, she had taken damnation to herself personally. How could a little girl hope to escape it? Why even a sinless newborn infant went straight to hell (albeit to the easiest room in it) if it died unbaptized. What chance was there for a child who, baptized or not, had been sinning for nine years with her hands, her tongue, her teeth, with every part of her? Damnation was under these circumstances as inevitable as death, and the imminence of death was a fact which Betty, in common with most well-brought-up Puritan children, had not been allowed to forget long at a time.

With Abigail, however, it was a different story. She was of a robuster sort, and though as relentlessly catechized as her small cousin, instinctively took damnation, death, and most other unpleasant things as something scheduled to happen to someone else, particularly to people she didn't like. Abigail had the smugness that had somehow lawlessly infected Puritanism in its later days, an attitude based on the unconscious assumption that the children of the elect would inherit salvation along with the family pewter. Thus fortified she was fitted to appreciate the passage in the Reverend Michael Wigglesworth's *Day of Doom* which describes the blessed in heaven as looking down with eternal joy on the torments of the damned. Abigail anticipated this prospect with relish; it must be rather like watching a hanging, this being one of the few pleasures which, because it was edifying, the Puritans did not deny their young.

But Abigail's state of mind would not, if detected, have been classified as innocence even by Calvinist standards, nor was it happiness. Placed in a less rigid society she might have been a gay little girl, but not here. Too much of her native gusto had been repressed by an environment as confining to her spirit as her neat long-gown was to her coltish legs. She was a child who longed to make far more noise in the world than she had ever been permitted to make. When of a Sabbath she sat in meeting, raising her eyes to her uncle standing black and impressive in his pulpit, she often quite simply and earnestly desired to yell. Wonderful to see all the faces turn to her instead of to her dull uncle with his sixthlies and seventhlies, wonderful, but impracticable. One has been strictly brought up, and terrible is the punishment grown folk can inflict on little girls who give way to their impulses.

So Abigail, though restive, had to date sat as decently in meeting as any. Much of the time she even listened to the sermon on the chance that there would somewhere be lusty talk of the devil, that arch-criminal in the everlasting crime-detection story conducted by the Church. It would be going too far to say that Abigail loved the devil. For all her bold spirit, she sometimes quailed before him and had bad dreams. Nevertheless she took a horrid fascination in hearing about him, and while Betty beside her twitched and swallowed her sobs, Abigail leaned forward to catch every word on this subject. There was in her a craving for fantasy which in a world that had banished Robin Goodfellow and Queen Mab received no other satisfaction than this.

It was, nevertheless, improper nourishment for the fancy of young Abigail. It was no better for her that she was being forced by her immature understanding of the creed back to the sadism of her infancy than it was for poor Betty that she lived in terror for her soul. Both children were about to take a terrible revenge upon a society that had with the godliest of good intentions used them ill.

2

Betty and Abigail had by 1692 lived in Salem Village for well over two years, assuming that they had come when Betty's father did, in November 1689. They already knew in the way that children do know these things that the community was not perfect in godliness, that it was inhabited by crabbed characters, many of whom failed to appreciate the quality of the Reverend Samuel Parris.

That the latter had his own perversities they were probably loyally unaware; and indeed, since such shortcomings, were born of a complicated series of frustrations, in the light of the everlasting mercy, Parris was perhaps as deserving of pity as the children in his charge.

His life had not followed an even pattern. Though he had once begun theological studies at Harvard, he had interrupted them to go into trade with the Barbados. There he had prospered so ill that by thirty-five he was looking for an opening in the ministry as providing a securer means of livelihood. Parris had real gifts as a preacher—his worst enemies would always admit to that—but the better churches liked ministers with a Harvard degree, and that he could not offer. It was probably a matter of profound humiliation that he got no better call than the one that came early in 1689 from obscure little Salem Village.

He kept the parish dangling for the better part of a year before he accepted. In fairness to Parris it must be admitted that he had other reasons than pride for doing so. Salem Village was by reputation one of the most contentious little communities in the Massachusetts Bay Colony. Although bickering was hardly uncommon in any Puritan community (living up to so severe a creed put a strain on anyone's good temper), here some quarrels had lasted so long as to amount to something like a state of bloodless feud. Worst of all, the village was capable of mistreating a minister most abominably. Since its founding in 1672 as a parish separate from Salem Town, no less than two ministers, the Reverend James Bayley and Reverend George Burroughs, had been hounded out of the parish by the acrimony, snooping, and the refusal on the part of many of the congregation to pay "rates" to the support of a minister they didn't want. Both times the minister had been upheld and the parish reprimanded by judgment of the General Court, but both ministers had left rather than struggle further with so flinty a congregation.

Although a third minister, one Deodat Lawson, had made out more peaceably, Parris could be forgiven a delay while he took stock of the situation. However, he had utilized this delay less to assure himself of the friendly intentions of his future parishioners than to bargain with them. He wanted unheard-of things, unheard-of at least in this village; for instance he expected clear and permanent title to the parsonage and grounds. It was as if the man confounded his gifts with those of the Mathers, and though the parish had a high opinion of his ability, it was not that high. In the end the plain farmers had outsmarted the exigent pastor. Parris came for the modest salary of £66, one-third to be paid in provision, would have the use of the parsonage only during occupancy, and was denied even such common courtesies as "the minister's wood spell"; he had to find his own firewood.

Late in 1689 Parris finally capitulated, and obviously rankling, had taken over the parish like a general taking over an army suspected of insubordination. He would not ordain his deacons, not even good Nathaniel Ingersoll, for twenty years the mainstay of the church and its most patient peacemaker, until they had submitted anew and under his eyes to probation. He searched his parish for signs of iniquity, and made church members in good standing, like Ezekiel Cheever, son of the famous school-master, do public penance for the most trivial and excusable of peccadilloes.

What he did not search with sufficient care was the ordering of his own household. He did not know, until too late, what the two little girls in his charge were up to.

CHAPTER II

YOUNG PEOPLE'S CIRCLE

There were in the Parris household two slaves, relics of his Barbados venture, the loutish John Indian and his consort, the ageless Tituba, said to be half Carib and half negro. The possession of these slaves lent prestige to the parsonage, for although there were other negro slaves in the community, there were not many. Thanks to the labours of this pair, Mrs Parris, a shadowy, self-effacing woman of whom history says little and tradition only that she was a truly good woman, was able to find time for numerous errands of mercy, and the children to live like little princesses, not to be sure in the sense of enjoying any pampered idleness, but in the sense that their chores consisted of those lighter household tasks that even a princess may learn.

All the heavier household work fell to the slaves. John Indian attended to the livestock and wood-lot, worked in the field, and even on occasion was hired out to give a hand in Deacon Ingersoll's ordinary, cater-cornered across the road from the parsonage. Tituba did the heavier, coarser household chores, boiled and pounded the linen when seasonal wash-days came, fetched water from the well, emptied the slops, scrubbed and sanded the floors.

All these things Tituba did, but not, one gathers, with energy. Her breeding had been in a softer, more languid clime; her life at hard labour in frosty New England was none of her choosing. She found subtle ways of easing her lot, and one of these was idling with the little girls.

Finding opportunity to do so was not difficult, for the children were often left to their tasks under Tituba's direc-

tion. The minister spent much of his time afield inspecting
the parish, and even at home usually sat safely out of range
in his study. Mrs Parris was in the kitchen more often, but
even she had frequent charitable errands abroad. Left alone
with the children, Tituba had long ago learned to amuse
herself in ways that would have got her a thrashing from
Parris had he got wind of them in time.

The sport may have started quite harmlessly, possibly
even within the hearing of Mrs Parris, with nothing more
questionable than reminiscences of life in the Barbados imparted within Tituba's lawful moments of leisure. But there
were presently occasions when, in the absence of the elder
Parrises, Tituba yielded to the temptation to show the children tricks and spells, fragments of something like voodoo
remembered from the Barbados. Once she started, Abigail,
thirsting for excitement, must have egged her on to further
revelation, conspiring with her to find occasion for the sport,
and Betty became a timid accomplice.

Betty's reactions to these sessions are not on record—no
more than anyone else's, for no one was ever to be wholly
truthful about what went on in the parsonage kitchen.
However, the child's painfully overdeveloped conscience
could not have missed the scent of evil in these enterprises,
and above all she knew the guilt of keeping a secret from
her parents.

Yet Betty did not give Abigail and Tituba away, no matter how guilty and frightened she became. For one thing,
daring Abigail had long ago become her leader in most
private matters; for another, Betty was devoted to Tituba,
whose special pet she was. The half-savage slave loved to
cuddle the child in her own snuggery by the fire, stroke her
fair hair and murmur to her old tales and nonsense rhymes.
Never from her own mother had the child received such
affection, for though godly parents loved their children as
much as any heathen, they would not risk spoiling them.
Basking in this warmth, Betty gave an almost hypnotic attention to the slurred Southern speech and tricksy ways of
Tituba. Well she knew in her upright Puritan heart that
she was tampering with the forbidden, but she could no

more resist than she could lift a hand to free herself from
the spell of an evil, thrilling dream.

Abigail knew more explicitly than Betty that what she
was doing was none of God's work; even her heart may
have known its secret pangs of guilt. But Abigail was so
constructed that up to a point the guilt only added zest to
the adventure.

2

It is possible that history would never have heard of Abigail and Betty except as half-legible names on lichen-
spattered stones had they kept Tituba to themselves. But
that they could not do. Tituba's fascination was too powerful to be monopolized by two small girls. Thanks to her,
the parsonage kitchen presently became a rendezvous for
older girls in the neighbourhood.

Winter had closed in on Salem Village, and winter was
dull. The bustle of harvest, the husking-bees, the solemn
thanksgivings followed by cheer at table were all over. The
occasional pleasure of a house-raising could not take place
once the ground had stiffened and the snows had come.
The Puritan calendar provided no alleviation for the tediums of winter; such pagan festivities as Christmas and
Mardi Gras, the one a splendid defiance against the death
of light, the other a heady foretaste of spring, were fiercely
forbidden.

For menfolk it wasn't so bad. This was the season when,
relieved of their heavier farm chores, they could take a musket into the forest to shoot wild turkey, deer, and a ma-
rauding fox or wolf; or they could fetch a line and hook,
cut through the ice, and fish. Housebound, they could turn
to the secondary trade that nearly every Puritan frontiers-
man practised in his spare time. Some cobbled shoes; some
fashioned trays and trenchers of good-smelling wood; even
if a man had no craft there were always odd jobs of car-
pentry and patching and mending to do about house and
outhouse. Men and boys were not often idle, not often
bored.

Womenfolk were not idle either, but their activity was the same monotonous round they had known the year long; such variation as they had came largely in summer when there were berries to pick, beer to carry to the men working in wood-lot and field. In winter every one of their scanty diversions was cut off. But for Sabbath meeting some of them would hardly have got out of the house at all.

Matrons were hardened to this monotony; the children underfoot gave point to their labours. But for young girls still unspoken-for, winter was unrelieved drudgery. It was not that in their eyes matrimony was a romantic condition. In the lusty society in which they lived, they saw matrons made pregnant nearly as often as milch cows, and knew all about the hardships of childbirth. Even so, without marriage or visible prospects thereof, they were without a sense of direction, and worse, without dignity. They had no place, no position. They lived at the mercy of smug matrons and dowagers, and how some of them resented those dowagers and matrons.

There was in Salem Village in the winter of 1691–2 quite a store of young girls, unattached teen-agers. The Puritans, sober in all things, quite properly looked on marriage as a serious business and did not favour it for the very young. Thus there were several girls about who had reached the age of sixteen, seventeen, and even twenty still manless and unprovided for, and these girls were instinct with repressed vitality, with all manner of cravings and urges for which village life afforded no outlet.

This winter life was particularly dismal. One calamity after another had been heaped on the Bay Colony—smallpox, Indian raids frighteningly reminiscent of the opening of King Philip's War, and the growing certainty that New England had lost for ever the near-independence it had enjoyed under the charter. God had manifestly turned His countenance from a people unworthy to be chosen as He had once chosen them. The devout were searching their hearts—and the conduct of their neighbours—for cause of this withdrawal. There were many who seriously believed that Doomsday was imminent. All signs pointed to its coming at the close of the century. Repent, they cried, for the Kingdom of God is at hand.

A conviction that the end was near did not at all prevent people from keeping at their labours. God would expect to find business going on as usual right up to the crack of doom. But the wholesome therapy of the daily chore was sickened for most people, even the phlegmatic who did not take the Book of Revelation so literally as others, by the pressing uncertainty of whether they could continue to claim possession of the land they tilled.

That uncertainty had come with the loss of the charter in 1684. Not only had the charter been as precious to Massachusetts theocracy as the tablets of the law to the children of Israel, providing the means whereby God could rule directly over His people, but it had direct personal value. Land titles had been issued under it, and these titles, according to the first royal governor, Sir Edmund Andros, had been invalidated by the revoking of the charter. Though Massachusetts, emboldened by news of a revolution in England, had overthrown Andros in 1689 and restored the old charter government, everyone knew that the latter no longer had any legal basis of authority, and that the problem posed by Andros had not been solved. For three years what had once been a vigorously self-propelled commonwealth had drifted rudderless, placing all its hope on its ambassador-extraordinary to court, the Reverend Increase Mather, who had been in England since 1688 trying to restore the charter. And now the rumour was that God had not prospered him, that Mather was giving up.

How intelligently teen-agers in Salem Village followed these political technicalities is questionable. But they were certainly not impervious to everyone's frantic anxiety as to what would happen to their land if the charter were really lost. Their elders, looking about them at acres cleared and tilled by generations of back-breaking toil, knew that they, become freeholders by grace of God and their own labours, were like to fall into a kind of servitude again. Some received the providence with prayerful humility, but more

fell into a despairing cantankerousness that made them hard
to live with.

Even teen-agers would rather not think too much about
facts so painful and about which they were so helpless. The
girls in Salem Village had been instinctively escaping from
the repressions of so dismal a background; their natural high
spirits, turning inward, were concentrating in a force that
awaited only the right moment to find explosive release.
Adolescence, the silly careless age in the eyes of adults, who
usually manage to forget its inwardness as thoroughly as
they forget that of their infancy, can be under such circumstances a history-making age. More than once history has
been wrenched from its course by teen-agers; to name one
example, by Joan of Lorraine. These girls were about to
make history of a peculiarly distressing nature. From the
Puritan flint in them—for in their environment they could
not be happy pagans, were as obsessed by the Puritan conviction of sin as John Calvin himself—was about to be struck
off the fatal spark.

It was given Tituba to strike it.

3

The girls who first discovered what sport was to be had
in the society of Tituba would be those who lived in the
immediate neighbourhood: the sixteen-year-old Mary Walcott and Elizabeth Booth, and Susanna Sheldon, two years
their elder. All these lived so close to the parsonage that it
was easy for them to watch for the coast to clear so that
they could slip over for a session with the gifted slave. If
they neglected their own duties in the process, that omis-
sion could not easily be held against them since a virtuous
reason can always be found for visiting a parsonage. Mr
Parris, they could say, happened to be out when they came,
but since he was expected back momentarily they waited
and meantime gave the cook a hand. Such an explanation
was so close to the truth as to forestall suspicion.

In any case the girls were in and out of the Parris household and learning much from Tituba. Probably what they

were chiefly after was fortune-telling. Not only were they at the age when the future is full of unsounded mystery, but in New England at large many people old enough to know better were currently solacing their uncertainties by practising what Cotton Mather called "little sorceries," by conjuring with sieve and scissors and candle. Even books of palmistry had been caught passing about in Essex County, and had been consulted by respectable matrons and church-goers.

Such conduct was of course forbidden, and the arts involved considered very black indeed. God who reveals all things in His own good time does not permit His providence to be tempted. Only the devil will stoop to such devices; therefore to attempt by magical means to see into the future is to traffic with the devil.

The girls had not been left in ignorance of these facts. Rare was the minister who did not preach periodically on the damnable guilt of what they were now doing; they were left in no doubt that hell-fire would be their portion on the part of divine authority, and that human agents would thrash them if they caught them at it. The hell-fire they managed to forget about—except in their secret hearts where an implacable conscience lay chained—and the human agents they had so far skilfully evaded. Perhaps they worried sometimes about the inescapable presence of Abigail and Betty, especially the latter, who showed symptoms of tears and fright when Tituba exuberantly progressed into really esoteric mystery. It was a nuisance always to have these children about. Still, Abigail was as bold as the best of them, and it was obvious that the conscience of Betty, however unhappy, was bound by the twin chains of her loyalty to Tituba and her subjection to the will of her domineering cousin.

Even so, these novitiates did not quite keep their secret. Each had a friend in some farther reach of the village, and when the latter came in on Sabbath or Lecture Day, it was impossible not to show off a bit, to confide details of the thrilling new art, and finally to find a way of smuggling the friend into the presence of the high priestess. Thus it was that the seventeen-year-old Elizabeth Hubbard, who worked for her aunt and her aunt's husband, Dr William Griggs, was initiated. Two older girls, both twenty, presently joined the unacknowledged sorority, Sarah Churchill, who worked for the family of that salty-tongued patriarch, George Jacobs, and Mary Warren, maidservant to John and Elizabeth Procter.

4

By far the most important of the newcomers, in the light of future events, was the youngest girl of all. She was Ann, daughter of Thomas and Ann Putnam, a sickly, highly strung twelve-year-old, who presently found her way to the household in company with the Putnams' maidservant, Mercy Lewis, a sly wench of nineteen.

Ann was what Abigail and Betty were not, something of a prodigy. She had the advantage of association with a mother who was not only literate but well-read, and through her mother she had been exposed to tragedy in a way that gave her a most unchildlike knowledge of the world.

The tragedy had its roots in events of two decades ago when Ann's mother, a girl herself at the time, had come to the village with her sister Mary, young bride of James Bayley. The latter, the first minister of the parish, having been called by a slim majority, was hampered and hectored by a minority of malcontents. The dissension gave small cheer to his wife, who during this period dragged herself through one pregnancy after another, bearing her children only to lose them, until at last she died herself. To her young sister's way of thinking, Mary had been deliberately done to death by the spite of Bayley's enemies, and by the humiliation of being constantly spied on at the parsonage.

Ann had nevertheless remained in the village. At sixteen she married into one of its most prosperous and widely ramified families; she became Sergeant Thomas Putnam's wife. But though she got thereby an affectionate and forbearing husband, she did not find peace. Obviously the malignance that had destroyed her sister was now pursuing her. She too bore babies only to bury them, and suffered so much in body and spirit that even when a living child was born to her in 1680, the younger Ann, and others after, she remained inconsolable. She was a Rachel crying for her children which were not, an Esther calling for vengeance.

Lately the elder Ann had felt herself close to uncovering the mysterious cause of her wrongs. The dead had walked before her. In dreams so vivid that they were more real than reality she had seen her sister Bayley, her sister's children, and her own standing before her in their winding-sheets, piteously stretching out their hands. It was as if they, cold these many years in their graves, had some urgent request to make of her, but though they spoke, she had never been able to make out the words.

Under these circumstances she judged it no sin to try to get more directly in touch with these importunate dead. Mr Parris, had she consulted him, could have told her differently. Just so had Saul reasoned in seeking out the Witch of Endor to raise the reluctant spirit of the prophet Samuel, and Saul was no sanctified character. But the woman saw no reason to go to Mr Parris about so private a matter. Instead she went to his kitchenmaid, to the local Witch of Endor, who was Tituba; or rather she sent her daughter and Mercy.

Ann, initiated to the mysteries of the Parris kitchen, speedily became in spite of her youth the aptest of Tituba's pupils, the natural leader in the unhallowed enterprises of the older girls. Her intelligence was quicker, her imagination livelier than any of the others, and thanks to her mother's obsessions she had already had some experience with arcana. With her mother she had pored over the Book of Revelation, puzzling her keen young mind to find local applications for its symbolism, for its red dragons, its beast that was and is not, Babylon mother of harlots, the star called Wormwood.

Another subject of study had of course been Wigglesworth's *Day of Doom*, that most characteristic of early Massachusetts best-sellers. From it Ann had absorbed a fierce,

unyielding sense of Calvinist righteousness. It was clear to
her that there could be no mercy for those whom God Himself had destined to damnation, that indeed hell for the
damned actually was mercy, most august divine mercy. A
little girl brought up to believe so literally in such concepts
would be unlikely to show more mercy than her God if she
by chance were called to testify in a local day of judgment.

If in this Ann resembled Abigail Williams, there was also
an important difference. Abigail, like many of the older
girls, was here for mischief; Ann had come on a serious,
even a tragic errand. The confidante of her mother since
her earliest childhood, Ann knew all about life and death.
Death she knew from her mother's tearful visits to the family graveyard where lay Ann's siblings and cousins. Life she
knew from the hysterical suspicion with which her mother
surveyed the conduct of many of their neighbours. Through
her Ann knew all evil; there was not a scandal or rumour
of scandal of the past twenty years on which the child
could not speak with authority.

Ann was now on the verge of adolescence, already subject to the preliminary strains of that difficult period, to
unexplained pains and heaviness in the limbs, to dizziness
and flashes of imagination so vivid that they sometimes resembled hallucinations. It was not good for her that it was
just at this time that she was exposed to an experience
which complicated her already unstable emotional set by
awakening a smothered sense of guilt.

In particular it was not good for Salem Village.

CHAPTER III

THE POSSESSED

One cannot pursue forbidden pleasures without paying a penalty, without suffering the consequences of a conflict between conscience (or at least fear of discovery) and the unhallowed craving. This was true of all the girls, but particularly of little Betty. Some time in January, apparently quite early in the month, the child began visibly to sicken.

Always sensitive, Betty had long been subject to sudden fits of weeping, but now came something new and progressively alarming. It started inconspicuously enough with an absence of mind not natural in one so young and essentially docile. Betty began to forget errands and chores, and what was disturbing was that the effect was not of naughtiness but of real inability to concentrate; or rather it was as if she were so rapt in some secret preoccupation that she could remember nothing else.

Sometimes her mother found her sitting all alone at her needlework, her hands poised but motionless, her eyes staring with uncanny fixity at an invisible object.

"Betty," the mother would say, and the child would start violently as if caught in an act of guilt, scream sharply, and being pressed for an explanation would give utterance to a meaningless babbling.

It came on even in prayer, in fact after a while particularly in prayer. When all heads were supposedly bowed, Parris would steal a sidelong glance of inspection and discover that Betty had remained upright, her eyes fixed in that deathlike stare. Better, he soon learned, to leave her be, for if he reproved her, she remained rigid as ever, but worked her mouth and gave off curious hoarse choking sounds, sometimes almost like the barking of a dog.

And this, alarming enough in itself, had the further disadvantage of setting off Abigail, who caught the affliction as if by contagion. She too was absent-minded, though in her case this was nothing new, and began to make babbling and rasping sounds. Also, having started, she presently went beyond Betty. She got down on all fours and ran about under the furniture, barking and braying, and sometimes fell into convulsions when she writhed and screamed as if suffering the torments of the damned.

The plight of both children became frightening and showed no signs of passing by itself. Even prayers were no help; indeed they made it positively worse, for Betty, as her disease progressed, screamed wildly at the mere sound of "Our Father," and Abigail covered her ears and stamped her feet and roared to shut out the sound of holy words. Once Betty, that most gentle of little girls, actually hurled a Bible from her. Later she came to herself and sobbed distractedly that she was damned.

The Parrises at first sought no publicity for their troubles; in fact they seem to have drawn a veil of privacy over the affliction in their household until nearly February. But so sensational a disturbance was bound to become known eventually, especially in view of the fact that the parsonage lay at the very centre of community life—beside the church and across the road from the seemly convivialities of Deacon Ingersoll's ordinary. People were always coming and going in the parsonage, and when the trouble became known, nothing could keep them from crowding in to see for themselves.

It was at this stage that something even more alarming happened. As the news spread, so did the contagion. First it struck near neighbours. Mary Walcott and Susanna Sheldon fell into convulsions at the Walcott house, and the seizures recurred. Then the affliction spread to the home of the Thomas Putnams, where both young Ann and Mercy Lewis got it. Ann's sufferings were horrible. People who watched her hardly expected her to live from one moment to the next.

Nor was even this the end. One girl after another succumbed to the malady until there was hardly a quarter in the village without its afflicted maiden. Around each there assembled a circle of awed watchers. Some came to give aid, to straighten out limbs twisted in convulsions, to hold the victim back from leaping into the fire; others came only to look on. Of these, some found a ghoulish pleasure in what they saw, and nearly everyone experienced an unconscious relief from the nagging cares that had weighed them down so long. It was curiously as if a kind of holiday had been declared. Even so, many watched the girls with a terror approaching panic; too well they suspected what had happened.

Not quite four years previously, about the time that Salem Village had opened negotiations with Parris, a similar providence had occurred in Boston. In the family of the God-fearing mason, John Goodwin, four young children, impeccably well-behaved until then, had fallen into just such fits and had scared the whole of Cotton Mather's North End with their crazed and often blasphemous capers.

Neither the concerted prayers of four ministers nor the hanging of the malefactor judged responsible for their fits, an Irish washerwoman known as the Witch Glover, had effected a cure. Mather had had to take the eldest child, Martha, into his home and conduct an elaborate series of psychic experiments before the children were finally restored to sobriety.

Remote as was the village from Boston, it knew all about the Witch Glover and the Goodwin children. Mather had published a report of his laboratory observations on diabolism under the title of *Memorable Providences Relating to Witchcraft and Possession,* and the book had had a wide circulation and made an immense impression; Parris himself had a copy. Also the Parrises had probably had first-hand experience of the case, since they appear to have been living in Boston at the time. The little girls might even have been taken to see the hanging.

None the less Parris, to his credit, refused to jump to conclusions on the basis of the resemblance between the cases. It was for a scientist, not for a minister, to pass on what ailed the children. Parris got his charges to a doctor and saw to it that the custodians of the other girls did likewise.

Call in

2

The nearest physician was Dr Griggs of the village. No doubt he was capable in simpler emergencies, broken bones, scaldings, severed arteries, even smallpox. But this odd epidemic was quite outside his experience. It was not his fault, poor man, that although his times had already evinced an awakening interest in scientific investigation, medicine itself had not yet struggled out of the apathy of the Middle Ages, that it had forgotten what little the Greeks had learned about hysteria, or that he was all in all rather less well-equipped to cope with the aberrations of young females than an experienced midwife.

He prodded and peered; he turned from the twitching bodies of the girls to thumb another of his books. He thought of epilepsy, looked it up and shook his head; whatever this was it wasn't epilepsy. He tried out his "physics"; they made no difference; the girls became rational or fell into gibberish without reference to his doses. Finally he ruled out all possibilities but one.

"The evil hand is on them," he said, the medical vocabulary not having yet been enriched by more soothing shibboleths such as psychoneurosis.

Expected though the verdict was, it appalled the village. Humane people had hoped against hope for a more naturalistic explanation, perhaps a little-known disease that would run its course and leave the girls in the end unharmed. They were encouraged in this hope by the fact that when a girl came out of her fits she seemed little the worse for her experience, no matter what extremes of agony she had endured in them; some even looked positively refreshed.

A few, a very few, distrusted the diagnosis. They were irreverent enough to point out that there was something strikingly apt about some of the antics of the girls, something very like what many young people would have liked to do if they dared. The girls availed themselves of the opportunity of their illness to rebel against every restriction placed on them by adult society. Before hunting witches, why not experiment with the effect of a good whipping?

So callous a suggestion outraged most people acquainted with the pitiful reality of the girls' sufferings. With the devil in command, the poor girls had no choice but to cast off discipline; such was one of the commonest symptoms of demoniac possession, and Cotton Mather, observing it in little Martha Goodwin, had regarded it as one of the most dangerous. These poor children—in spite of the advanced age of some, everyone called them "the afflicted children" because of Betty and Abigail—needed the prayers of the parish, not its derision.

That they might be assured these prayers, Parris proclaimed a state of emergency and appealed for help to the ministers of the North Shore. When Dr Griggs had relegated the affliction from the physical world to the spiritual, he had thrust the responsibility for its treatment upon the ministry. It was now plain that the devil was at work in Salem Village, and since even the devil cannot produce results on this scale without human accomplices, it was equally plain that he had commissioned witches here. But if it was no surprise to Parris to learn that witchcraft existed in a community that had consented to his rates and his rights with such ill grace, it was not seemly for him to work single-handed to search out the black sheep in his own flock. Accordingly he appealed for help.

By this time February was well advanced and had brought with it a thaw that made the ways nearly impassable with flood and slush. Yet so grave was the emergency that half a dozen ministers from Beverly, Salem Town and round about sludged their nags through the mire and got to the haunted village to pray and consult with Parris.

From Salem Town came the Reverend Nicholas Noyes;

officially he was only second pastor of the First Church; but its senior pastor, John Higginson, was old now, and more and more left practical details to his younger colleague. This was a circumstance which was to have important results, for Noyes, that rarity among Puritan ministers, a bachelor, was of a fiercer, more unforgiving temper than the older, mellower man. Noyes could indeed be gentle with the sinner who repented and renounced his sin, but for the sinner who denied his guilt he would have no mercy.

John Hale rode over from Beverly and watched the girls with a mien even more troubled than most. In very truth this affliction gave him a sense of guilt. It had happened that twice within a decade he had been called upon to deal with charges of witchcraft against women in or near his parish, and both times Hale, a man slow to believe evil, had used his influence to clear the accused.

Now that he looked at these girls and learned how widespread this plague had become, he questioned whether he had on those earlier occasions defended or wronged the innocent. Had he then acted firmly and refused to give way to his natural sympathy and to the plausible explanations offered him, this might never have happened. The very women he had defended, Dorcas Hoar and Bridget Bishop, might well be the cause of this awful providence. Not that Hale jumped to a new conclusion on the subject. The situation was too confused and awful for prompt and easy decision. But he pondered and prayed and steeled himself to accept the humiliation of a public reversal of his former position should God require it of him.

Arrived in Salem Village, the ministers celebrated publicly a day of fast, and then meeting privately with the girls, applied the therapy of prayer. The results were discouraging. Some girls sat dully insensible to the exercise; others shrieked as if touched with hot iron at every sound of a sacred word. Abigail in particular was beside herself on such occasions and in meeting set up such a hullabaloo as to make a devil's travesty of divine service. Now indeed the hellion in Abigail had his will; it was the child good people stared at, not the minister. Even in her silence they kept an uneasy eye on her, bracing themselves for her next war-whoop.

Faced with so impossible a situation the ministers resolved perforce upon a more drastic course of action. Hale came to this decision reluctantly, for he knew what misery it would entail; Noyes came to it with unflinching purpose and Parris with something like zest. The latter was in a delicate position in that the outbreak had first occurred in his own household, in the person of the little ones entrusted to his care. It was for him to demonstrate by the energy of his prosecution that it was from no negligence on his part that such a disaster had come about; besides there was something in his composition to which so dramatic a struggle with the powers of darkness made a direct appeal.

by minister

Anyway, the decision was reached. The girls must be induced to name their tormentors; the witches must be ferreted out and brought to justice.

3

Meanwhile, how was it with the girls? No one can ever know in precise detail. For one thing, history has an annoying way of failing to record the complete data any responsible psychologist would require for a diagnosis; for another, it was not given these girls ever again to tell the simple truth. When some tried—at least three were to do so —they were baffled by the fact that the truth was no longer simple, no longer explicable even to them, and for most people no longer credible.

Nevertheless the general pattern of their conduct is clear enough; in modern terms they all of them, in one degree or another, had hysteria. Of course hysteria itself is no simple phenomenon, and it was here inevitably complicated by the varying emotional patterns the different girls brought to it. Some of them may have verged on the psychotic. Certainly Ann Putnam's mother, from whom the girl took her emotional colouring, had her paranoid tendencies. Recognized insanity was to appear in the Parris family; though, as the child in whom it was to appear was yet unborn, it may have had no bearing on the case of little Betty. On the other hand there were girls who could sometimes take possession calmly. Mary Walcott was to sit placidly knitting through a Dionysiac frenzy on the part of her companions. Two of the older girls retained sufficient hold on reality to be shocked by the excesses of the others and to make a dishonoured attempt to denounce them.

There was nothing new, nothing at all peculiar to Salem Village in the outbreak. Similar examples of mass hysteria and on a far more enormous scale had occurred repeatedly in the Middle Ages, and always like this one in the wake of stress and social disorganization, after wars or after an epidemic of the Black Death. There had been the Children's Crusades, the Flagellantes, the St Vitus' Dance, and again and again there had been outbreaks of witchcraft. Sweden had recently had one, and on such a scale as to make what was going on in Salem Village look trivial.

Nor has susceptibility to "demoniac possession" passed from the world. A rousing religious revival will bring out something like what Salem Village was experiencing; so will a lynching, a Hitler, so will a dead motion-picture star or a live crooner. Some of the girls were no more seriously possessed than a pack of bobby-soxers on the loose. Their affliction was real enough, deserving of study and treatment, but not of the kind of study and treatment it was about to receive.

In the long run what was remarkable here was less the antics of the girls than the way the community received them. It was the community—extended in time to include the whole Bay Colony—that would in the end suffer the most devastating attack of possession, and not only the ignorant, but its best minds. The nearly universal belief in devils and witches could not alone explain the capitulation of reason which took place. The fact was that the commonwealth no less than the girls craved its Dionysiac mysteries. A people whose natural impulses had long been repressed by the severity of their belief, whose security had been undermined by anxiety and terror continued longer than could be borne, demanded their catharsis. Frustrated by the devils they could not reach, they demanded a scapegoat and a full-scale lynching. And they got it.

4

The girls at this point were having a wonderful time. Their present notoriety was infinitely rewarding to childish natures beset by infantile cravings for attention. Hitherto snubbed and disregarded, they were now cosseted and made much of. They could hardly have attracted more notice if among them they had married the king and all his court.

They were as of the present given over to a primal orgy, a kind of ghost dance and were therein released by their affliction of all the tediums and inhibitions placed on them by their betters. Yet though in their secret hearts they were exhilarated by these exercises, they were as yet wholly without plan or guile. When the ministers asked them to name who afflicted them, they drew a blank. The girls fell dumb. No one afflicted them; it had just happened.

Their impotence dismayed their guardians. Witchcraft was afoot and could not for the safety of the common-wealth be allowed to go unchecked. But the witches could not be identified without the help of the girls. When country folk approached the ministers with old recipes for detecting a witch by other means, they were sternly reprimanded. Idle superstition could be permitted no place in so serious a situation; only the best scientific methods were to be used. The girls must somehow be made to pull themselves together and concentrate on the problem; certainly God in His mercy would give them power to name their tormentors.

Investigation was now conducted on a new plan. The simple "Who torments you?" had been proved ineffectual. Leading questions were now put to the girls, not only by Parris and Noyes but by people throughout the village. Though there had until now been only sporadic witch cases in Massachusetts, suspicion of witchcraft was endemic, not only here but in the country from which these people came.

Names of old suspects were now suggested to the girls and their reactions sharply studied. Parris for his part found his mind turning to Tituba. Now that he looked back he recalled that Betty and Abigail had been with the untutored slave more often than was good for them, and that he had seen the older girls hanging about his kitchen.

So the questions were put, and locked though the girls were in their own private world, in the hypnoid state to which they periodically achieved they could not indefinitely remain impervious to the power of such persistent suggestion.

Even so, when the girls at last began to talk it was not in response to suggestion but because—or so everyone believed —of an unhallowed experiment instigated by Mary Sibley, aunt of Mary Walcott. Goody Sibley induced Tituba and John Indian to try an old country recipe for witch cake. All unknown to Parris, who, characteristically, did not know what was going on in his household in an emergency, the slaves mixed rye meal with the urine of the children, baked it in the ashes and fed it to the dog.

Tituba had not seen much of the girls since the outbreak had begun. In particular her own nursling Betty had shrunk away from her, though Tituba was as perplexed and concerned as any about the child's condition. In her solicitude she followed the ritual to the letter and was most unpleasantly rewarded. For Parris did discover what happened, and tragic little Betty, torn all this time between devotion and duty, gave way to what sounded like an accusation.

"Tituba . . . she . . . oh Tituba!" sobbed the child, and went off into delirium so dreadful that her parents thought it would be the end of her. The other girls, faced with this evidence, agreed to the charge, and when at last three male-factors were brought to judgment, it was Tituba's name that headed the list.

CHAPTER IV

TITUBA

Salem Village breathed easier when the identity of the three suspects whom the girls were induced to name became known. Any community playing at a grim game of nominating characters most likely to be picked up in a witch hunt would have hit on the likes of these. They were Tituba, Sarah Good, Sarah Osburne.

Tituba, marked as she was by her exotic colouring (suspicion was to turn automatically to other negro slaves in the community), was an inevitable suspect. It is only fair to add that if Salem Village contained anyone at all who deliberately practised the black arts, it was she. That the girls did not indict her earlier, in fact not at all until after little Betty's outburst, can only have been due to a not unreasonable fear of what Tituba under cross-examination might say about them. Guilt is an indispensable ingredient in the witch's broth of hysteria; the latter's tics and spasms usually originate in a moment of near discovery. Though the girls, whose seizures had long since become involuntary, were as hazy as anyone about their exact origin, they had not yet discovered that they were impregnable in their martyrdom, their word proof against anyone's word, let alone that of a poor slave. At this point, still young in possession, a saving grace of reality made them tremble at possible revelations by their accomplice.

Sarah Good was from their point of view less formidable than Tituba, but from the community's even more of a nuisance. Her husband, William, being landless, supported his family by hiring himself out as a labourer, and whoever took him usually took Sarah and her several children as well. Much as labour was needed in the colony, people had long ago developed a reluctance to incur the presence of Sarah in their homes, for she could be shrewish, idle, and above all slovenly. During the late epidemic she had been accused of spreading smallpox, if not by malefaction, at least by negligence. She had lately become something of a tramp, begging from door to door, being often not only rebuffed but followed to see that she did not bed down in the haymow and set the place afire with her evil-smelling pipe.

Nothing in the records suggests that any in the community felt pity for this forlorn outcast. Pity in truth was not a Puritan virtue. Dedicated to industry, accustomed to measuring godliness by the prosperity meted out as a reward, Puritans at large had scant patience with the poor. God, who balances His accounts so exquisitely that one who has a toothache can know for a certainty that he has been caught sinning with his teeth, had not inflicted poverty on Sarah Good without just cause, and it is not for the godly to question God's will. The only concession to Sarah Good was that her children had been absorbed, at least temporarily, by sundry families.

Hard times had toughened Sarah. She was a powerful hag, capable of giving the constable some bad moments when he came to fetch her to jail in Ipswich. Withal, her matted hair was so grey, her face so seamed and leathery that people seeing her alone estimated her age at seventy. Actually she was much younger; one child, Dorcas, was still under six, and she was even now carrying another.

The third suspect, Sarah Osburne, was of an entirely different social order. She not only had property but was even moderately well-to-do; the sturdy frame of her house with its fine oaken panelling stands to this day. She had, however, lost caste. When her first husband, Samuel Prince, died she had taken William Osburne into her home as overseer, and according to rumour had lived with him in all senses of the phrase. Her recent marriage to him had not appeased the feeling against her, and Goody Osburne, no doubt incensed by all the tattling, had become scandalously remiss in her church attendance. Now in 1692 she had not been seen in meeting for fourteen months; true, as she would querulously remind you, she was bed-ridden; but that was a recent affliction, and her offences against decency were very old.

The testimony against these women was taken from the girls; on the basis thereof formal complaints were sworn out, and on 29 February—for 1692 was a leap year—warrants were issued. The accused were taken to Ipswich Prison, and preparations made in Salem Village for their examination, a preliminary inquest to decide if evidence warranted their being held for trial.

2

Court cases were in Massachusetts heard by the "assistants," members of the General Court of the colony; two magistrates, John Hathorne and Jonathan Corwin, were sent out from Salem Town to conduct the examination. The former accepted his assignment assertively, with every appearance of zeal; the latter did not. Corwin was a quiet man, and in this emergency less sure of himself than Hathorne, or at least less outspoken.

Neither was without practical experience, since both were of the General Court, but neither had had any formal legal training, nor for that matter had anyone else currently administering the law in Massachusetts. The one professional school, Harvard, had been founded to provide training for one profession only, the ministry; recently it had made some sketchy provision for medical training, but a Law School had not been thought of and would not be for time to come. The Puritans had a low opinion of lawyers and did not permit the professional practice of law in the colony. In effect the administration of the law was in the hands of laymen, most of them second-generation colonists who had an incomplete grasp of current principles of English jurisdiction. For that matter, this chosen people, this community which submitted itself to the direct rule of God,

looked less to England for its precepts than to God's ancient and holy word. So far as was practicable the Puritans were living by a legal system that antedated Magna Carta by at least two millennia, the Decalogue and the tribal laws codified in the Pentateuch.

Given this background, or at least their interpretation of this background, the fine old English concept that a man is innocent until proved guilty would not enter the heads of these magistrates, or at least not of John Hathorne. Trial by jury was indeed to be recognized, but, as matters were to work out, not the principle that the judge is bound by the jury's verdict. Neither Hathorne, Corwin, nor any of the magistrates that were to follow them saw any reason to provide an accused witch with right of counsel, and their notions of evidence and of courtroom etiquette were, to put it mildly, peculiar.

Yet they by no means took their duties lightly. The two men assigned to conduct the preliminary examinations had been in Salem preparing themselves carefully for their responsibility.

First they had to set themselves clear as to the nature of witchcraft and how it was to be recognized. To this end they ransacked their Bibles—and all of Massachusetts with them—and ran into a dismaying difficulty. Nowhere does the Bible define witchcraft; it simply names the offence, usually in the same breath with sodomy, lying and idolatry, and lets the matter rest. Indeed the very word "witchcraft" was hardly mentioned in earlier editions than the King James; its prominence there was largely a compliment to his majesty's known interest in demonology. (He had in practice a shrewder, more sceptical grasp of the subject than the men of Massachusetts would easily achieve.) Thanks to semantic accident, one unequivocal statement had been thrown into relief: "Thou shalt not permit a witch to live." Hence, however reticent the Bible might be about the details, there could be no doubt about God's will on the subject, nor was there any doubt in the minds of most intelligent people in Massachusetts as to the reality of witchcraft. Their belief, rooted in the folk-ways of old England, was powerfully reinforced by the conspicuous place occupied by the Miltonic devil in the Puritan cosmology. To doubt the devil was a blasphemy on a par with doubting God Himself, and to deny acts of malefic witchcraft was to deny the devil.

Yet for the magistrates to cope with this emergency they needed a more practical guide than either the Bible or books of theology afforded. To this end they assembled a small reference library. They sought out the chapters on witchcraft in Bernard's *Guide to Jurymen,* Glanvil's *Collection of Sundry Tryals in England and Ireland,* Keeble's *Common Law.* They studied the precedents contained in Baxter's *Certainty of the World of Spirits,* R. Burton's lurid *Kingdom of Darkness,* and finally in the very last word on the subject, their own Cotton Mather's *Memorable Providences.*

Fortified by this reading, the magistrates came to Salem Village agreed on certain principles of evidence. They would accept as proof of guilt the finding of any "teat" or "devil's mark," that is to say any unnatural excrescence on the bodies of the accused. They would accept as ground for suspicion of guilt any mischief following anger between neighbours. And most important of all, they would accept the doctrine that "the devil could not assume the shape of an innocent person in doing mischief to mankind."

In reviewing the cruder tests for witchcraft sanctioned by tradition, they were somewhat inconsistent. Though they resolved to abstain from the water test, recently practised in Connecticut but denounced by Increase Mather as superstitious and unchristian, they proposed to retain another which really up-to-date divines had as little use for—the touch test.

The principles that the magistrates accepted were to set the pattern not only of the examinations, but of the trials to follow. Searching for the devil's mark would be carried on in prison; juries of the suspects' sex would strip the bodies of the accused and examine them minutely, running pins through any abnormality they found. The clause about "mischief following anger" was eventually to set almost the entire colony to compiling a quaint and atrocious spite history. A memory for petty quarrels now became a virtue; magistrates everywhere were to have their hands full recording circumstantial accounts of squabbles which in the past, often the very distant past, had been followed by the breaking of a cart-wheel, the loss of a scythe, the sickening of a hog, the drowning of an ox.

But by far the most important principle accepted by the magistrates was the premiss that the devil cannot assume the "shape" of an innocent person, the admission of the so-called "spectral evidence." Thanks to this arrangement, hallucinations, dreams, and mere fancies would be accepted in court as factual proof not of the psychological condition of the accuser but of the behaviour of the accused. This was, as many good men and women were to discover, the sort of "proof" against which there is no disproof. Let an accuser say, "Your shape came to my room last midnight," and the accused has no defence at all; no conceivable alibi can be furnished for the whereabouts of a "shape," one's airy substance.

People accused and held under such evidence were to have only one recourse. It was Tituba's small but solid claim to fame that she found it first.

3

Tuesday, 1 March, was the date set for the preliminary hearings. So spectacular an event had never before occurred in the simple annals of Salem Village, and most people celebrated the occasion by taking a holiday and riding to Ingersoll's ordinary to watch for the magistrates to arrive and see what happened next.

The local constabulary and some of the guard set up a watch on the road from Salem Town, and when towards noon the magistrates came into sight, they fell into formation beside them and escorted them to Ingersoll's, pennants flying and drums athrob. The martial solemnity of the spectacle was beautiful and touching to see. Salem Village knew how to carry itself in the war which the devil had declared.

But when the magistrates descended at the ordinary, they decided not to go in. Although Deacon Ingersoll had fitted up his great chamber to serve as courtroom, it would not hold a fraction of the people who milled about the lawn in grave excitement. Not only had nearly every able-bodied man, woman, or child of Salem Village come, but so had people from Beverly, Ipswich, Topsfield, and even Salem Town. It was no part of the plan to hold Star Chamber proceedings on so urgent a public matter; Massachusetts' controversy with the devil was to be conducted openly, in full view of the populace. It was accordingly decided to open the meeting-house for the purpose. No sacrilege would be involved; in a commonwealth so dedicated to the will of God, the least municipal function had its sacramental character, and in consequence throughout New England the village churches were also the place of town meeting. Where better could the grand campaign against the devil be opened than here?

The few necessary practical arrangements were quickly made. A bar of justice for the prisoners was provided by turning the minister's chair about. The pulpit was moved back to make room for a large table fetched from the ordinary, and seats were set behind it for the magistrates and their secretary. Ezekiel Cheever performed that office on this occasion; Corwin himself, always inclined to leave the actual prosecution to Hathorne, also took notes. Extraordinarily copious notes in the case of Tituba. Parris, who wrote a neat round hand, stood by for the nonce; he was, however, itching for the assignment.

When all the officials had taken their places and the afflicted girls had been seated facing them in the foremost benches of the auditorium, the throng was permitted to fill up the rest of the church; they came in dressed in their decent Sunday best, and for all the tremendous excitement of the occasion, in their Sunday sobriety, and they filled the place to the last available square inch.

A hush settled over the house. Outside in the bright noonday a chill March wind rattled at the leaded casements and wailed devil songs under the eaves. In deathly silence the people waited for the first of the witches to be brought before them.

She came between two constables, each of whom kept a tight grip on either arm, for this was a sinewy witch and hard to handle. Already the story had got about of how she had fought off the jailer in Ipswich, and how this morning, riding thence, she had flung herself from her horse and all but given Constable Samuel Braybrook the slip. Now Sarah Good walked up to the bar with something like a swagger. Few looking at the unsavoury crone could doubt that one so agile in chains and on horseback would be equally agile on a broom.

4

But Goody Good would in no wise own up to the broomstick. All charges she faced with a peppery denial. She did not hurt the children. "I scorn it." She did not employ familiar spirits. "I scorn it." Then looking about her she said maliciously, "You bring others here and now you charge me with it. You brought two more."

But the magistrates were not to be deflected from their inquiry into the ways of Sarah Good. They produced testimony against her. Why, for instance, did she not go to church. "For want of cloosel" she snapped. Villagers testified that when she was turned away from a house on her begging expeditions, she went muttering, and that often after such mutterings cows died. Once she had been directly charged with malefaction in this connection and had retorted to the accuser that it was all the same to her if all his cows died. She had called children vile names and had retired mumbling from the Parris house shortly before the children fell ill.

"What is it that you say when you go muttering away from a person's house?"

"If I must tell, I will tell. It is the commandments I say. I may say my commandments, I hope."

She was invited then and there to say her commandments; at a loss she mumbled something like a psalm, a

garbled, nearly unrecognizable psalm. Contemptuously the
magistrates dismissed her and called for Sarah Osburne.

Hearing the name Goody Good roused herself for a part-
ing shot. "It is Gammer Osburne that doth pinch and afflict the children!"

Then she was marched away to temporary duress in Ingersoll's ordinary. She fetched her evil pipe from out her
rags, got her a coal from the fire and puffed stoically.

Gammer Osburne was not fit to be out of bed. Nevertheless she had been taken from it yesterday to the cold
comfort of Ipswich Prison, and this morning got somehow
on the back of a nag and ridden hither. To get her into
court at all the constables had to support her.

Now, leaning heavily on the back of the minister's chair,
she looked away from the cold eyes of neighbours that for
years had had no use for her and made her tremulous bid
for sympathy. She was, she said, "more like to be bewitched
than that she should be a witch." And she told a rambling
story of something she "either saw or dreamed"; a "thing
like an Indian, all black . . . pinched her on her neck and
pulled her by the back part of her head to the door of the
house."

Gammer Osburne presumed in hoping to join the society
of the afflicted, those honoured girls who sat down in front,
going into fits if one of the accused looked their way. In
poor Osburne, whose affliction was in no wise feigned, there
was neither the energy, the dramatic fire, nor the narrative
ingenuity to carry conviction. Nevertheless she would admit to nothing, either to acquaintance with the devil or
with Sarah Good. The magistrates made what they could
of her testimony, then had her removed and sent for Tituba.

5

Whatever Good and Osburne had tried to say had been
punctuated by yells and writhing on the part of the girls;
still, they had not been excessively tumultuous. But when
Tituba was set on the bar above them, they went into a
really frightful access of demoniac possession. And indeed

the devil in each of them had every reason for terror of what might come out if Tituba confined herself to the facts.

But Tituba had had some rough handling since Parris's discovery of the episode of the witch cake. Her master had been remorselessly at her to get the truth out of her, and yet the simple truth, so far as Tituba could now piece it together, was exactly what he would not accept. He would listen to no word which reflected discredit on his child whose pitiful outcries even now rang in his ears. When Tituba fell into sullen obduracy, he thrashed her. And he continued to thrash her until the terrified slave hit on the formula that pleased him.

When Tituba at last had painfully found the "truth" which would appease her master, she would in no wise depart from it. Thus when the trembling black woman took her place on the terrible eminence before her masters and began to respond to the questions of the magistrates in her own idiom and her slurred, Southern voice, a beautiful peace came over the courtroom. The girls, beside themselves at first, became quiet as so many sleeping babes. Not that they were asleep; on the contrary they were hanging with rapt attention on Tituba's every word; for Tituba was "confessing."

She was confessing, that is to say, within the frame of reference her betters had created for her. With her slave's adaptability, her only weapon, she caught at every cue the magistrates offered and enlarged on it. Presently she became subtly aware that she, the despised slave, was grasping something like power over these white-faced enemies. From the throng before her emanated something oddly like sympathy and admiration. All unwittingly she exercised the same spell over the people of Salem Village and even over the magistrates that she once had exercised over a pack of silly girls. All they wanted of her was what the girls had wanted. And Tituba was the one to give it to them.

Expanding in this unexpected warmth, this perverse geniality in the Puritan spirit, Tituba for three days told Salem Village exactly what it wanted to hear. Little by little she released every restraint upon a richly endowed imagination

—though she still kept her wily lookout for cues. And though what she did was instinctive and unpremeditated, had she deliberately plotted to avenge herself on a society that had enslaved and abused her, she could not have done better. For in her apparently witless wanderings she laid down a pattern which would wreck the peace of mind of Massachusetts for months and even years to come.

Against the etched silver and black of New England's waning winter, the private world of Tituba stood out in radiant relief. She talked to the court of red cats and red rats, and these cats and rats could talk and said to her, "Serve me." She told of a Thing she could describe only as "something like a cat"; it had a woman's face and it had wings, and it was Osburne's creature.

She talked most often of a tall man—not once was she trapped into mentioning the devil by name; the tall man came to her often and tempted her with "pretty things." Pretty things! The colours of the tropics blazed a moment in Tituba's mind as she looked out at this drab assembly and at the blanched faces, all exactly alike. When since the Barbados had she seen pretty things? There had been only the silken, honey-coloured hair of little Betty.

The things that Tituba had seen, the cats, the rats, the dogs, the hogs, all had one refrain. "They told me serve them and that was a good way." The tall man "he tell me he God and I must believe and serve him six years. . . . The first time I believe him God he was glad."

Service to these Things had involved various duties. The shapes wanted her to pinch the children. "I would not hurt Betty. I loved Betty. Then they haul me to pinch Betty and the next Abigail." Sometimes when she resisted such orders, Good and Osburne came too and forced her to obey. By such means had her spectral shape been made to go to the Griggs' home and pinch Betty Hubbard, and to attack Ann Putnam with a knife.

At this point everyone stole a sidelong glance at Ann, now sitting quiet and pale and staring up at Tituba spellbound. What a mercy of God that the child was still alive! The story had gone like wildfire through the village one night that the child was in her death throes, fighting off a witch who was trying to cut her head off, and all about her helpless because the witch was invisible to all but Ann. What a mercy that the child sat here unscathed and that the witch stood before her in humility and repentance so that her demons were bound and could no longer lay hands on innocent children. It was a Sign. The angel with healing in his wings now hovered over Salem Village; the end of this dreadful possession had come.

But if the devil had done, the magistrates had not; at least Hathorne had not. Corwin sat hunched over his notes, intent only on getting the facts straight; the court had hardly heard the sound of his voice. But Hathorne was determined not to let the case rest until he had exacted the last bit of information from Tituba.

This Tall Man, it had come out, had brought a book. What names were signed there? Tituba, who could not read, either spectrally or otherwise, searched her memory. Goody Good had done so, she said at last; her Shape had told her so; "but Goody Osburne would not tell. She was cross to me."

How many names had she seen in the book? At Tituba's answer a gasp went over the house, for Tituba had counted nine names. The case then was not yet closed. Who were these others? But only two of them had appeared to Tituba, and even these she could not name. One was the "Tall Man of Boston," whose face he had never let her see; another a woman she had noticed sometimes in Boston wearing a silk cloak and white hood.

Had there been witches' sabbaths? Oh yes, and Tituba had been to them. Transportation had been airborne and in company with the Man, a hog, two cats, and Osburne's sphinx-like familiar. But as to the time and place Tituba was vague. "I was going and then come back again. I never saw Boston. I never went to any town. I see no trees, no town."

Her testimony was unleashing new devils of suspicion on Salem Village. Even the girls, quiet during the early part of this examination, had during its recesses begun to whimper and moan again.

"Who hurts the children now?" demanded Hathorne.

But Tituba could not be tricked into forgetting her role as a brand plucked from the burning. "I am blind now. I cannot see." Second sight is not for a witch who has renounced her calling.

One thing she had accomplished. Had Osburne's yarn of being tormented by "something like an Indian—all black" been taken seriously it might have led to the arrest of John Indian. But so skilfully had Tituba drawn red herrings over this trail that the allusion was never thought of again. John Indian for his part saw the light. Hardly was the examination over than he succumbed to full demoniac possession, tumbling and rolling about the floor and roaring, as people said, "like a beef creature." Most often these fits came while he was at work in Ingersoll's ordinary, there being always a good audience there. And in his lucid intervals he was always ready to serve a stranger as a kind of guide to the witchcraft. John Indian took an honest pride in his position; not every man can boast of a witch for wife.

Meanwhile on 7 March the magistrates shipped their first haul of witches to Boston for safe keeping until the trial. The women could not have found much pleasure in each other's society, since each had been glibly accusing the other. The brief exhilaration of Tituba's gaudy day in court faded in the company of her resentful colleagues. The querulous voice of poor sick Sarah Osburne grew daily fainter until at last on 10 May she died. Sarah Good gave birth; just when, no one bothered to record. In fact for all the records show she may have brought a suckling babe to prison with her. All that interested the authorities was that she let the child die. Anyway it did die, the prison with its fetid air, its cold floors and its meagre fare serving ill as a crèche. But Sarah Good was left her pipe, and when good people of Boston came to the prison to look at the witches much as they might look at caged animals, she begged tobacco of them.

CHAPTER V

GOSPEL WITCH

Now that the witches had been detected and taken, most of Salem Village would gladly have been excused from hearing any more about the matter. Sap was rising in the sugar bush. The fields were thawing and drying out in the intermittent sun. It was time that sensible people turned their attention from the show which the devil had brought to town and got down to the real business of the year, to ploughing and planting.

Besides, there were some who from the first had had no patience with this notion of a witch hunt.

The pious Mrs Parris was not one of these, but she did protest successfully against making any further use of her little girl as a kind of spiritual bloodhound. Younger than the other girls, Betty had not their knack for coming out of possession refreshed and hale; on the contrary she had fallen into a truly piteous state, weeping, talking wildly, accusing herself as much as Tituba, almost as if the child supposed herself to be one of the witches.

Accordingly the mother prevailed on her husband to send the child out of reach of contagion, to Salem Town, to the home of Stephen Sewall, brother of Samuel. Here, removed from the thrilling events of the village, from the fatal solicitude of neighbours who dropped in hourly to question the girls and watch them for symptoms of possession, and above all from her companions in affliction, Betty slowly began to recover. Her new guardians were kind, they were prayerful, and for all that they were enormously impressed by her gifts, they were strict. Under their care Betty reverted little by little to the drab life of an ordinary little girl. It was duller that way, but it was safer.

If Mrs Parris's desire to protect her child was understandable, there were others whose aloofness from the whole affair could not always be so innocently accounted for. There were actually people who seemed not to believe in witches; or at least if they did not go to such atheistic lengths, they scouted the possibility that any such chimeras were indigenous to plain, workaday Salem Village. They proposed less mystical explanations for the afflictions of the girls. Even close connections of the girls shared this scepticism. It was rumoured that when Joseph Putnam, youngest brother of Sergeant Thomas, heard that the latter's daughter was beginning to prophesy and accuse, he went to the girl's mother.

"If you dare to touch with your foul lies anyone belonging to my household, you shall answer for it!" he was reported to have said. It was as if the man confounded the sacred revelation of spectral evidence with common gossip.

"Bitch witches" was the word old George Jacobs had for the afflicted girls, one of whom was his own maidservant, Sarah Churchill. John Procter, who had the prophesying Mary Warren on his hands, was reporting that he had cured her fits by plumping her down at her spinning-wheel and promising her a thrashing if she stirred from it, in or out of possession. It irritated him that after he had thus "cured" her, the magistrates had sent for the girl over his protest to testify in court where, as Procter drily remarked, "She must have her fits forsooth."

Even those props of the village church, Deacon Ingersoll, his wife, and his thirty-year-old spinster daughter Sarah, had some misgivings about the ethics of witchhunting. Their ordinary being the community centre, they were in a position to see and hear nearly everything that went on. When John Indian was not underfoot, it was one of the girls. Little Abigail in particular now asked nothing better of life than to escape from the parsonage to perform before whoever happened to be in the ordinary, especially if they were men. Although the Ingersolls were unfailingly gentle with so young a child, they kept a sharp eye on the older members of the sorority and did not hesitate to reprove them when they irresponsibly bandied respected names. The girls responded meekly. One of them in a later crisis was to find that Sarah Ingersoll was the only person she dared confide in.

Out in the farmlands, not far from the home of the Procters, lived Martha Cory, who, exposed to her first view of demoniac possession, simply threw her head back and laughed. Such levity gave offence, and it gave more when it was learned that Martha had tried to restrain her husband Giles from going down with the rest of the village to watch the examinations. This Giles was even at eighty a great powerful brute of a man, slow of comprehension, but quick of temper, and so born to trouble as the sparks fly upward; his life had been punctuated by lawsuits and worse. So Martha had tried to keep him home. When words failed to dissuade him, she used her wits. She took the saddle from his horse and hid it.

"But," as she wryly commented later, "he went for all that."

2

These people, and a great many whose motives were above all suspicion, would have thanked God when Tituba's examination finally ended on 5 March if that were the end of witchcraft. That it could not be, however, every thinking person was uneasily aware. Tituba's testimony had put Hathorne in the position of a district attorney who, supposing that he has closed a case with the apprehension of certain malefactors, discovers that the latter are unimportant representatives of a powerful gang still at large and unidentified.

Though the magistrates no longer held court for a space, everyone knew that they were by no means idle. They were conferring with Noyes and Parris and the afflicted girls. "Who afflicts thee?" they were again asking; and now with special urgency, "What tall man of Boston hath appeared to thee?" But again the girls, though distressed at intervals, were dumb, or at least inarticulate, especially on the subject of the tall man from Boston. Few of them had been so far afield—Tituba was far more of a cosmopolite than they—and even the elder Ann Putnam was little versed in Boston gossip.

Their silence was baffling, for to the magistrates the existence of a wizard in Boston was the most disturbing aspect of the case. At any cost he must be found and brought to justice, were he of high or low degree, and in running him down they had only these poor girls to aid them.

Friday, 11 March, was observed in Salem Village as a day of fasting and prayer. Again the ministers of the North Shore came down to consult with Parris, and to pray with his distressed flock. And so mightily did they wrestle with the angel of the Lord that the eyes of one of the girls were again opened to the invisible world. Ann Putnam saw and named another witch, and people gasped at the name. It was, to everyone's disappointment, not a tall man of Boston, but a local woman, and this time not a tramp or slave but a respectable matron, a member of the congregation in good standing and a tireless attendant of meeting. It was, in fact, Martha Cory.

3

The natural enemies of the feminine teen-agers were, as has been reported, the older matrons and the dowagers. Many of these were stalwart countrywomen, used to lifting heavy loads, to planting their big feet in muck, to assisting in the birthing of cows and the slaughter of pigs. Their buttocks were broad and their hands were coarse, and since they lived close to the sources of life, so on occasion was their speech. The latter-day caricature of your prim, mealy-mouthed Puritan had not yet been invented. There was nothing at all Victorian about the countrywomen of Salem Village.

Young girls, still on the threshold of the biological experience that these matrons knew so lustily and well, or else,

as seems probable from the later record of some of them,
getting furtively and sinfully what their elders enjoyed lawfully, shrank from the pitilessly realistic appraisal in the eyes
of the latter. "She'll be over it when she takes to wearing
clouts." "Get her a man and the wench'll settle down." Such
comments were an intolerable invasion of the privacy of the
very young. One is never more delicately an individual than
in the teens, or more resentful of crude generalizations that
ignore the precious individuality.

Martha Cory was just such a countrywoman, and she
was, to boot, a stout professor of the faith. Though it was
only a year since she had been received into the village
congregation from her former communion in Salem Town,
she was already a personage. But not too popular a personage. Opinionated, outspoken, Martha Cory had the misfortune of being always right, and no one ever forgives that.
In this crisis, however, she had at last put herself in the
wrong. Her scepticism about the whole course of the witchcraft was said to border on downright heresy. Neighbours
had been muttering about her already, and when Ann in a
vision clearly identified her as a witch they said, "I told
you so."

Nevertheless, as an "old professor" and a constant attendant at meeting, Martha Cory had to be given special
consideration. Accordingly on the afternoon following the
day of fasting, Edward Putnam and Ezekiel Cheever set
out to have a private word with her. Before they did so
they took a precaution; they asked Ann to take a good look
at Martha's spectral shape and tell them what she had on,
this being in the interest of correct identification. But not
for nothing had Ann been Tituba's disciple. Her tranced
eyes strained into nowhere; then she shook her head.

"I am blind now; I cannot see." Ann explained that the
wily Martha, perfectly aware that she was about to be interviewed and for what purpose, had cast this spell on her.

They found Martha alone in the kitchen. She looked up
at them from her spinning-wheel and smiled.

"I know what you have come for," said she, and there
was in her tone and smile that note of mockery that had

got her disliked. "You are come to talk to me about being a witch."

Martha had always had an annoying trick of taking the words out of one's mouth. Her visitors, who, whatever their suspicions, had come only anxious to be fair, to warn her, and talk things over with her reasonably, wished that this once Martha could have resisted that temptation. After what Ann had told them such a remark was disturbingly like clairvoyance.

But in the next breath Martha incriminated herself beyond redemption.

"Did she tell you what clothes I have on?" Her visitors could only look at her. "Well, did she tell you?" insisted Martha.

Curtly they admitted to the details of their conversation with Ann. Confronted with their damning implications surely an innocent woman would have been stricken. But Martha actually laughed, and then sat smiling at them "as if," they reported later, "she had showed us a pretty trick."

They had not, however, come to crack jokes with Martha. They brought up their business; sternly they pointed out to her the dishonour that would come upon the church if one of its members were proved a witch. Martha became serious too. She had had her bellyfull of loose talk going on about her, she said, of being put on by malicious gossip. What did they as fellow professors of the faith propose to do to stop the mouths of scandalmongers?

Cheever and Putnam looked at the woman with mounting aversion. All their earlier doubts in her favour were being destroyed by her mockery, by her wicked prescience. Her present display of righteousness they found insufferable. And now, as if this were not enough, Martha gave way to undisguised blasphemy.

"I do not believe that there are witches," she said.

She could say that, they asked, when three proved witches had already been taken in the parish?

Martha might have with justice replied that the witchhood of these three had by no means been proved. Legally Tituba and her companions could not be held guilty until the trial had taken place and a jury had found them so. But Martha, for all her intelligence, had no better acquaintance with jurisprudence than any other Puritan. She too confused examination with trial.

"Well, if they are," she said, still with that irritating smile, "I could not blame the devil for making witches of them, for they are idle slothful persons and minded nothing that was good." But what, she demanded, did such people have to do with her, a professor of the faith, a gospel woman?

"Woman, outward profession of faith cannot save you!"

Outraged, the visitors left her. It had been worse than they feared, and now they had no compunctions about her. The sooner the body of the church was cleared of this corrupt branch the better. Why, she was worse than Sarah Good, worse than Osburne; they, at least, though unrepentant had not denied the reality of witchcraft. In all Salem Village they knew no one capable of such outright atheism.

On 19 March a warrant was sworn out for Martha's arrest. That day, however, fell on a Saturday, and it was not until Monday that she was actually taken. So it came about that she was able to astound meetings of the Sunday with a prodigious display of her craft.

4

Deodat Lawson, minister in Salem Village after George Burroughs, preached at both these meetings. He had come down from Boston to observe the plague that had broken out in his former parish and to investigate a report that the girls had information that his wife and daughter, dead these three years, had been done to death by sorcery.

He reached the village early Saturday afternoon, put up at Ingersoll's ordinary, and at once began his investigations. Mary Walcott was there and a witch was biting her: Lawson heard her shriek and on her invitation examined her wrists by candlelight. It was true; he could see the marks plainly. But Lawson was a cautious man, and when he recorded his observation of the toothmarks in the notes he began to take at once, he took pains to insert the word "apparently."

During the evening he went to the parsonage for a consultation with Parris. Once in the house, however, it was nearly impossible to do anything but look at Abigail, who was in full possession. He found the child running through the house saying "Whish! Whish!" and flapping her arms in an attempt to fly.

When he thought to settle down with Parris, ignoring the child awhile, there being women to tend her and the fluttering and whishing a comparatively harmless type of diabolism, the child froze his attention upon herself by going into a dramatic and ominous bit of shadow play.

A Shape had entered the room. None but the child could see it, though everyone looked to where Abigail's round eyes were focused. And when the child called it by name, Lawson's heart misgave him, for this was not Tituba nor Osburne nor even Goody Cory, but a woman he had admired and even revered for her charity—for her seeming charity.

"Do you not see her? Why, there she stands!" shrilled the child. And now Lawson, really aghast, not at all inclined to make mental reservations involving the word "apparently," saw the child strain to push an invisible and dreadful object away from her.

"I won't! I won't! Oh, I won't!" yelled Abigail. "I am sure it is none of God's book! It is the devil's book for all I know!"

With his own eyes he saw a human soul in the very act of resisting the devil, or anyway the devil's disciple. Heroic little girl, how she fought, and how helpless they were to rescue her from the agonies with which the hellish Shape punished her resistance. How marvellous was God's providence that to a little child it was given to fight for them all, beating off the power of darkness with her own fists.

Presently Abigail lost all control of her actions. She ran into the fireplace, came out with firebrands and hurled them about the house. Then she dashed back and tried to fly up the chimney.

Lawson came hollow-eyed to the pulpit next morning;

he had been on his knees half the night, wrestling with the
angel, imploring God's mercy and his blessing on this poor
village which the devil had cursed, imploring that God
save harmless these little ones, these innocent children who
were the commonwealth's sole bulwark against diabolism.
"Suffer little children," the Lord had said. How true it was
now, and how clear that of such indeed was the Kingdom
of Heaven.

Part of this prayer was answered, for Abigail came to
meeting in the morning holding fast to the hand of her
aunt, rosy and cheerful after a sound night's sleep. She
walked down the aisle with eyes downcast, ignoring with
the modesty of the truly great the looks of awe that her
elders were casting her way.

But when Lawson strode up to the pulpit, and standing
there let his eye rove over the congregation, he saw what
appalled him. The Witch Cory had also come to meeting.
In full knowledge that on the morrow she would stand here
in ignominy facing a hellish charge, the woman had come
to church and taken her place among good Christians.
That she should dare so much was an affront to all decency. The congregation could hardly keep its eyes off her;
the afflicted girls were all but forgotten in the scandal of
her temerity, but not for long. Martha could have come
only for the express purpose of defying God before his very
altar. Now, before the eyes of the congregation, she began
to work on the children. Invisibly of course; all that the
naked eye could see was the sturdy bulk of the woman sitting upright and quiet as any decent body; but all the while
her incorporeal essence, her Shape, darted among the children, pinching and choking.

The poor girls wailed so piteously that Lawson could
hardly get through his first prayer. And after the psalm was
sung, Abigail was beside herself.

"Now stand up and name your text!" There was authority in her clear voice. Every face in the congregation turned
to gape at her. Martha alone looked straight ahead of her,
and even now the woman had the effrontery to smile. The
minister, looking tenderly down at Abigail, obeyed her. "It's

a long text!" sneered Abigail, or at least the devil in her sneered.

Lawson entered his sermon, but the tricksy sprites released by Martha Cory would not let him preach in peace. He was hardly well launched when the spirit rather unexpectedly descended upon a hitherto inconspicuous young matron, Mrs Gertrude Pope.

"Now there's enough of that!" rapped out the young woman to the parson.

Not even the Quakers had often dared make more disturbance in meeting, and they had been hanged for it. Yet not a hand was laid on the children and the matron. The minister looked at them sorrowfully and went on as best he could. The young people knew not what they did; one could only pray. Perhaps there would be peace at the afternoon service if Martha did not come.

But Martha did come. There was indeed no way of keeping her out. The warrant had not been served and could not be served on a Sabbath, and until it was, whatever the mockery of the situation, Martha had as good a right as any to take her place in meeting. Useless to reason with the woman or appeal to what a witch might have of a sense of propriety. Martha affected to believe that she was doing God and Salem Village a service by her presence here.

"I will open the eyes of the magistrates and the ministers," the woman had retorted when they reminded her that she must return to this place to-morrow to stand before her accusers.

So Witch Cory returned and sat on her bench, square-set and immovable as a rock, ignoring the children, ignoring the sidelong glances of her neighbours. But she was paid for it this time; she was publicly exposed.

"Look!" rang out the voice of Abigail suddenly. "There sits Goody Cory on the beam suckling a yellow bird betwixt her fingers."

Eyes shifted from the massive substance of Goody Cory on her bench to the beam overhead where her Shape sat swinging its stout legs. As was to be expected, most people saw nothing more incriminating than a cobweb. The sharp

eyes of Ann Putnam picked her up, however, and saw the
bird flutter from the beam to the minister's hat hanging on
its peg in the pulpit. She whispered this observation to her
neighbours and jumped up to make the announcement
public. She was pulled down and hushed. A craving for
order was beginning to assert itself even among the Putnams. These were subtly aware of the sentiments of people
who blamed the disorder less on Goody Cory than on the
girls and their parents. In any case not even the inspired
Abigail interrupted the parson thereafter.

5

After such a prelude the good people of Salem Village
made sure of their seats early Monday morning, and when
at noon the magistrates arrived from town, accompanied by
Nicholas Noyes, the house was full. The officials took their
places and summoned the defendant.

Martha, escorted by the constables, came down the aisle
and mounted to the bar. There was nothing cowed about
this woman; she turned to the magistrates confidently, as
if she had actually looked forward to this opportunity of
expressing herself about current events. She had every intention of taking the offensive in this examination, and to
this end, after the Reverend Nicholas Noyes had opened
the meeting with "a very pertinent and pathetic prayer,"
Martha asked leave to pray too. As every minister knows,
a prayer is a superb device for airing an opinion.

The magistrates did not fall into the trap; curtly they
told her that they were here not to hear her pray but to
examine her, and Hathorne went at once to the point. He
did not even ask for her plea; what with the girls yelping
on the front benches, such a query was superfluous. He
simply asked her why she afflicted them.

"I don't afflict them," said Martha.

"Who doth?"

"I do not know. How should I know?"

She added, her self-righteousness asserting itself, that

what they accused her of would be impossible to her. "I am a gospel woman."

"She's a gospel witch!" screamed out one of the children. All the pack took up the cry. "Gospel witch! Gospel witch!" And there was pandemonium and such earsplitting racket that Hathorne waited for it to quiet down. Presently out of the tumult came the clear voice of little Ann Putnam testifying. She herself at her father's house had seen Goody Cory and another praying to the devil. That was where Goody Cory directed her prayers.

The girls had fallen quiet to listen. In this rare lull the magistrates turned to Martha and Martha to the magistrates.

"Nay," she said to them, "we must not believe these distracted children."

The dry reasonableness of the remark affronted Hathorne. Distracted children, he exclaimed; who then distracted them? Let anyone who had eyes look and see. Indeed the answer was only too plain. Even while Martha proclaimed her innocence her devils had not been able to resist devising new tortures for the girls. What Martha did now they all did. If she shifted her feet they did so too, and fell to stamping with such force as to rock the meetinghouse. If she bit her lips, they yelled that she had bitten theirs, and came running up to the magistrates to show how they bled.

"What's the harm in it?" asked Martha when they ordered her to stop biting her lips.

Wearied, the prisoner leaned against the minister's seat; the motion sent such a tearing pain through Mrs Pope's bowels that she flung her muff at Martha, and missing, threw her shoe and fetched her a clout on the side of the head.

The girls' eyes and ears opened and they saw and heard that which the rest of the assembly shuddered to think about. One saw the Black Man whispering in the ear of Martha. The ears of others picked up the throb of a spectral drum, and when they looked out the window they saw the witches of all Essex County assembling to take their unblessed sacrament before the very meeting-house.

"Don't you hear the drum beat?" cried one. "Why don't you go, gospel witch? Why don't you go too?"

Good people sat shivering in the audience, hardly daring to let their eyes shift to the windows. The situation was getting frightful past bearing. Though Tituba had referred to witches' sabbaths, she had been vague about the place. Who could have dreamed that it would be here—and now; that the devil had grown so bold that he could marshal his own before a consecrated house at the exact moment when the forces of light were assembled within to give him battle?

Yet what was really appalling was the question of who might be out there on the church lawn serving the devil. The witch-hunt had seemed simple enough when it was a question of the three derelicts who had first appeared. Now the problem was assuming incalculable dimensions. No degree of respectability could be proof against suspicion now. Look at Martha Cory there on the platform; outspoken as she was, she had not been liked; yet until now few had connected her with witchcraft. Look at the one whom Ann Putnam had named in court to-day, one outwardly so gentle that it seemed impossible she could be guilty. Perhaps they had heard Ann wrong; perhaps Ann herself had mistaken the Shape.

Yet witches rioted on the lawns outside the meeting-house, and they were witches still unnamed and untaken. God guide these magistrates to find them!

The magistrates propounded to Martha some questions out of the catechism. Her answer about the godhead struck the attentive Lawson as odd, but, a scrupulous man, he remarked afterward that there was "no great thing to be gathered from it."

Martha's great blundering husband Giles was called to testify. He faced the judges in unwonted humility; within the year he had been received into Noyes's church in Salem Town, and he took his devotions seriously. Besides, ever since that business of Martha's hiding his saddle to keep

him from the examinations, he was inclined to think that
there was something in what people said of her. He answered Hathorne carefully, trying his clumsy best to report
the exact truth of what he knew of Martha. The truth,
however, was unimpressive, unconvincing even, in a setting
like this. What it boiled down to was that Giles found it
hard to pray when Martha was about and was in turn
bothered by her own fluency in prayer. Once he had found
her late at night kneeling mysteriously silent on the hearth
and could make nothing of it. Neither, when he reported
the incident, could the magistrates.

Rather contemptuously they dismissed him, and a rustle
of speculation went over the house. What was the old man
concealing? Might not his very stupidity be a mask for
something else?

"You can't prove me a witch!" cried Martha before she
was led away to prison to be held for trial. But such a statement was beside the point. What she couldn't prove, what
no one at all accused of such a thing could prove, was that
she wasn't.

6

Martha Cory had hardly time to acquaint herself with
her new surroundings and the questionable society of Good,
Osburne and Tituba, before she was joined by an uncom-
monly small witch, Dorcas Good, five-year-old daughter of
the pipe-smoking Sarah. Her Shape, it seemed, had been
running about the country like a little mad dog, biting the
girls in return for what they had done to her mother. So a
warrant was duly sworn, the child, a "hale and well looking girl," fetched in from Benjamin Putnam's by Constable
Braybrook, and off to prison she went. She would come out
of it eventually; five-year-old witches were not hanged,
anyway not in Massachusetts, but she would not come out
"hale and well looking," or ever be so again.

CHAPTER VI

"WHAT SIN UNREPENTED OF?"

A day or so before Martha Cory's examination, Israel and Elizabeth Porter, man and wife, both comfortably well along in middle age, saddled a horse at their home at the head of Frost Fish River and plodded down the muddy lanes to call on an ailing neighbour.

The Porters were of the local gentry; at least Elizabeth was, since she was the sister of Magistrate Hathorne. They were also connected with the Putnam family; young Joseph Putnam, the same who had the audacity to intimate that common gossip was playing a large part in the witch-hunt, was their son-in-law.

The couple rode south on the Ipswich Road as far as Orchard Farm, and then turned sharp right into an intersection. There was something symbolic about the sharpness of this turn. It carried them away from the old gentry as represented by Orchard Farm, still in the hands of the distinguished Endicott family, into what might be called the new gentry, the four sons and four daughters of old Francis and Rebecca Nurse, who among them were cultivating a farm of three hundred fine rolling acres which had been cut off from Orchard Farm, and who had established there so self-sufficient a little community as to constitute almost a village within the village.

Not that anyone in Salem Village was likely to refer to the Nurses as "gentry." Old Francis had been a simple yeoman like any other—he was a traymaker by trade—and some felt that he had gone beyond himself in attaining to such estate. Indeed he had not yet really attained it. He and his sons and his sons-in-law were in the process of buying it in twenty yearly instalments from the Reverend James Allen. They had begun in 1678 and now in 1692 they had six more years to go before the title was theirs. The family, working together like soldiers, had prospered, had never defaulted on a payment; there was no doubt of their eventual ownership. Yet villagers could not bring themselves to speak of the "Nurse place." It was always, even in court records, "the Allen property." Though social mobility upward, to adopt the ponderous modern phrase, had been going on in Massachusetts since its settlement, as a concept it was not yet fully recognized. On the contrary the Puritan tendency was to support old English tradition by a belief that God had ordained the class structure and meant that people should stay at approximately the level where He placed them at birth. Accordingly, though no one could deny that the Nurses were decent, God-fearing people, their conspicuous prosperity had something questionable about it; their cheerful self-sufficiency could be and was resented.

Their progress had not been without its difficulties. Orchard Farm, flanking the creek called Cow House River, was still occupied by old Zerubel Endicott, and the latter intensely objected to the presence of a community of *arrivistes* established within sight of his own home. What was particularly galling was that the land was by right Endicott property. Allen had got possession of it by marrying an Endicott woman who died soon after. A decent man, so felt old Endicott, would have found a way of getting the land back to the family instead of opening it to strangers. He found a chance to express himself on the subject when he discovered that a wood-lot in the north-west corner of Orchard Farm was also included in the Allen claim. When he caught the Nurses cutting wood in the overlapping land, he sent his men to drive them off and brought suit against Allen. The Nurses could leave the suit to their landlord, but the right to cut wood they defended in their own way. There had been at least one brawl in the wood-lot, and though it was of no great consequence, it caused talk and confirmed people in their opinion that the Nurses were getting above themselves.

The battle of the wood-lot, the lawsuit itself, were old history by March 1692. The Porters had not come to discuss land claims; they had come to discuss the welfare of Rebecca Nurse, seventy-one-year-old matriarch of the Nurse family.

Rebecca was in the eyes of those who knew her well the very essence of what a Puritan mother should be. Deeply pious, she was so steeped in Scripture that the country roughness of her speech—she had a Chaucerian fondness for triple negatives—was often shot through with a poetical Scriptural quality. It was not merely a matter of lugging in texts, but a deep, instinctive poetry of feeling that overflowed into her simple, pregnant speech. When Rebecca spoke it was as if one of the grand women of the Old Testament were speaking, Naomi or Ruth amid alien corn (Rebecca herself remembered her birthplace, Yarmouth, England), or the beloved Rachel, or indeed her own namesake.

In her home life she had resembled the wise woman of Proverbs, and her children she had reared with loving devotion to both their spiritual and temporal welfare. Now in her old age they rose up and called her blessed, not only her four sons and four daughters, but what was perhaps the supremest tribute, her three sons-in-law and four daughters-in-law.

This is not to say that she was altogether a saint. Even the Bible women, as anyone can discover by examining Scripture closely, had their off-days. The years had made Rebecca hard of hearing and infirm; when she was ill and did not clearly understand what was said to her, she could sometimes lose her temper. It happened rarely, but the Porters could remember a fairly recent occasion when a neighbour's hogs had got into her precious flax garden and Rebecca had flown out at the neighbour in terms not distinguished for their charity. Uneasily the Porters remembered also that the neighbour had died soon after and that his wife had never stopped talking about the coincidence,

as if there were some sort of cause and effect involved. Yet
what was really remarkable about the event was its rarity
with Rebecca. What man or woman had not sometimes
flown out at an irritating neighbour?

2

A row of lilacs grew tall by the side of the fine old house
where Francis and Rebecca lived. So early in the spring
there were no blossoms, but the buds already showed green,
and on the brown lawn by the tall well-sweep a robin
bobbed and chuckled.

The visitors dismounted at the front of the house. They
paused to admire the fine old oak door, studded with nail
heads, and the sundial carved into the wall above it. The
dial bore the initials T.B. and the date 1636; this was the
Townsend Bishop house, one of the oldest and nearly the
finest in the parish. God had blessed Rebecca and Francis
when He gave them so manorial a shelter in their old age.
Or had He? The Porters remembered their errand and almost dreaded the opening of the door by Sarah, the un-
married daughter.

Usually at this hour Rebecca would be astir by the enormous fireplace in the broad kitchen. She would be bending
over her pots or winding the flax she raised herself, or rock-
ing a cradle. There was always a new baby in her family,
and in old age Rebecca's arms still craved the soft feel of
baby bodies, so she was always finding an excuse to borrow
a grandchild for the day.

But to-day none of this activity was in progress. Mother
lay ill upstairs, Sarah told them softly. She looked at them
keenly; she knew why they had come, for the Nurses were
not so self-sufficient as to be ignorant of gossip; but she
knew also that they had come in charity. She waited only
until Rebecca's brother-in-law, Peter Cloyce, and a friend,
Daniel Andrews, could be fetched to serve as witnesses in
the forthcoming interview—the clan would not under present circumstances permit even a friend to speak to Rebecca

without their protection—and guided the party up the narrow, twisting hall stairs into Rebecca's chamber.

Rebecca lay flat in bed, her eyes fixed on the little fireplace in the inside wall. It was built into the same great chimney as the kitchen hearth beneath her, and since her room was just under the eaves, on bright days when the sun stood exactly right, sunlight fell through the chimney upon the firedogs. This was a day of shifting sun and shadow. Rebecca, her eyes upon the hearth, watched the sunbeams come and go.

Deaf as she was, intent as she was, she did not hear the approach of her guests. They looked down at her a moment unobserved. She had been ill several days with a stomach complaint; her hands laid on the patchwork quilt in unwonted idleness were waxy white and wasted; so was her soft, crumpled old face. "Weak and low" as she was, had they done right to come on such an errand? Might it not be better to go away with nothing said and leave Rebecca to the vigilant care of her children?

But when Rebecca saw them her face lighted up. She let Elizabeth prop her up on the pillows and eagerly inquired for the news of the day. How was it now with the afflicted children, she asked, and sighed when they guardedly told her. Poor little girls; she blamed herself for not having been to them in their distress, but besides the fact that she had been ill these "seven-eight" days she was a little afraid to do so "by reason of fits that I formerly used to have."

Her visitors were watching her closely. Did she know why they had come? Was there in her any of that fatal prescience that Martha Cory had shown in a similar interview? No, there was not the least sign. Whenever two or three were gathered together in Salem Village nowadays, the subject always turned to the afflicted girls. Rebecca spoke as anyone might speak.

"I go to God for them," she said softly. Then she stared into the little fireplace where the sunlight flickered again.

"But I am troubled, oh I am troubled at some of their crying out. Some of the persons they have spoken of are, as I believe, as innocent as I."

The Porters looked quickly at each other, then at Rebecca's kin. The time had come to speak plainly. Rebecca herself had been "cried out" on; Ann Putnam had named her first, but hesitantly, as if not quite sure; then another had picked up the scent until now the pack was in full cry. When Abigail Williams had in Deodat Lawson's presence thrust the "devil's book" from her, it was the Shape of Rebecca whom the child saw holding it out to her.

All this they explained to Rebecca, but not without difficulty, for it was hard to keep their voices steady, and besides Rebecca not alone from deafness but from amazement found it hard to grasp what they were trying to tell her.

"Well, if it be so, the will of the Lord be done," said the old woman, and from her tone and the look in her eyes, they knew she understood at last.

She sat a moment stricken beyond speech, staring ahead of her almost as if she were tranced. Then words welled up from the heart of her simplicity, piety and grief.

"As to this thing I am innocent as the child unborn," said Rebecca, "but surely, what sin hath God found in me unrepented of that He could lay such an affliction on me in my old age?"

The Porters were too deeply moved to reply. It was with them as with Pilate with Christ; they could find no fault in her. But they would not like Pilate wash their hands of her; as they went back to the horse, their hearts sore with pity for what lay ahead for one so gentle, they agreed to make a record of their impression and present it to court as testimony for Rebecca.

They did so, and Daniel Andrews and Peter Cloyce witnessed it for them. There were good and brave people in Salem Village still. It was beginning to take courage to gainsay any statement made by the delirious Ann Putnam, junior or senior.

3

During Martha Cory's examination, Rebecca Nurse's name had been bandied about before two or three hundred witnesses as freely as if she were already at the bar. Accordingly no one was surprised when the following day, 23 March, a warrant was issued for her arrest. What was surprising was that one outwardly so harmless should be accused of such multifarious criminal activities. All the time that Rebecca's physical part had lain helpless in bed, her Shape had flown about the country abusing nearly every girl on the roster of affliction, and adding for good measure one Sarah Bibber, a scandalmongering matron who had been hovering at the edge of "the circle" from the first, watching for her chance to be admitted as a practising seeress.

Even this was not all. What the elder Ann Putnam had lately seen was truly dreadful; if she could prove her charges, Rebecca would be convicted not alone of sorcery but of murder.

Yet when this culprit took her stand at the bar on the morning of 24 March, there was that about her which moved even Magistrate Hathorne to compassion—and to doubt. She was, poor witch, so very old and so frail, hardly able to stand after her illness, and yet so patient as she strained her ears to grasp what was required of her. Besides, the magistrate's sister had been talking to him.

Tremulously Rebecca made her plea.

"I can say before my eternal father that I am innocent, and God will clear my innocence."

"Here is never a one in the assembly but desires it," said Hathorne, and not before had he addressed a witch so kindly. "But if you be guilty, I pray God discover you."

The testimony began. Goodman Kenny reported that once when she came to his house he had been seized with "an amazed condition"; Edward Putnam that she had tortured his niece in his presence.

"I am innocent and clear and have not been able to get

out of doors these eight-nine days," said Rebecca to this. "I never afflicted no child, no, never in my life."

Who could look at Rebecca and not believe her? Hathorne gave way to his misgivings. Could not these children have made a mistake? As late as Monday Ann Putnam had not been sure that it was Rebecca whom she saw.

"Are you," he asked, "an innocent person relating to this witchcraft?"

He was answered immediately, unmistakably, and not by Rebecca. One of the girls fell into convulsions, and then another, and then all the girls together set up such a "hideous screitch and noise" that Deodat Lawson, who had left the meeting-house after the preliminaries to work on the Lecture Day sermon he was to deliver that afternoon, heard it at a distance and was amazed. Within the meeting-house among the spectators there was more than amazement; there was panic. An infection of demonism was running across the whole assembly; people shrank back from the touch and look of neighbours, no longer sure who was witch and who bewitched.

Above the clamour shrilled the voice of the elder Ann Putnam. "Did you not bring the Black Man with you? Did you not bid me tempt God and die? How often have you eat and drunk to your own damnation?"

It took some time for the uproar to subside enough for Hathorne to proceed, and it was ample time for him to repent his moment of weakness.

"What do you say to them?" he demanded.

It was doubtful if Rebecca heard him. Even Parris, who had taken the office of secretary to-day, was finding it impossible to distinguish among the manifold cries and accusations and to set them down in order.

"Oh, Lord help me!" cried poor Rebecca and spread her hands helplessly. Her very gestures became an accusation against her, for the girls immediately spread theirs, and thereafter whatever move Rebecca made they duplicated. Watching the devil's choreography, the most impartial spectator could no longer credit Rebecca's plea of innocence. Words may lie, but deeds cannot. Before the very eyes of the court, she was demonstrating her witchcraft.

Hathorne, looking at her closely, saw further evidence of guilt. Would not an innocent woman weep before such a scene, as many women were weeping throughout the auditorium? Yet Rebecca was not; there was a reason for this; tears are not possible to a witch.

"It is awful for all to see these agonies," said the magistrate very slowly and distinctly to arrest the woman's dazed attention, "and you an old professor thus charged with the devil by the effects of it, and yet to see you stand with dry eyes when there are so many wet."

"You do not know my heart," whispered Rebecca.

"You would do well if you were guilty to confess. Give glory to God."

But Rebecca, frail as she was, wavering at the stand, yet possessed the Puritan's steadfastness. She would not seek the solution already discovered by Tituba; she would not confess. She was "clear as the child unborn." She had no wounds, "none but old age"; she had no familiar spirit, "none but God alone."

"Would you have me belie myself?" she asked.

Hathorne read her the most serious charge, that which the elder Ann had sworn to. It was no matter of pinching and biting; it was murder. Little children in their winding sheets had been appearing to Ann, calling her aunt, telling her dreadful things; it was Witch Nurse who had done them to death.

"What think you of this?"

"I cannot tell what to think." But the intelligence as well as the courage of Rebecca was asserting itself; she gave voice to a hypothesis which would not in the end be forgotten. "The devil may appear in my shape."

"They accuse you of hurting them, and if you think it is . . . by design, you must look on them as murderers."

But nothing could shake the denial of Rebecca. Towards noon Hathorne ordered her led away, for the meeting-house had to be made ready for the Lecture Day sermon that Lawson was to preach in the afternoon. Parris gathered up his notes and in the peace of his study began to put them together. It was a thankless task; he was an able and diligent secretary, but there had been so many interruptions in this examination, and above all such uncontrolled commotion, that he despaired of ever getting them complete or in the right order.

4

Ploughing was getting off to a slow start in Salem Village; there was too much else to do. On Monday most of the community had neglected work to listen to Martha Cory's defence. Now on Thursday they had returned to hear the examination of Rebecca Nurse. When court adjourned at noon many flocked to Ingersoll's ordinary to gossip over cider and cakes; others spread picnic lunches in Parris's pasture, but almost none went back to work. The Lecture Day sermon would be too solemn an event to miss. The magistrates were staying over to attend it. Several ministers had come from neighbouring towns, and of course the afflicted girls would be present. The drama of the previous Sabbath raised high expectations of the part they would play in the service. A few villagers, unable to bear more, decided on second thought to go home; some of these, mostly Rebecca's kin, even resented the pastor's failure to control manifestations of diabolism in the House of God. But the majority stayed and took their places in meeting in a blend of dread and anticipation.

Yet after all, the service was quiet and seemly. The girls, at peace again now that the newest witch had been carted off to Salem Prison, and not visibly the worse from their painful experience of the morning, sat as decently as any. If there was any drama at all it came from the pulpit.

Lawson had chosen a thundering text, Zechariah iii, 2: "And the Lord said unto Satan, the Lord rebuke thee, O Satan. Even the Lord that hath chosen Jerusalem rebuke thee. Is not this a brand plucked from the burning?"

It was a stirring text and consoling. Salem itself, first of the cities of the wilderness, was the Jerusalem which the Lord had chosen; the Lord would not abandon His own to Satan; He would rebuke and destroy the terrible adversary.

Lawson reminded them of the nature of Satan, who, though a spirit, was still fortified by the power he retained from his late angelic estate, and could torture the body. In carrying out this purpose, however, he needed human mediums; these he sought among "the adopted children of God . . . for it is certain that he never works more like the Prince of Darkness than when he looks most like an angel of light."

He saw heads nod in agreement throughout the congregation. Lawson had hit on the answer to the question that had most troubled the devout: how was it that those who had been considered true professors of the faith, Martha Cory and Rebecca Nurse, could be guilty of this thing? It became perfectly clear when one thought it over; what could Satan hope to accomplish with slaves and tramps whom no one respected? If his aim was to undermine the whole community he would naturally work with his whole force upon the respectable and outwardly devout. What pressure he must have exerted to seduce these poor women, and what a pity that he had so hardened their hearts that not even Rebecca could be induced to confess!

"You are therefore to be deeply humbled and set down in the dust, considering the signal hand of God in singling out this place, this poor village, for the first scene of Satan's tyranny, and to make it (as 'twere) the rendezvous of devils. . . .

"I thus am commanded to call and cry . . . to you. Arm! Arm! Arm! Let us admit no parley, give no quarter. Prayer is the most proper and potent antidote against the old Serpent's venomous operations. . . . What therefore I say unto one I say unto all—Pray! Pray! Pray!"

The sermon made so deep an impression and Lawson thought so well of it that, taking a leaf from the book of the print-hungry Cotton Mather, he sent it out for publication along with a "brief and true narrative" of the witch case which he had been compiling during his visit.

Yet not everyone was converted to Lawson's view. John Procter, coming to town Friday morning to pick up his "jade," Mary Warren, whom he had again been forced to let attend an examination, gave voice to some very strong and very public remarks about the girls.

"They should be at the whipping-post!" he said. "If they are let alone we should all be devils and witches."

In his eyes the wrong people were being called to the stand. If one must have witches forsooth, look for them not among decent women of good reputations but among the obviously bedevilled, the girls themselves.

"Hang them! Hang them!" shouted honest John Procter.

You can't say things like that. Not in public, not in Salem Village of 1692.

CHAPTER VII

JOHN PROCTER'S JADE

Rebecca Nurse was the eldest of three sisters who were still sometimes referred to in the aggregate as the "Towne girls." The other two sisters, considerably Rebecca's junior, were both matrons of vigorous character. Mary, wife of Isaac Esty, lived in Topsfield, and Sarah, wife of Peter Cloyce, was a villager and attended the village church.

The church had, however, seen little of Sarah or any of Rebecca's other kinsmen since her arrest. The attitude of both Parris and Noyes had alienated the family of the accused. Both pastors had an interest in the case, Noyes because she was nominally still a member of his congregation, Parris because since Rebecca's removal from Salem Town she had found it more convenient to attend meeting at the village church.

Rebecca's family had been stunned by the failure of either pastor to show any charity to the old woman in her hour of need; they had been less merciful than Hathorne, who at least had had his moment of pity and doubt. There was no doubt in these men, much less pity; at a word from the girls they had dismissed Rebecca's whole life of faith and good works as irrelevant at best, and at worst mere hypocrisy. For them no examination or trial was needed to prove her guilt. Parris believed that with his own eyes he had seen her torture his niece for refusing to contract with the devil. After catching the woman red-handed, how could he deal with her but severely? There would be a time for pity and comfort when Rebecca had cleansed her soul by confessing her crime. Parris and Noyes visited her in prison and prayed for her, but always to one end, that she acknowledge her witchcraft.

To Rebecca's family was not given the grace to understand this solicitude. To them the ministers' attitude was brutal. Never again would they willingly listen to such men; they would, for thanks to Rebecca's rearing they were devout and now craved more than ever the comfort of the word of the Lord, journey miles afield rather than sit under a pulpit which contained Parris.

Yet 3 April was Sacrament Sunday; Beverly and Topsfield were hard to get to. Sarah Cloyce, deeply afflicted in her sister's affliction, hungering and thirsting after righteousness, let her neighbours persuade her to come to receive the sacrament in the village church.

The congregation assembled quietly that day; the Lord had laid His hand on the demons of the girls and they were still. There might indeed have been no disorder at all had not Goody Cloyce created it. But when Parris named his text, Sarah did what was unthinkable; she got up, stalked down the aisle and went out, slamming the door behind her.

"Have I not chosen you twelve and one of you is a devil?" Parris had read. In the quiet meeting-house the words had rung out with terrible clarity. But Sarah's exit and the manner of her going gave an even more ominous significance to his next words, his proposition, which he read as soon as the reverberations of the crashing of the door had died down.

"Christ knows how many devils there are in his church and who they are."

After service few could speak of anything but Sarah's behaviour and what it portended. Her friends defended her. She had become suddenly ill. She had not slammed the door purposely; the high wind had wrenched it from her hand. But others regarded such explanations as mere naïveté; there was a darker meaning which would be revealed in God's good time.

It was revealed very promptly, before they had done talking about it. The girls had fallen into their fits again and now pointed out a horrid sight, invisible to all others:

a company of witches gathered nearby to receive the unholy sacrament of red bread and bloody wine.

"Oh Goody Cloyce, I did not think to see you here," cried
one. "Is this a time to receive the sacrament? You ran away
on the Lord's Day and scorned to receive it in the meeting-
house. Is this a time to receive it?"

It was enough. A complaint against Sarah was sworn out
on Monday, a warrant on Friday, and on the following Monday, 11 April, Sarah herself was facing the magistrates.
She faced them at first, before her energy ran out, with
such spirit that there were moments when it was she rather
than the magistrates who conducted the examination.

"When did I hurt thee?" she demanded of John Indian.

"A great many times."

"Oh, you are a grievous liar!" cried Sarah.

But to make such a reply is only to drive a nail in one's
coffin. John Indian at once fell to the floor and tumbled
about there bellowing with pain. It was obvious to the dull-
est that the devil of Sarah's own spite was at work on him.

Presently Sarah asked for water and sat down. Her move
was a ruse and promptly exposed as such; she had merely
gained time to listen to something the Black Man was whispering in her ear; the girls saw him bend over her, and also
saw Sarah's familiar, a yellow bird, flutter about her head.
There could be no defence in the light of such evidence.
Sarah was held for trial and sent to join her sister Rebecca
in Salem Prison.

"It's no wonder that they are witches; their mother was a
witch before them," remarked young John Putnam of this
reunion.

He was paid for that remark. The shapes of Rebecca and
Sarah issued one midnight soon after from prison, fell upon
his eight weeks' child and tortured it "enough to pierce a
stony heart" until it died.

2

Sarah Cloyce was not alone at the bar on 11 April, nor
was the place Salem Village. The hearing had been trans-

ferred to the larger meeting-house in Salem Town to suit the convenience of several Very Important Persons who had come, mostly from Boston, to study the situation at first hand. These included Deputy Governor Thomas Danforth, Samuel Sewall, his brother Stephen, and three other members of the General Council.

Their presence here was proof that authorities in Massachusetts were by no means disposed to look on the outbreak as a parochial affair and purely the business of Salem Village. It was local only as the first appearance of a malignant contagion is local until it spreads and becomes epidemic. That this plague was spreading was already disturbingly obvious. Respectable church members had been caught in the act of witchcraft; a wizard was known to be practising in Boston. The existence of "the tall man of Boston" had now been corroborated by other evidence than Tituba's. At the witches' sabbath where Sarah Cloyce had been unmasked, one of the girls had caught sight of "a fine grave man," though who he was she couldn't say. The failure to identify this malefactor was one of the magistrates' most nagging problems.

Such villagers as may have hoped that the visitors had come in a spirit of sceptical inquiry were doomed to disappointment. If anything, the distinguished members of the Council watched the girls less critically than did villagers who had the advantage of acquaintance with these girls before they became so famous. Certainly Samuel Sewall did not want either for critical intelligence or for a generous measure of warm humanity; the diary in which he was keeping his account with God and which would one day be to theocratic Boston what that of his contemporary, Samuel Pepys, would be to Restoration London, was characterized by a gift for shrewd observation. But to-day his shrewdness was directed to one end—to catching the witches at their crimes—and his sympathy was all for the girls, those innocents whom the forces of hell were so cruelly abusing. Neither he nor his associates had any innovations to suggest in the procedure initiated by Hathorne and Corwin, who of course were also present. How else could you conduct a witch-hunt but in this way?

The examination opened, to be sure, more tamely than most. The girls, apparently awed by their new surroundings and the extreme dignity of the assembly, contained themselves warily at first. In fact they left the initiative in the examinations of both Sarah Cloyce and the next witch to John Indian. But once it was borne in on them that the dignitaries responded exactly as did the farm folk they knew, they were off and into such a hullabaloo that Parris got hopelessly behind in his note-taking. Only Mary Walcott was calm; she had brought her knitting with her, and became so intent on it that she clicked her needles no matter what devils rioted about her. Every so often she glanced up to confirm someone else's story; she corroborated Abigail's announcement that two witches were sitting in the laps of unnamed magistrates, and John Indian's warning to a dog under the table that the wizard Procter was astride him.

For by now the law had caught up to John Procter.

3

Initially it had caught up with his wife only. The first crying out had occurred on Monday, 28 March, a few days after Rebecca Nurse's examination and John Procter's outburst against the girls.

"There's Goody Procter!" one of the latter had cried in Ingersoll's ordinary. "Old witch! I'll have her hang."

For all John Procter's recent reckless talk about the girls, he and his family held a high place in the esteem of the community. Accordingly the several witnesses to this crying out responded with unwonted scepticism. They looked about them, remarked that there was nothing to see, and told the girl who had spoken that they believed she was lying.

Had the girl run true to form she would have reacted to this reproof by going into convulsions. Instead she sheepishly came out of her trance. "It was for sport," she ad-

mitted. "I must have some sport." Later when Elizabeth
Procter was taken anyway, Goody Ingersoll, Daniel Elliot, and William Raymond put the episode on record to
present as testimony for the defence. They might have
spared themselves the pains. The magistrates, committed
to "spectral evidence," would waive as irrelevant and even
frivolous any testimony based on the fact that other people
could not see what the girls saw. One might as well in a
modern court testify that water is free from bacilli on the
grounds that it looks clear to the eye; the girls were the
microscopes which God Himself had provided for the laboratory work of detecting witches.

But though the magistrates would not honour such testimony, the fact that it had been offered did seem to have a
chastening effect on the girls. When Elizabeth Procter took
the stand they eyed her in silence. But for John Indian,
Elizabeth might have left the place without a count against
her.

"There is the woman who came in her shift and choked
me!" he yelled suddenly.

The ice was broken. The girls began to mutter and moan
and to go into the preliminary stages of their mediumistic
trance, and then to produce the din that Sewall called "awful." Elizabeth was sighted on what was now the classic
perch for a witch, the beam, and half a dozen said that she
had been after them to sign the Book.

"Did you not tell me that your maid had written?" cried
little Abigail. The "maid" was Mary Warren, who signifi-
cantly was not present.

"Dear child, it is not so," said Elizabeth. "There is another judgment, dear child."

It was as if she, the mother and stepmother of John
Procter's brood, thought she could reason with one so young
and tender. But there had never been anything tender
about Abigail; to-day her demon was rampant; even after
court it set her in a poltergeist frenzy in pursuit of her uncle,
still labouring at his notes over the long table, until finally
the poor man could only record that the demons loosed

upon the girls were beyond control, and fold up his report unfinished.

Thanks to this diabolic meddlesomeness, the contribution of John Procter to the situation is obscure. He had come unsummoned to stand by his wife. At one point, while he was raising his stentorian voice in order to make himself heard above the tumult, young Abigail turned on him with an air of pleased discovery.

"Why he can pinch as well as she!" exclaimed Abigail, and she, unfortunately, was heard.

Procter had never been given to holding his tongue in a crisis. Certainly his voice boomed out again and again during the scene that followed. But either Parris could not hear him through the uproar, or he considered everything he heard irrelevant. The magistrates, intent upon the reactions of the girls as their true source of information, turned to him only in reproof.

"You see, the devil will deceive you," one of them said. "The children could see what you was going to do before the woman was hurt. I would advise you to repentance, for the devil is bringing you out."

Procter was learning that he had spoken more truly than he knew when he said that the girls if let alone would "make devils of us all." He must have accompanied his accused wife to Salem confident that now that some of the soberest minds in the colony, notably Danforth and Sewall, were investigating the witchcraft, common sense would prevail. Instead he now saw something like witchcraft of a most unexpected and disturbing nature. The common sense of these men had abdicated before the crazed fantasies of wenches in their teens. Had these men no eyes to see? Had they no daughters or sisters that they should not know how silly a female can be in the silly season of her teens, to what lengths she can go in her craving for attention? Procter knew how to handle the witches; look at Mary Warren, who knew better than to come to court to-day. Just give him a chance to demonstrate his therapy on the rest.

But Procter's reasoning was like blasphemy to the magistrates. With them the devil had indeed taken over; this was

his hour and the power of darkness; he came in the form of
a stern mad logic, a closed circle which admitted no intru-
sion from the world of objectively observed reality. Or
rather it was a logic which admitted of only one reality, the
affliction of these girls and their testimony as to its cause.
The girls had pointed out Procter as "a most dreadful wizard"; he must be put away with the rest.

And so he was. Later in the day six accused were ridden
away to Boston to await trial in prison there: Sarah Cloyce
and her sister Rebecca; the Procters, man and wife; Martha
Cory and puzzled little Dorcas Good. Their estate, however,
was not so miserable as that of the three who had gone
before them. They were good friends and good neighbours,
and with the exception of the little girl were people of ma-
ture experience and character. They could discuss their
common plight together, reason it out, and make plans for
bringing Massachusetts officialdom back to its senses. God
would be with them, for they were innocent, and none
doubted it about the other.

Dorcas, clinging to the constable, looked about her in a
kind of sober eagerness as they skirted the broad Lynn
marshes to Noddle's Island, and then crossed the harbour
by ferry to Boston Town. No one else in the village, no one
she knew, had ever had the advantage of a trip so far from
home. But the journey's end was a shock. Of all the fine
buildings in Boston, brick and frame, the constable picked
out the meanest to stop at. It smelled ill, and in it waited
Dorcas's mother in a foul humour.

4

For Mary Warren's absence from court there had been
sound reason. John Procter had after all made one convert
to the cause of common sense, and it was the girl he called
his "jade."

Procter, a titan of a man, as commanding of figure as he
was downright in manner, had long ago won the respect
if not the love of his maidservant. Her affection, to be sure,
did not extend to his present wife. Mary felt that Elizabeth

did not understand her husband, that she was making his life miserable, an observation for which there may have been some grounds in that Elizabeth was currently suffering the first stages of pregnancy.

Yet Mary was in the present crisis too loyal to her master to testify against his wife. Besides, good sense may impress a hypnoid subject as well as fantasy. Living at close quarters with Procter's sanity, Mary had well before the examination begun to emerge from her dream. Older than the other girls, serious in her pieties, she now looked about her and saw that she had fallen into strange company.

The taking of Procter with Elizabeth gave Mary a kind of shock treatment which completely restored her sanity. She might in her secret heart rejoice to see the wife put away, but the husband, never. Besides, Mary, left at home with Procter's five children, was in a difficult position. The three older children were old enough to speak to her in plain terms for her part in bringing about such a misfortune, and their comments were reinforced by the opinion of the neighbourhood at large. Procter had been a good neighbour; few who knew him either here or in his native Ipswich would believe ill of him. Other people might be witches, but not in the name of common sense John Procter.

If this were not enough, Mary may have had another and extreme object-lesson in the misery fantasy may bring into the world. Under the law witches were to be treated like enemy aliens found guilty of conspiring against the government under which they lived; not only their lives but their goods were forfeit. Neither, to be sure, could be taken before trial and conviction, but in Procter's case a zealous sheriff overlooked this technicality. Well before the trial he "came to their house and seized all the goods, provision and cattle that he could come at, and sold some of the cattle at half price and killed others and put them up for the West Indies; threw out the beer out of the barrel and carried away the barrel, emptied a pot of broath and took away the pot and left nothing for the support of the children." The youngest of these were three and seven respectively.

So suggestible a nature as Mary Warren's could not look

on such events unmoved. Looking at the other girls with
whom she had spent so many tranced hours, she now saw
them as a pack of undisciplined children who had somehow
beguiled an entire community into playing a wicked game
with them, such a game as a five-year-old might invent.
"It was for sport." One of them had admitted it and *apropos*
of the Procters. Well, here was their sport, an orderly household suddenly deprived of its mainstays and little children
weeping. If this was sport, Abigail Williamson and Ann
Putnam could have it. Mary Warren was through.

Mary was not, however, of such stuff as heroines are
made of. She did not at this point seek out Mr Hathorne or
the Reverend Samuel Parris to make a formal announcement of her change of heart. She might in the end as well
have done so; she could not keep her views to herself, and
what she confided to her friends presently reached the ears
of the afflicted girls and immediately after, the magistrates.

The girls, Mary was saying, "did but dissemble. . . . The
magistrates might as well examine the keeper's daughter
that had been afflicted many years and take notice of what
she said as any of the afflicted persons." She added details
from personal experience; in her affliction, she was reported
as saying, she had seen "the apparission of a hundred persons, for she said her head was distempered that she could
not tell what she said, and when she was well again she
could not say that she saw any of the apparissions at the
time aforesaid."

That Mary's heresy had been suspected so early as the
time of the Procters' examination was indicated by Abigail
Williams's question about the maid's having signed the
Book. Not long after, Mary's whispering campaign against
her former colleagues became so afflicting as to send some of
them into possession. In this state their eyes were opened
to the truth. Satan, alarmed at the efficiency with which the
girls were exposing his secret agents, was now penetrating
the accusing circle itself. Through the medium of the Procters he had got Mary to put her hand to the Book. She, so
lately one of the tormented, had now become a tormentor.

In such an emergency there was only one thing to do.

A warrant was issued for the arrest of the renegade. So it happened that on 19 April Mary was given the opportunity that she had not had the courage to seek directly. She was taken before the magistrates and asked to explain herself.

5

The courtroom into which Mary Warren was led should have been familiar enough. The magistrates had returned to Salem Village; from the stand Mary could overlook her own bench where she worshipped of a Sunday and into the faces of people she had known all her life. And yet there was a difference; the people were eyeing her strangely, not at all in the pitying awe with which most of them had looked at her when she was fighting off imaginary devils and telling what she now knew to be untruths. She looked in vain for a sign of sympathy and encouragement. There was none. Mary all alone turned and tremulously faced the magistrates.

Hathorne bent forward; his voice was kind, for this was not the common run of witches, but a girl already tormented beyond endurance and more to be pitied for frailty than condemned for deliberate wrongdoing.

"You were a little while ago an afflicted person; now you are an afflicter," he said. "How comes this to pass?"

Mary found her mouth gone almost too dry for speech. It had formerly been so easy to speak in this meeting-house; she had been buoyed up on a warm current of solicitude and belief. Now it was as if these familiar people before her had been turned to stone; stonily they awaited her reply, and in their eyes she read their disbelief of what she had said and must say.

Yet the magistrate seemed kind, and desperately she turned to his kindness.

"I look up to God," she quavered, "and I take it to be a mercy of God."

"What!" rapped out Hathorne incredulously. "Do you take it as a mercy to afflict others?"

In the front benches just below Mary sat the girls. Initially she had not been afraid of them; she knew them all, and all their tricks. But now these began to cry out and gasp and writhe, and when they did so there was something new. Hitherto when that had happened, Mary had been part of it; her body had writhed with theirs; her voice had been a part of the howling and yowling; it had been a kind of warm communion, tormenting and yet inexplicably satisfying. But now that she was apart from it, it was all different —different and yet terribly the same. In spite of herself the suggestible Mary began to quiver too; she could not control herself; she felt her fits returning.

But even as she sank to the floor her voice rang out in a despairing cry. "I will speak! . . . Oh, I am sorry for it! I am sorry for it! Oh Lord help me! Oh, good Lord, save me! I will tell! I will tell!"

What she would tell and what she was sorry for no one could make out. She became speechless; her jaws locked. For a while she struggled on the stand and then fell into a fit so sore that she had to be carried outside. It was not Mary but one of the girls who interpreted the situation to the spectators. Mary, she explained, had started to confess, but the shapes of Martha Cory and Elizabeth Procter had fallen on her in fury and choked her off.

Nothing could be done with the girl at the time. The magistrates let her rest across the road in the ordinary while they examined two other witches and one wizard who had also been brought to court on 19 April. When they had disposed of these cases they took Mary aside for a private interview. This was an unusual concession, but then Mary was an unusual and above all a pitiful witch. In her present struggle they saw a symbol of Christ fighting off the devil in the wilderness.

In that private interview Mary became briefly coherent. "I will, I will speak, Satan! She saith she will kill me! Oh, she saith she owes me a spite and will claw me off. Avoid, Satan, for the name of God, avoid!"

Even this outcry was not informative; on the basis of the spectral insight of the other girls the magistrates gathered that "she" was Elizabeth Procter, though Mary herself did not name her. There was nothing to do with the girl but confine her in Salem Prison with the others who had been heard that day.

There Mary remained several weeks. Her prison record was curious. When she was let alone for a space she was as rational as anyone, and in discussion with her fellow prisoners reasserted her scepticism in the value of fits, anyone's fits, as a means of getting at the truth. Had John Procter been there, Mary might have been able to keep it up even when the magistrates came to interview her, as they frequently did. But Procter was far away in Boston, and by herself an emotional servant girl was no match for magistrates and ministers trained in the rigid discipline of theocratic logic. Even Joan of Arc broke at times under the stress of the Inquisition, and poor Mary was no Joan. However an interview started, she always ended by "confessing" to whatever the magistrates desired to hear at the time; in the end she "confessed" to so much that it would have been better if Mary had never ventured into her brief heresy and so drawn to herself such intensive inquiry.

Even so, such reports as the magistrates kept of their private conferences with the girl between 21 April and 12 May show a pattern of stubborn, recurrent sanity on the part of Mary, an attempt to tell the real story. Though she was early induced to admit that Procter had brought her the Book, she denied that he had tried to force her to sign it by threatening to run hot tongs down her throat. No, said Mary, and probably truthfully, that threat had been made only to bring her out of a fit.

She cited a conversation that had the ring of truth.

"If you are afflicted, I wish you were more afflicted and you and all," Procter had said.

"Master, what makes you say that?"

"Because you go to bring out innocent persons."

"I tould him that could not bee," reported Mary in the magistrates' spelling. She added lamely, "Whether the devil took advantage of that to afflict them I know not."

Even then Mary stubbornly refused to make a direct accusation of her master, though she succumbed early to the temptation to make a witch of her mistress. She reported suspicious objects that she had seen in Elizabeth's house, a mysterious ointment, a poppet stuck with pins, books that she could make nothing of. Once Mary had opened one and spelled out the word "Moses," but the phrase that followed she could not make out and regarded darkly.

The shape of Elizabeth paid her off for these revelations. One day in the presence of the justices the girl fought off her apparition.

"I will tell! I will tell!" she cried. "Thou wicked creature, it's you that stopped my mouth. . . . Oh Betty Procter, it is she. It is she I lived with last. . . . It shall be known, thou witch. Hast thou undone me body and soul?"

Other fantasies streamed from her once she started. In her visions she accounted for the supernatural causes of the death of a man from a vessel in Salem Harbour, the falling of a man from a cherry tree, and the casting away of a ketch.

At last, on 12 May, she gave up trying to defend Procter from the charge of wizardry. There was something blissful about her surrender. Dreamily she reported that she had felt a Shape hovering above her; she had reached up and pulled it down, and lo, there was John Procter in her lap.

Shortly after this catharsis, the magistrates pronounced Mary cleansed of her sin and allowed her to rejoin the girls in their place of honour in the courtroom. Mary never again played lead in their demonstrations, but neither did she again lapse into the dangerous, unbelievable world of reality.

6

Mary got no honour from her abortive act of courage, not even from fellow heretics who agreed with her that the girls "did but dissemble." Some of these, seeing her return to the "circle" and go on as before, were to say that the whole incident was a plot designed to make the proceedings more credible.

Yet surely no one was "plotting," least of all the hapless Mary. The community at large had become bewitched, magistrates no less than the girls—bewitched by a kind of mad hypnosis, expressed in panic on the one hand and crusading fervour on the other. At such moments the voice of reason always sounds like blasphemy and dissenters are of the devil. The wonder was not that Mary's defection was denounced, but that it should have been treated with mercy.

About a month later there was a parallel though less conspicuous defection. Sarah Churchill, the other twenty-year-old, fell prey to compunction after her explosive master George Jacobs was seized, and in this condition was accused by the girls of becoming an afflicter. In court Sarah made no visible attempt to hold out; she collapsed on the stand and "confessed" at once.

But afterwards she went in private to Sarah Ingersoll and distractedly sobbed out her story. Nothing in her confession, which had further incriminated poor Jacobs, had been true; she had belied herself. She had "confessed" only out of fear of torture and hanging.

"If I told Mr Noyes but once I had set my hand to the Book, he would believe me," wailed the girl, "but if I told him one hundred times I had not he would not believe me."

Sarah Ingersoll soothed the girl and then set her jaw and made note of the conversation to present as testimony in court. But she acted quietly, and though her deposition was duly filed with the rest, neither ministers nor magistrates gave it any weight. Sarah Churchill had "freely confessed," she had been forgiven and like Mary Warren restored to the accusing circle, her character as witness no whit impaired by anything said about her or said by her. The accusing circle had become a vicious circle from which no girl had any chance of breaking free—until the climate of opinion should change in Massachusetts. And of that there was as yet no sign.

CHAPTER VIII

THE WEIRD SISTERS

Spring was coming to Massachusetts. First had come the March peepers, chorusing at night in the marshes, then the hoarser, deeper grumping of the frogs. In thickets at the meadows' edge showed the velvety pearls of the pussy willows, silver and rose; and the alder catkins swelled and shook down their yellow pollen. At the roots of the maples standing in the swamps, the skunk cabbage pricked up its bright green ears, and deeper in the woods unfolded the fern fiddleheads and the speckled jack-in-the-pulpit.

Then the real flowers came, violets blue and white in Parris's pasture, and about the brook cowslips as sunny as if the place did not lie under a spell. The lilac buds swelled larger and began to show colour about the low overhang of Rebecca's roof. A few warm days would bring the apples out; cherries were already exploding into blossom, white against naked black limbs.

All at once grass stood ankle deep in the meadows. No one had seen it come; one day it was simply there. Over it skimmed the bobolinks in abrupt, dipping flight, shedding liquid drops of music behind them. The redwing blackbirds squealed and chirred, and from an alder twig a catbird mewed and poured down golden mockery on a farmer breaking ground with his plough.

It is fitting that theocratic Massachusetts should have a physical substructure of unyielding, durable rock. This does not lie so close to the surface in fertile Salem Village as in the crabbed hills about Salem Town, but it is close enough. The plough stuck suddenly under a stone, the reins fell from the ploughman's hands, and he fell to his knees in a furrow.

"Devil take it!" he exclaimed.

Had he been a papist he would then have crossed himself. God help him, what guest had he invited? Looking about him he saw a visible change come over the genial afternoon. The wind had shifted to the east and now carried to him the smell of kelp on the rocks of the point, uncovered by low tide, and the raw chill so familiar to Salem people just when they think warm weather has come at last. A little yellow bird flitted towards him.

He stared at the bird. Had not just such a Thing hovered over the heads of Martha Cory and Sarah Cloyce? Their birds had not been visible to most; his eyes had not then been opened. What portent was this that now that he had called the devil he too saw the dreadful Bird?

"Avoid, Satan, avoid!" he shouted, and hurled a clod at the Thing. It missed, and the bird skimmed back to the meadow where the bobolinks chimed. But now a toad looked at him from the sod with jewelled round devil's eyes. That devil he could trample and mash and he did.

It would not have surprised him when he got home to find a constable waiting, warrant in hand, but there were only his wife stirring a pot over the fire, and his youngest, sitting on her stool, murmuring to something cuddled in her arms, a grotesque little cornstalk doll dressed up in oddments from his wife's work-basket.

A doll? God save him, a poppet! The constables had been looking for them lately. Elizabeth Procter had one, and now that Bridget Bishop. He snatched the thing and hurled it into the fire, and wife and child jumped at the fury in his voice.

"Who gave her that? What bitch witch made it?"

One might give the man a name. There were simple people taken in witchcraft, and not in Salem Village only, who under examination confessed to just such incidents as their part in letting the devil in. For now the plague was going through the village like a forest fire, and more dreadful than a fire since every effort to control it served only to spread it further. Already it was enveloping Topsfield and Salem

Town. It was a time when it was a brave man—or perhaps a stolid, unthinking man—who dared trust his neighbour, his wife, his mother, or for that matter his own wits. The devil had in Massachusetts obliterated the line that divides fact from fantasy. The one could no longer be distinguished from the other; the very concept that they could be different things was being forgotten.

It was a time when any insect bite might be fatal, for the devil might be in the insect and the mark he left identifiable as the witchmark where the familiar spirit was given suck. Now that there were not only witches but wizards, young girls lived in dread of a spectral rape by the incubus and of giving birth to a demon child. That such had already taken place was demonstrated by the person of little Dorcas Good; obviously a child of human get could not become a witch at an age so tender; let those sentimentalists who said that Dorcas was too young to be in prison think of the facts in the case and hold their tongues. Young men and older were haunted by the spectres of not unshapely matrons who at midnight hopped over the windowsill or dropped down from a beam and got into bed with them. Bridget Bishop, conspicuous because her Shape like her body affected a "red paragon bodice," and the trim Susanna Martin were making these unwomanly advances to honest men and true who in the proper time would not hesitate to offer such testimony in court.

It was hard under such circumstances to attend to chores, to set about planting. Even Indian wars, at least as known locally, had not been so disruptive of routine, for when Indians were about one could still plough and harrow, the musket slung over the shoulder. But muskets were no protection against this sort of thing. If a passer-by hove into view, it was necessary to drop the task in hand and inquire, how goes it with the girls? Who has most lately been cried out on? And when the magistrates sat in court there was no resisting the sick fascination of what went on there, though it cost a whole day at a time away from work.

And now court came oftener and oftener, and more witches came to each. Three came with Mary Warren on

19 April; eight three days later, and more soon after. God send that they all come soon and that the matter be disposed of and life allowed to go its normal course again. Yet there seemed to be no hope of that. "Confessors" were coming in now; and though each witch who confessed gave glory to God, it was to men an awful judgment, for never did a witch confess without incriminating others yet unsuspected.

2

The three who had been indicted with Mary Warren on 19 April were Giles Cory, Bridget Bishop, and Abigail Hobbs. Old Giles, slow of wit, and in his old age humble before his betters, had accepted the theory that the fits of the girls proved the guilt of his wife Martha, had indeed denounced such of his sons-in-law as defended her. Now he stood in court and in bewilderment saw the same phenomenon converging on him.

"What!" exclaimed Hathorne. "Is it not enough to act witchcraft at other times, but you must do it in the face of authority?"

"I am a poor creature and cannot help it," said Giles humbly.

But presently the magistrates aroused his old spirit. They touched on the one chord calculated to shock the old man to life, to the independence of his youth.

"What was it frightened you?" they asked, *apropos* of something Goody Bibber had been saying about a black hog.

Giles straightened his bowed shoulders and eyed them man to man.

"I do not know that I ever spoke that word in my life," he snapped, and something too snapped in him, something that set his slow intelligence to functioning. Here were the girls squalling and tumbling and crying that he did it; well he didn't. Just so had they howled and cried out on his wife. How had it come that he had believed not his wife but these wenches? It would take Giles Cory, remanded to prison, a long time to work this thing out, but once he had done so, nothing would ever again shake his conviction. And he would not again humble himself before anyone.

There had always been talk about the next witch, Bridget Bishop. For one thing she was a flashy dresser; her "red paragon bodice" set her style, and for best (one does not wear paragon for best) she had a great store of laces. These she liked to vary, and sometimes brought pieces to Samuel Shattuck of Salem Town to have dyed. The latter, a dour Quaker, who because of his faith had in the past had his own brushes with theocratic authority, had always thought there was something questionable about the quality and style of these laces, and now stood ready to give his reasons.

But the real gossip had centred around Bridget's conduct as tavern-keeper. She had had two ordinaries, one formerly in Salem Village, another currently outside Salem Town, on the road to Beverly. It was an old complaint that she permitted young people to loiter at unseemly hours playing at "shovel-board" and making an uproar that disturbed the sleep of decent neighbours. One of these had once burst in on Bridget and hurled some of the game pieces into the fire.

It was natural that one who stood out in such vivid relief against the sober habit of her community should be accused of witchcraft. Indeed, this had first happened some years ago. Bridget had been accused of malefaction in the death of a neighbour and might have been condemned but for the intercession of John Hale, who testified that in his opinion the deceased was crazed and had made away with herself. In the current fever, memories of the old episode had been revived. Hale himself was giving much thought to the matter and praying that if the devil had deluded him before the Lord would now open his eyes to the truth.

Bridget in court was a cool one.

"I do not know what a witch is," she said flatly when they asked her why she was one.

She was undone like all the rest by the plainest evidence. In asserting her innocence she rolled her eyes to heaven, and immediately all the girls rolled theirs. It was ghastly to see the glaring whites of so many eyes; even among the spectators some sensitive people found themselves to their horror yielding to the same irresistible compulsion. No one who saw the providence could doubt that a devil was about working for Bridget.

Yet when Hathorne asked her if it did not trouble her to see the girls tormented, her reply was an insolent "No!"

Bridget was taken to Salem Prison, and there took the first opportunity to cross-examine the still vacillating Mary Warren and record a deposition of the conversation.

If Giles Cory and Bridget Bishop were firm in their fashion, their companion was not, or rather she was firm in an opposite direction. She was Abigail Hobbs, a wild creature who had long shocked people in Topsfield, her home, by her ramblings about the woods at night. One of the accusers reported that she was unafraid because "she had sould herself body and soule to ye old boy." Her own mother, Deliverance, decent wife of William, had once said of Abigail that "she little thought to be mother of such a dafter."

The disorder of the courtroom had no terror for this Abigail; it was her element, and she entered into the spirit of things by plunging at once into headlong confession. She described with gusto, as if it had been a kind of distinction to be present, the unholy meetings in Parris's pasture, named nine witches who had attended with her, and identified the Boston woman in a silk mantle whom Tituba had seen.

The other girls fell silent when the confession began, just as they had done when Tituba had set this precedent. Presently they gave Abigail their active support by nodding their heads, and afterward several went out of their way to assure the magistrates that this witch was a pitiful creature, that they were intensely sorry for her. They might have accepted her as a recruit to their ranks, but the judges did not see it that way. She was, for all her docility on the stand, too outlandish a personality; even in their credulous ears some of her exuberant confessions rang false. Besides, when they interviewed her privately in prison she cheerfully confessed to real abominations, among them murder.

"Were they men or women you killed?" they asked her.

"They were both boys and girls."

"Was you angry with them yourself?"

"Yes, though I do not know why now."

What could any society do with a girl like that but lock her up? The magistrates declined to augment the circle of accusing girls by the addition of this specimen, and sent the girl to prison with the rest.

3

The day after Abigail Hobbs's great moment in court nine warrants, an unprecedented number, were sworn out, and by ten in the morning of 22 April all but one of these (Mary English could not at the time be found) had been fetched to Ingersoll's ordinary, and the examination began.

The records of the hearing of two of these, notably Edward Bishop, stepson of Bridget, and his wife Sarah, have somehow been lost. However, it is plain that Edward was just such another as John Procter; he had recently had the temerity to whip John Indian out of his fits, and with such success that he had publicly recommended that a similar cure be tried on the girls. Now the law had him and would keep him, along with his wife.

Deliverance and William Hobbs, parents of wild Abigail, were sent for as a result of their daughter's fantasies. Deliverance looked about the courtroom in panic. The shrilling that the children set up the moment she came in unnerved her, and so did their cry that her Shape had been sighted on the beam just above her head.

"I am amazed! I am amazed!" whispered poor Deliverance when asked what she thought of this.

She made an effort to give the information required of her. "Last Lord's Day in the meeting-house I saw a great many birds and cats and dogs, and heard a voice say 'Come away.'" Again she heard "a kind of thundering." From this excursion into natural history Deliverance lapsed by almost imperceptible degrees into confession; that is, she began to agree to any statement put to her by the judges.

"Have you signed any books?"

"It is very lately then—the night before last."

Goody Wild had brought her the book, she said, apparently almost at random, and her helpless testimony rambled on in this fashion, both in court and later in prison. She agreed to every previous witch's witchhood and once made a brief sensation by reporting that she had seen the Shape of Mercy Lewis as well. But then she remembered the honoured position of Mercy and caught herself; Mercy's Shape had never hurt her. With more conviction she reported on the misconduct of her daughter Abigail; the girl had long ago thrown over parental control and had been much in the disreputable society of Sarah Good.

Thus Deliverance. Her husband William was of sterner stuff.

"Can you now deny it?" demanded the magistrates, having confronted him with his wife's confession and the lamentable state of the afflicted.

"I can deny it to my dying day!" roared William, and he did.

The matron Sarah Wild had little chance to defend herself after the implication of Deliverance Hobbs's confession. Mary Black, a negro slave attached to the household of Nathaniel Putnam, missed her chance to follow in Tituba's footsteps by her bewildered incomprehension of what people wanted of her.

"Do you prick others?" she was asked.

"No, I pin my neckcloth."

When the girls came running up to show their hands all bloody from malefaction, Mary Black still did not grasp just what it had to do with her. But being led away to prison was no more baffling than many other incidents in her life of servitude; it was unpleasant in prison, but at least she had there the rare luxury of sitting with her hands folded in her lap.

With the seventh prisoner something unprecedented happened. The girls looked at him—he was Nehemiah Abbott, nearly one hundred years old by his reckoning, a "hilly faced man" with strands of white hair falling over his eyes —and admitted that they had made a mistake.

"It is not the man," said Mercy Lewis positively.

The other girls were less sure. They asked that he be led to a window and there crowded about him, pawing over his scalp in search of a wen some of them distinctly remembered. There was no wen. The man was discharged. A wave of relief went over the spectators in the courtroom. It was not that anyone cared much about old Nehemiah, but the painstaking care taken by girls and justices was very reassuring. Innocent people might be taken in the witchcraft; but when by God's providence their innocence was discovered, they were sent their way unmolested.

4

The last witch of the day was Mary Esty, fifty-eight-year-old sister of Sarah Cloyce and Rebecca Nurse, youngest of "the Towne girls." In court she displayed neither the tremulousness of Rebecca nor the explosive temper of Sarah, but carried herself with such grace, courage and good sense that Hathorne gave way to one of those moments of doubt which were his saving grace.

"Are you certain this is the woman?" he asked the girls. After all, they had made one mistake with old Abbott, and since Mary had come to the stand they had fallen into one of their moods of quiescence; they were eyeing her in silence.

Such a question, however, never failed to act as a signal to release the full dynamic of demoniac energy. The girls quivered and whimpered as it entered into them, and then howled with pain. The court saw the familiar, damning choreography; Mary Esty was standing with her head a bit to one side; a spirit forcibly twisted the girls' heads into this position, thrusting them sometimes at so unnatural an angle that it seemed as if their necks would break.

"Oh, Goody Esty, Goody Esty!" shrilled Ann Putnam

above the gibbering. "You are the woman! You are the woman!"

What, asked the magistrates, did Mary think of all this.

"It is an evil spirit," replied Mary judiciously. "But whether it be witchcraft I do not know."

She was imprisoned with the rest, but her quiet self-possession and her gentle manner continued to make their impression. Her very jailers spoke up for her, and the magistrates were impelled to interview the girls again, asking them one by one, "Are you certain this is the woman?"

The girls were no longer certain. Though their fits continued apace and they had in them sensational revelations which were resulting in half a dozen arrests a week, most of them admitted to the magistrates that they were no longer visited by Mary Esty.

On 18 May, at a most wonderful season when the trees are in full young leaf, that tender, immaculate leaf that they know only in May, Mary was released from prison and allowed to go home to Topsfield. It was a deeply satisfying homecoming. There was never a neighbour but was happy with her and as convinced as she that the same good sense and courage that had won her release would also win that of her sisters, and of such improbable witches as the John Procters.

It is not on record just what Mary did with her time when she got home; but she would not have been a true Puritan housewife had she not addressed herself to the business of housecleaning and baking. For more than this she did not have time; she was given just three days.

She had not been home two of these before Mercy Lewis was taken violently ill. From paroxysms of agony she would lapse into comas when she lay with her jaws locked. Again she would revive enough to make her pitiful prayers.

"Dear Lord, receive my soul," watchers would hear her murmur. And again, as the pains mounted, "Lord, let them not kill me quite."

Everyone who saw Mercy's affliction was sure the girl was dying. The news ran across the country and the magistrates heard it with peculiar misgivings. It had happened

that of all the girls Mercy alone had not cleared Mary Esty;
they had disregarded that fact because Mercy had not expressed her dissent with impressive conviction, was in any
case one among many, and the one whose presence some
people deplored among the girls; there had always been
something a little sly, a little mean about Mercy. If she
said yes and Ann Putnam said no, it was young Ann whom
people would believe.

Even now, though Mercy's incoherent outcries were
plainly directed at Mary Esty, the authorities would not act
on this girl's say-so alone. Ann Putnam and Abigail Williams, who as the youngest of the girls were also presumably the most innocent, were stationed at Mercy's bedside to
see what they could descry, and when they made positve
identification of Mary Esty, still other girls were brought in
to check their accuracy. It fell to Mary Walcott to make the
most complete diagnosis. Not only did she see Mary put
chains about Mercy's neck and choke her, but she was able
to question her and learn exactly what happened. She had,
volunteered the Shape of Mary Esty, who plainly lacked
the discretion of Mary in the corporeal state, blinded the
eyes of all the other girls so that they, not seeing her, had
supposed her innocent; but Mercy she had not been able
to blind, so now, for obvious reasons, she had to kill the
girl.

This disclosure was completed towards midnight. By
now the strength of Mercy was at so low an ebb that it was
clear she would not live until morning if she were not relieved. Accordingly the constables were sent after Mary.
The Estys had long since blown out their candles and gone
to bed when there came a pounding and shouting at the
door. Mary accepted the situation with her usual calm. She
dressed, let herself be lifted to the pillion behind the constable, and did not in prison resist the jailer when he trussed
her up with irons. Exactly as this took place, or as exactly
as one could figure with hour-glasses, Mercy came out of
her convulsions and fell into deep, natural slumber.

The magistrates would not again be brought to risk the
life of these poor girls by false sympathy for one accused.

God had opened the eyes of babes and sucklings (though that was an odd term to apply to the strapping Mercy Lewis) what he had hidden from them.

On the other hand the Shape of Mary Esty had not stirred abroad for the last time. It would appear again, long after, in a most dramatic and disturbing context.

CHAPTER IX

SMALL BLACK MINISTER

The fluent revelations of Abigail and Deliverance Hobbs and of a number of other confessing witches who appeared in court soon after were equipping the magistrates with material for a natural history of witchcraft as practised in Massachusetts.

For one thing the spot favoured by Essex County malefactors for their witches' sabbaths was now definitely established. Earlier there had been uncertainty. Tituba had never been sure where her wild rides had taken her. Twice the girls themselves had glimpsed the witches in session on the lawns of the church, but these must have been sporadic gestures of bravado, for after Abigail and her mother the place became unmistakably identified as Parris's pasture.

This, one gathers, was not the pasture attached to the parsonage grounds, for whose permanent possession Parris had bitterly and vainly contested, but another nearby which Deacon Ingersoll had more recently deeded to the minister in an effort to soothe the latter's outraged feelings.

The pasture itself, though rich in grazing and approved by cattle, had always had something unnerving about it. It was haunted by a plague of spade-foot frogs, which in spring and summer set up such a diabolical clamour that it was nerve-racking after dark to go within earshot of the place. Even before the present trouble began, honest people did not willingly go near it, for it is well known that frogs, like toads, are capable of diabolic affiliation. Does not the Book of Revelation, required reading now for anyone concerned with the awful providence of the witchcraft, speak of "unclean spirits like frogs" coming from the mouth of the Apocalyptic Beast? And now the testimony of the witches was proving that the place was as evil as it sounded. The voices of the frogs were raised to hymn the horrid rites they saw nightly celebrated about them.

At midnight from this place a horn was sounded. To people of good conscience its blast was inaudible, but those who were in compact with the devil heard it though they were at the farthest reaches of Essex County. And then in Andover, Salisbury, Salmon Falls, the damned mounted their sticks, sometimes two or three to a besom, rose into the air, and skimmed the treetops until they came down in the pasture like a flock of cackling birds.

The elfin adventure, as reported by those who had renounced it, did not lack for homely detail. After grounding their sticks in Parris's orchard, witches from the remoter places drew bread and cheese from their pockets and had a snack by the brook before going on to the abominations of the sabbath.

The abomination of the rites consisted in their mere existence and in their dedication to the devil. Aside from that, they were surprisingly staid revels, not for a moment to be compared to the pagan obscenities which characterized such gatherings in Europe and old England. These witches had been after all only recently conforming Puritans, and they still looked it. They sat as orderly in the devil's meeting as they had in their own, and partook of Communion in quite the usual way, even though here the bread was red and the wine just what the papists had always said it was—real blood.

They even listened to a sermon. Often it was a practical, go-getting campaign talk. Witchdom was what Puritanism in its later phases was not, an evangelical faith. Each communicant was urged to bring in at least one more convert before the next sabbath.

On other occasions the sermons were based on inspirational messages. The devil's spokesmen promised release from the psychological and social rigidities of theocracy, and a more abundant life in the new land. Once the Church had been overthrown (and it was not for nothing that the devil had opened operations in a minister's household and was holding his sabbaths hard by the meeting-house) "all would be well." There would be maypoles, the pagan delights of Christmas, Shrove Tuesday, cockfights, gaming—all the hellish old-world pleasures which New England had renounced. And there would be no more shame, no more judgment, and no resurrection. All men would be equal and all men would "live bravely."

Of such simple, earnest stuff were the Massachusetts witches, and this was the ideological content of witchhood. At least this is what the witches confessed to. Maybe they didn't confess to everything. At least none but Abigail Hobbs confessed to murder. Murder was committed, but always by someone else.

2

The witches continued to come in with monotonous regularity. Among those brought to justice in Ingersoll's ordinary on 2 May were Susanna Martin, who had long in her native Amesbury attracted legend as the lightning rod attracts lightning, and Dorcas Hoar of Beverly. The latter, whom once the Reverend John Hale had defended and now defended no more, lashed out bitterly at the girls.

"Oh, you are liars! And God will stop the mouths of liars."

"You are not to speak after this manner in court!" said Hathorne.

"I will speak the truth as long as I live!" cried Goody Hoar, though in this boast, as later events were to prove, she overreached herself.

The likes of these were receiving only scattered attention from the general public, for it was now in the air that the leader and organizer of the witches was about to be exposed. These meetings in Parris's pasture, these services that were not of God, these campaigns to proselytize the whole of Essex County to "ye ould boy" did not conduct themselves; nor could the devil in person, preoccupied as he was with international affairs, give the matter much active supervision. He had like any wise executive delegated his authority to a trusted aide, and this person, master-mind of the district, was now being run to earth.

The first clue to his identity had been given by little Ann Putnam. On 20 April the girl had seen witches alighting in the pasture to celebrate their sabbath. Then those who were with her, among them her father, heard her cry out sharply.

"Oh dreadful, dreadful! Here is a minister come! What, are ministers witches too?"

She did not recognize the newcomer, whom, indeed, she had never seen in the flesh, so while with distended eyes she watched his behaviour, she courageously questioned him.

"Oh dreadful, tell me your name that I may know who you are."

She kept after him so insistently that finally he obliged, gave her not only his name but a partial list of his crimes. Witches were peculiar that way; none could keep a secret no matter how much it was to their interest to do so. Probably professional pride was involved, for this one made a point of explaining that "he was above a witch for he was a cunjurer." Having gone so far, however, the Shape took no further risks. When the child tried to repeat his name he choked her. Ann was like to die when a Shining One, identified by the onlookers as another character out of Revelation, though of course it was not given them to see him, came to her rescue and broke the hold of her tormenter. Then only could the girl gasp out the name. It was such a name that the father shuddered to hear it. The mother, however, was neither surprised nor shocked; the elder Ann Putnam had suspected his deviltry for a long time, to be exact, for a decade.

The next day honest Thomas Putnam got out paper, quill, and inkhorn and wrote a letter to the magistrates. He wrote guardedly; best not to entrust a disclosure so scandalous prematurely to writing. For the present he dared do no more than hint. He began by expressing his gratitude for their "care and pains" in behalf of his little girl, "for which

you know we are never able to make you recompense."
Then he got to what was uppermost in his mind. It was his
duty "to inform your honours of what we conceive you
have not heard, which are high and dreadful . . . of a
wheel within a wheel at which our ears do tingle."

Putnam need not have been so cautious. That very day,
and before his letter could reach the magistrates, the spectral minister was indiscreet enough to revisit the village
and let himself be seen and publicly exposed by Abigail
Williams.

It happened first outside Ingersoll's ordinary.

"There he stands!" yelled the child, and Benjamin Hutchinson struck out where she pointed. Once he hurled a pitch-
fork into the road and evidently hit his mark, for Abigail
heard the minister's greatcoat tear.

When Abigail went into the ordinary, into the great
chamber where good people were assembling for the Lecture Day sermon, the minister had the effrontery to follow
her. Fortunately for the child, so did Hutchinson. The latter
slashed about with his rapier at Abigail's bidding, and again
had the satisfaction of hitting home. Abigail saw the Shape
of the minister dwindle into a grey cat, and then saw Goody
Good swoop in to gather the cat in her arms before any
other could see it.

Once the metamorphosis and flight of the godless minister had taken place, the Lecture Day service followed its
decent course, but afterward the room filled up with Shapes
coming in through the windows as thick as horse-flies. Abigail, joined now by Mary Walcott, saw the Hobbses, an
unidentified Indian, and all manner of Things. Eleazur
Putnam helped Hutchinson fight them off. Between them
they killed "a great black woman of Stonington and an Indian who came with her" and another. The floor ran with
blood, but it was spectral blood and as such invisible to the
killers, as were the corpses. Indeed the latter were quickly
removed. Looking out the window the girls saw the witches
assembling to mourn their dead.

Even when Abigail tired of her spectral sport and trotted

across the road to supper at the parsonage, she continued to receive visitors from the invisible world. In a vision she learned that "the little black minister" at whom Hutchinson had been hurling pitchforks was not only the master-mind of local witchcraft but a murderer. According to Abigail's cryptic report he had killed three "wives . . . two for himself and one for Lawson." Her announcement had the effect of releasing the hapless women from their graves. Their spirits sought out Ann Putnam, laid aside their winding-sheets and showed her gaping wounds sealed up with wax.

Even then the magistrates delayed action, for it was a horrifying thing to have a minister, the highest figure in his community, fetched on such a charge. They would avoid such scandal while there was the least doubt. Providentially, however, the revelations of Ann and Abigail coincided with a disposition on the part of some of the newer witches to confess. They now had in their hands Deliverance Hobbs, who by her past reputation was the most decent of the "confessors," certainly several cuts above Tituba and Deliverance's own wild daughter, a woman on whose word they could rely. In Salem Prison, now the lodging of accredited confessors, they consulted Deliverance who, after her terrifying day in court, was their obedient servant. The woman could now see Shapes when anyone mentioned the subject. Asked to focus her powers on this problem, Deliverance saw what they expected her to see: the small "black minister" who had once been in Salem Village, presiding over the unholy sacrament in the capacity of grand wizard of all Massachusetts.

3

The Reverend George Burroughs had not seen his late parish of Salem Village for nearly ten years, nor did he care about seeing it again. Not indeed that he was finding life easy in Maine. Ever since the overthrow of Andros and the odd philanthropy of some Bostonians in selling arms to the Indians, the "eastward" country had been beset by the devil-worshippers of the wilderness and by their allies, the French. As recently as 27 January of this year, Burroughs had joined several others in sending to the General Court in Boston a cry for help, lest the settlements be utterly exterminated. "God is manifesting His displeasure against this land," Burroughs had written. "He who formerly hath set His hand to help us . . . doth write bitter things against us."

Even in his urgency, however, Burroughs was probably happier in this rough, precarious life than he had ever been in the physical security of Salem Village. Danger of this sort draws people together. He could face it better than the senseless bickering that had made his life a burden in the Village.

He was, moreover, superbly endowed to cope with hardships. Though small of stature, he was possessed of an extraordinary strength and agility which had won admiration back in his student days, when he had been one of Harvard's first athletes. Even the Indians might well respect his capacity and endurance. In their eyes the swarthy, sinewy little man with the sleek black hair resembled a *coureur de bois* from Canada more than he did an English parson. There was something of the exotic, something Celtic about Burroughs, and this was perhaps his undoing.

But just now, early in May 1692, he had no thought of being undone. He had settled in the comparative safety of Wells with his third wife, her daughter, and his own seven children, the eldest a lad of seventeen. Here he could resume the good life, working among his books of which he had managed to conserve a goodly store in spite of his several uprootings, preaching on Sunday and Lecture Day, and taking time between to work his fields, fish the streams and hunt in the forest. In giving so much the Lord had blessed him. What more in such times could a man ask of life than what had been given to George Burroughs?

But what the Lord has given the Lord can take away. He who once gave Satan a free hand to test Job may do so even with other men; Burroughs was about to undergo a test more searching than that of the ancient patriarch.

One day while he sat at meat, men sent in answer to a summons from Salem strode into his house, hauled him from the table, and rode him off to Salem. It happened so suddenly that wife and children stared after him blankly. The man had not been allowed to finish his meal, much less to pack his belongings or make an orderly farewell. The only explanation had been the unfolding of a warrant making incomprehensible allegations.

Sudden as the blow was, however, the Burroughs family must have heard enough of what was going on in Salem Village to grasp the situation, once they thought it over. The witchcraft was the major news event of the Colony; even the charter was now of only secondary interest in comparison, and though Maine had another sleepless preoccupation in its troubles with the Indians, its people had certainly heard of the witchcraft, especially in such accessible communities as Wells. It would have been strange indeed if rumours had not reached Burroughs of what was going on in his former parish, and if he had not discussed them with his wife and children. What would not have occurred to him was that in discussing the fate of his old parishioners he was discussing his own.

News filtered up the coast after Burroughs had gone. Mrs Burroughs, the third Mrs Burroughs, left alone with a pack of children not of her bearing, heard it with tightened lips. The fantastic charge written on the warrant was proved; it was established in court that the man she had married was a wizard, ringleader of all the witches and wizards in the Colony. His very property was forfeit and sooner or later the sheriff would take it. Well, she would take it first. Mrs Burroughs, a woman of action, picked up everything of value in the house, found a buyer for the books and let out the money for interest. Then she took her own daughter and moved out, leaving the children of witchcraft to shift for themselves.

It is no part of a woman's duty to provide for the get of a wizard, convicted and condemned. Who knew what devils might be in them?

4

The magistrates, whose reluctance to admit that a minister could be on the roster of witchcraft had caused them to wait nearly two weeks after Ann Putnam's accusation before sending for Burroughs, permitted another delay after they got him. Though he was brought to Salem on 4 March, it was not until Monday, 8 March, that he was examined.

During the interval Burroughs remained in an upper chamber of Thomas Beadle's house, and was apparently not forbidden to receive visitors. He had, in Salem Town at least, some defenders. Captain Daniel King urged Elizur Keysar to go call on him. "If you are a Christian, go see him. . . . I believe he is a child of God, a choice child of God, and that God will clear his innocency."

Keysar, sure that Burroughs was the worst of the lot, was unwilling "to meddle or make with it." Nevertheless later in the day his business took him to Burroughs's chamber. He was there disturbed by the fixity with which the latter stared at him and not surprised when later in the day he began to see visions. These took the form of Things "something like jelly" in his chimney; they did "quaver with a strange motion," and there was a light "about the bigness of my hand." He called his maid and wife, and when they could make out nothing at all, realized that Burroughs had put the evil eye on him.

Before Burroughs's appearance before the magistrates on 9 May, he was given a chance to consult with a jury of his peers. The ministers of the vicinity met with him privately to sound him out on doctrine. They got from him several damaging admissions. He could not remember when he had last served the Lord's Supper—this from one who had so lately been seen administering the red bread—and only his eldest son had been baptized. The elders shook their heads over this statement, for it was an implicit confession of Anabaptist leanings and further confirmation of the old observation that the most serious forms of witchcraft begin in heresy.

When they moved from doctrine to items of common gossip they had less success. Burroughs denied that his house in Casco had been haunted, but "owned there were toads," denied that his family had been "affrighted" in the house by a white calf, or that he had forbidden his first wife, the one Salem Village had known, to write her father Ruck without his permission.

These matters cleared up for what they were worth, the ministers had a jury strip their colleague and search his body for witchmarks. But here they had to give him a clean bill of health. Burroughs's lean body was perfect. There were no "unnatural excrescences" at all, unless you counted his muscles, which, however, did seem to be of more than reasonable development on a body so small.

No effort had been spared to make the examination itself a public procedure of utmost dignity. A special session of the magistracy had been called, Sewall sitting with Hathorne and Corwin, and William Stoughton presiding. No one more eminent than the latter could have been chosen to that position, for Stoughton was both magistrate and minister. From Harvard he had gone to England during Cromwell's time to take a church; returned to Massachusetts during the godless days of the Restoration, he had applied himself to the business of government. He was a true granite man, just and inflexible in his decisions, and except that there had been some uncertainty as to where he stood during Andros's time, respected throughout Massachusetts. In him Burroughs faced one who would be invulnerable to personal considerations or false pity.

Burroughs, poor man, hardly knew whom he faced. Dazed by so abrupt a translation from such modest eminence as he had achieved in Maine to this ignominy, imperfectly acquainted with the trend of events in Salem Village since he had left it, he looked about the courtroom in bewilderment. The situation was vaguely reminiscent of an event that had occurred in 1683 when he, having resigned his pulpit, had tried to leave. He had got no farther than Ipswich when he had been collared by a constable and

brought back to the village on the charge of having left a
debt unpaid.

This charge, Burroughs well remembered, had been
brought by John Putnam. Burroughs and his family had
had the misfortune to live for some time with this branch
of the Putnam family, the parsonage being out of repair.
It had been a misfortune because in the old quarrel about
the management of the church, most of the Putnams were
of the Bayley faction, and now that Bayley had gone were
prepared to resent his successor. Naturally the John Putnams had made the most of the new minister's presence in
their household to inquire minutely into his manners and
to publish their findings to the village. They had in particular denounced his treatment of his wife; he had refused
the poor woman the harmless recreation of gossip. He had
indeed, not improbably in defence against the Putnams'
pumping of his wife, made her sign a paper promising to
give away none of his secrets. When after less than a year
in Salem Village this Mrs Burroughs had died, the Putnams
blamed the husband's severity, considered him little better
than a murderer.

The warrant under which Putnam had had him arrested
was connected with his wife's death, though the charge had
been no more serious than failure to settle incidental ex-
penses connected with the funeral, notably for two gallons
of canary and stuff for suiting. Burroughs had faced the
court not without dignity. He had no money, he acknowledged, "but there was his body." The court had on that
occasion declined to hold his body. There was a pettiness,
a meanness about the episode which shamed even the minister's opponents. How in the name of common sense could
a parson whose parish had left him nearly penniless be expected to pay all his bills? But to top everything, Deacon
Ingersoll came forward with evidence that Burroughs actually had paid this one. John Putnam was made ridiculous
—never a politic thing to do to a Putnam, however—and
Burroughs was allowed to go his way in peace.

Now, brought back on so much more deadly a charge,
Burroughs looked about the courtroom in search of the

friends who had stood by him during the parish quarrels
and had saved him harmless during that earlier brush with
the law. Where were they? He could not see them, and
indeed if any of them had come to-day they were avoiding
his eye. It was perhaps expecting too much of human nature to look for tokens of friendship at such a time. Those
most responsible for having originally brought him to the
Village church were painfully aware that if this charge were
proved, they would be exposed as those most responsible,
however ignorantly, for bringing witchcraft to the village.
There was nothing they could now do for him but pray.

The afflicted girls, who had been moppets or mere babes
when he saw them last, he carefully and by instruction for-
bore to look at. When he was presently ordered to do so as
a part of the test, the hush was broken. The girls shrieked
as his devils went into them and fell writhing to the floor.
Not even in an Indian raid had Burroughs seen anything
quite like it. He was hardly less moved than old Giles Cory
or Deliverance Hobbs had been.

"It is an amazing and humbling providence," he stam-
mered when Stoughton solicited his opinion. "But I understand nothing of it."

When the testimony against him was brought forward,
Burroughs listened with the helplessness of a man who
hears voices in a nightmare. He was, it seemed, wanted for
murder; not physical murder in such a manner as can be
tested by reference to time and place, but spectral murder,
a thing of shadows. It transpired that whenever a soldier
from the village had died in the Indian trouble in the "eastward country" where Burroughs lived, not the Indians but
he was held responsible; he had bewitched them. This information came from Ann Putnam, niece of the vindictive
John. Other victims were his first two wives, both of whom
floated into the assembly to corroborate the charge. True,
Burroughs could not see them, nor could Stoughton or
Sewall or any other except Susanna Sheldon and probably
Ann Putnam, who on their appearance went into convulsions and had to be carried out. Yet no one doubted their

presence, hardly at the time even Burroughs, though he could and did deny what they were saying.

The minister heard tributes to his strength. He was used to such praise, but now he heard his prowess exaggerated quite out of recognition; that story, for instance, about his inserting two fingers ito a barrel of molasses and lifting the barrel thus above his head. It did no good to deny such feats, however; there had always been an eyewitness, and the eyewitness swore not only to the story but to his conviction that only diabolic assistance could have given such power to so small a man.

A whole succession of fantasies, some of them rather prettily imaginative, were contributed by a young woman whom Burroughs could not place at first. When he heard the name Mercy Lewis he remembered her as the little girl whom he and his first wife had taken into their home in Maine and had brought to Salem Village with them, and whom Burroughs had eventually left with the family of the Thomas Putnams. She had been a sly piece, the kind of child who listens at door jambs, and now Burroughs discovered that she was so gifted in spying as to have kept it up when he was no longer there.

Mercy testified that he had taken her to his study and asked her to sign a "new fashion" book and that when she refused he had conducted her to a mountain-top and tempted her by showing her the kingdoms of the earth.

In vain for Burroughs to say that far from inviting Mercy to autograph his books, he would have thrashed her if he had caught her laying hands to one of them, or that he had never taken her to any mountain-top whatsoever. His denials had only a physical frame of reference; his accuser, this young paranoid, who plainly, and in Burroughs's opinion blasphemously, identified herself with Christ, was talking of Shapes, and what Burroughs' Shape had been doing he was not competent to testify. He had never seen his Shape.

Yet it existed and had been doing what it should not. Abigail Hobbs and Mary Warren, the latter not yet released from Salem Prison, were brought forward to identify him as the leader of the unholy sacrament in Parris's pasture. It was this "black minister," said the latter, who gave the blast on the spectral trumpet to summon the witches at midnight.

Not all Burroughs's study of theology or of Ramist logic could avail him against this manner of reasoning. He was committed and sent to prison to await trial. There he divided his time between writing "solemn and savory" letters of paternal admonition to his children and acquainting himself with the experiences of his fellows in witchcraft. From these he acquired considerable sophistication. When he next faced court he would not be so ill prepared.

CHAPTER X

PURITAN KNIGHT

During these troubled days in early May, the Frigate *None-such* from England was beating its way closer to the New England coast. It carried two notables, one of whom was now urgently needed to unsnarl the legal tangle created by the arrest of so many witches. This was the new royal governor, Sir William Phips; his companion was Increase Mather, president of Harvard, pastor of the Second Church, father of Cotton, and for going on four years ambassador-extraordinary from Massachusetts to England.

As the two stood at the rail together, straining their eyes for sign of landfall, they were not thinking of the witchcraft. They had not heard of it, and anyway their minds were taken up with problems that looked weightier.

Mather's mind was on the charter he was at last bringing Massachusetts; it was not the old charter restored but a new one, and there was the rub. He had not been sent to fetch a new charter; that he had done so, consenting to compromise after all these years of fruitless attempts to revive the old privileges, would be regarded in some theocratic quarters, as he was well aware, as desertion. Mather had already anticipated this viewpoint. He had drafted a document describing his work in England, first at the court of King James, then of William and Mary, and setting forth the reason for his capitulation.

"It is not so bad," he had written of the new charter, and the words so clearly fitted the lameness of his achievement and the low state of his present enthusiasm that his pen had paused here. Then he resolutely pushed it on to round off a proper period. "Take it with all its faults and it is not so bad but when I left New England the inhabitants . . . would gladly have parted with many a thousand pounds to have obtained one so good."

He reviewed the good, the incontestably good points of the charter; actually it gave privileges "in some particulars greater than those formerly enjoyed." It did not meddle with local government; laws would be made and local taxes levied as in the past by the General Court, whose representatives the people would continue to elect. All the general privileges of English citizenship, threatened by Andros, and the land titles had been confirmed to the people. Let them remember, if they were disgruntled by other provisions, by how narrow a margin Mather had saved them (not that he asked thanks) from a supreme humiliation. William, soon after coming to the throne, had sent to the colonies a circular letter confirming the last royal governors in office. But for the alertness of Mather's friends in informing him of this move and his own energetic action, the letter would have gone to Boston, and Boston would have been placed under the unthinkable obligation of recalling the deposed Andros from his confinement in Castle Island and setting him up in the Town House again. Whatever Mather had done or had not done, he had saved Boston from that.

Something like a smile passed over Mather's austere, yet not unhandsome face (in his wig he looked not unlike the late John Milton) as he recalled how he had presented the fact of a revolution in Boston to King William. It was a moment calling for all his diplomacy. Even if England had just consummated a revolution, now referred to, since it had succeeded, as "glorious," that was no indication that England would take a sympathetic view of revolutions irresponsibly set in motion in Boston.

"I presume your majesty has been informed of the great service which your subjects in New England have done for your majesty," he had begun in an interview at Hampton Court on 4 July, and this tone, skilfully evasive of any hint of apology, any suggestion of irregularity, had been accepted.

But Mather's smile faded as he thought of what other provisions the charter contained. What would the godly say when they learned that the electorate was no longer to be limited to members of the Covenant but broadened to include propertied members of every Christian sect this side of papistry? This was a revolutionary innovation, whose consequences would be incalculable. Hitherto the limitation of the privilege of voting to the elect had been the very corner-stone of theocracy. It had been a wise and humane provision designed to keep the faithful in control even when, as had long ago become the case, they were heavily outnumbered by lesser men without the Covenant. God who had not designated the majority of men to salvation surely never intended for the damned to rule. Yet now, under the new charter, it very much looked as if they might.

Mather was heavily aware that this was the aspect of his compromise that would require the most explaining. Not even the provision that Massachusetts, used now for five decades to electing its own governors, must hereafter submit to an appointee of the Crown would raise such furious opposition as this dangerous broadening of the electorate. Though Mather was too tough a soldier of the Lord to shrink from difficulties, he faced the task ahead of him without pleasure. Elisha Cook and Dr Oakes, sent to work with him in the later stages of negotiation, had refused to sign a charter containing such provisions and had gone home ahead of him to denounce him for doing so. Mather too would have rejected it if there had been any possible alternative, but there was not. The upright Puritan had not spent these years at court, at two successive courts, without learning something of statecraft and compromise. Politics, he now knew, was a matter of tacking with the wind, and God who sends the wind must have willed it so. Having failed to get the whole, he would not reject the half. To do so would be to condemn Massachusetts to drift rudderless indefinitely. It had already drifted too long. Who knew what sickness of spirit might not be bred there if some measure of security were not restored?

Yet Mather, leaning on the rail of the *Nonesuch* in a kind

of resolute despondency, knew that if it were not so patently
God's will he would hardly have gone home at all. Was it
in fact still home? The most stimulating years of his life,
first, soon after Harvard as a student at Trinity College in
Dublin, then as a chaplain in England until the Restoration
drove him home, then more recently as ambassador at
court, had been spent in the old country. After London,
though it still bore the scars of plague and fire, what was
Boston but a mean country town where cows grazed and
pigs rooted in the thoroughfares? And how pitiful were the
pretensions of little Harvard compared to the seasoned
scholarship of Oxford and Cambridge! How much better
to leave Harvard and Boston with it to his eager son Cotton,
who having known no other, supposed that here was a university and here a metropolis.

But there is no discharge in God's holy war. Mather stiffened his back and looked at the portly figure beside him.
His heart lightened. Let his enemies say what they would
about the charter, they could not deny that he was bringing
them a proper governor, one after their own heart, in Sir
William Phips. And he was quite literally bringing Sir William; in reward for signing the charter, he had been given
nearly a free hand in naming the Crown's appointees. Sir
William as governor and William Stoughton as deputy governor had been his choice.

2

Sir William was no stranger. He was a New Englander
born and bred, and what is more, a man of the people. He
had not been born to high degree but had been elevated to
it as the climax of a remarkable success story. There was
an element almost of the fabulous about him. When young
girls, like those in Salem Village, sought by unhallowed
means to learn the identity of their future husbands, what
they were inevitably hoping for was something like Sir William, a shepherd who would rise if not like David of old to
kingship, at least like William of the moment to knighthood.

He had been born on 2 February 1650, at what Cotton

Mather called "a despicable plantation on the River of the Kennebeck." His father had been a gunsmith from Bristol, and his mother, obscure otherwise, demonstrated the soundness of her stock by giving birth to twenty-six living children, twenty-one of them boys. William had grown up in the wilderness of Maine, innocent of all learning except the ways of wood and shore, the lore of the Indians and the calling of a shepherd.

During adolescence he had begun to experience unrest, a sense that he had been "born to greater matter." In this mood he apprenticed himself to a ship's carpenter, and having mastered the trade, went to Boston to seek his fortune. As one step in this enterprise he undertook, at the age of twenty-one, to learn his letters; as another he married a "lady of good fashion," whose friends thought that she was lowering herself in marrying a rough-handed ship's carpenter so recently and so imperfectly literate. But the future Lady Phips, widow of Captain Roger Spencer and daughter of John Hull (as such she was a connection of Samuel Sewall's), did not see it that way. She adored her husband and did not require his boastful assurance that he would be captain of a king's ship and would one day give her "a fair brick house in the Green Lane of Boston." She laughed at such talk; she needed no such gauds to be content. But she got them anyway, and more besides, a ladyship, a jewelled cup, and many honours and responsibilities, some of them sorrowful.

High adventure won the honours. Phips had built a ship, sailed to the Bahamas, and raised the treasure of a Spanish galleon sunk on a reef called the Baileys. He had done so against the machinations of a mutinous crew who, when they found the long labour of such engineering tedious, proposed to drop their captain on an island and go after the quicker returns of privateering.

His men gave no more trouble when the first Spanish chest was heaved over the side of the ship; at first glance, it appeared to be a lump of rock, being encrusted six inches deep with limestone, but when the crust was broken, there was the treasure, bushels of pieces of eight. Thereafter the men worked with a will and hauled up six tons of silver bullion, quantities of gold, pearls, and all manner of jewels, in all a treasure valued at £300,000.

It was not the least of Phips's achievements that he got such a crew and such a treasure safely back to England. He got them there by promising his men a just recompense, a promise that he doubtless kept as he kept all others, for the bulk of the fortune went to the Crown and his backers, his own share coming to only £16,000. That was ample for Phips to give his lady the fine house he had promised her, and besides, the Duke of Albemarle sent her a princely gift, a gold cup valued at £1,000, and King James gave her a ladyship by making William Knight of the Golden Fleece.

The distinction was conferred in 1687 when Massachusetts was smarting under the rule of Andros. In all these excitements Phips had by no means forgotten that he was a New Englander. When James, having dubbed him knight, asked him what boon he would ask, Sir William promptly requested the restoration of New England's privileges.

"Anything but that!" said the king. Instead he made his new knight high sheriff of New England. The honour came to nothing because Andros had no use for Phips or Phips for Andros, but when Boston sent the former packing in 1689 and entered into its brief independence, the colony sent Phips on a successful expedition against Nova Scotia, and on a second, less glorious one, against Quebec.

During that time Phips had received baptism at the hands of Cotton Mather and membership in the Mathers' own Second Church. The act was proof of his loyalty to New England, for he could have lived royally in old England, and churches there had invited him to membership.

But, had said Sir William, "I knew that if God had a people . . . it was here, and I resolved to rise and fall with them."

He had, however, returned to England in season to help Mather complete his negotiations. It was this circumstance that had given the latter his inspiration. So long as a royal governor must be, Sir William was the right candidate. And so it was.

Now after several weeks with him in the close quarters of the frigate, Mather might have been excused an occasional misgiving. That this flower of Puritan knighthood was not to the manner born was painfully clear. Sir William's temper was quick; when words failed him he used his fists, and even the admiring Cotton Mather was to call him a man "of an inclination cutting rather like a hatchet than a razor." Also, when words did not fail him, his speech was salty and savoury, rather outside the divine's ordinary experience.

Still, vigour in speech may be forgiven a man so vigorous as this. There was no meanness in the man; with his quick temper went a quick forgiving; he never held a grudge. Hatchets were after all more suitable to the wilderness than razors, and his problems were of the wilderness. The delicate task of convincing Massachusetts of the merits of the new charter was Mather's responsibility; the chief problem that awaited Sir William was that for which he was best fitted, the subduing of Canada, which was, in Cotton Mather's words, "the chief source of New England's misery." Sir William, searching the horizon for the landfall, was full of plans in this direction; that another sort of crisis was awaiting his action he had no idea.

3

It was the afternoon of 14 May that the *Nonesuch* was sighted taking its course around the islands in Boston Harbour. When the news reached Lady Phips, vigilant these many days upon her widow's walk, she nearly fainted with joy. By candlelight the frigate was at anchor and the new governor and his companion were being escorted to the Town House. There was no firing of volleys, for this was Sabbath eve; however eight companies of militia attended Sir William to his house and Mather to his and there were joyous reunions at both places.

Then Massachusetts rested on the Sabbath day and kept

it holy, except possibly in Salem where two more witches were picked up; and on Monday the governor set out for the Town House to begin his duties. This time there was more demonstration. Not only the eight Boston companies but two from Charlestown escorted him and stood at attention while he and his councillors were sworn in.

At last the aged Governor Bradstreet, the head of the makeshift government ever since the overthrow of Andros, was relieved. Or rather, his deputy, Thomas Danforth, was, for Bradstreet, old and ailing, had much of the time not even been able to get to meeting of a Sabbath, much less to move about supervising the business of the colony. Thereby hung a tale, for had Bradstreet been in full possession of his faculties at the onset of the witchcraft, matters might have gone somewhat differently. He was a man likely to have scant patience with the sort of evidence called "spectral" had he been able to attend the examinations. As it was, he was only remotely aware of the situation, and decisions in the handling of it had been left to Danforth. Now it was Stoughton who took the office of deputy governor, and in the Burroughs affair Stoughton had already demonstrated his respect for spectral evidence. What viewpoint Sir William would take remained to be seen.

Sir William had no viewpoint. The last thing he had expected when he arrived in Massachusetts was to find the place overrun with witches. He had been bracing himself to attack a tangible enemy; the necessity of dealing first with an invasion from the invisible world caught him unprepared. He was nearly as bewildered at the prospect as had been poor Burroughs.

There was, however, nothing of the sceptic, the Sadducee, about Sir William. A sailor on the Spanish main has seen too much of the devil to question his power. That spirits could scald innocent people with brimstone, stick them with pins, thrust them into the fire and drag them "out of their houses and over the tops of trees for many miles together"—these being some of the details laid before Sir William—seemed to him deplorable indeed but not at all improbable. He had this intelligence directly from the friends of the afflicted who now came to him, as he reported later, "with loud cries and clamour," demanding his protection. This could be accomplished only by his setting up proper courts to try and condemn the witches. For lack of such courts, because of confusion as to the exact legal procedure to be followed, Massachusetts prisons were filling up with witches, some of whom had not ceased to practise their arts under close confinement and could not be expected to do so until they were put to death.

Sir William, as innocent as any in the colony of legal training, turned to his councillors and was relieved to learn that they had already devised the proper machinery for trying witches. What was needed, it seemed, was a special court of Oyer and Terminer. When on the last Wednesday in May the governor's council set up a General Court, the latter promptly appointed judges to try the witches and arranged that their sittings should begin on 2 June.

This accomplished, Sir William departed with a clear conscience to attend to the more comprehensible difficulties offered by the French and the Indians, happy to be able to leave Massachusetts' more spectral problems in the able hands of William Stoughton. The affair, thank God, would be cleaned up and disposed of without him.

In departing he granted a boon to the afflicted girls. Unthinkable that so many of the witches already taken up should be allowed to work on these poor martyrs from their very prisons. Certain experiments had encouraged the authorities to believe that if the witches were chained such malefaction could be circumvented; besides, some of the prisons were flimsy places and chaining was almost necessary to ensure confinement. Accordingly the governor authorized the wholesale making of chains for this purpose; the expense would be charged to the several accounts of the witches.

CHAPTER XI

DEMOCRACY FOR WITCHES

During the whole of May, before the court of Oyer and Terminer could be set up to put a period to the painful business, witchcraft expanded at a terrifying rate. Long ago it had burst the immediate neighbourhood of Salem, town and village. Reading was represented now, Gloucester, Beverly, Lynn, Malden, Amesbury, Billerica, Marblehead, Boston, Charlestown, and towards the last of the month a warrant was issued for the first of what was to be a long and somewhat distinguished line of Andover witches.

The witches thus summoned were anything but a homogeneous group; the only thing that most of them had in common was having been "cried out" on. Otherwise they afforded nearly as wide a variety in race, religion, and class as did Massachusetts itself. There were whites and there were negroes; there were church members in good standing, members of no church, and there were Episcopalians (but oddly enough apparently no Quakers, though it was hardly a generation since one might as well confess to witchcraft as to the heresy of Quakerism). There were pauper witches and propertied witches, witches of every degree both high and low.

There was, in short, a democracy among witches not to be found among law-abiding theocrats. The devil had not spoken idly when he promised one of his followers that under his rule all men should be equal. The fallacy in his promise was that barring the King and Queen of Hell, both now in the hands of authority (and were not such titles an infringement on the promised equality?) no one was elevated in his service; his followers were merely degraded to a common level.

The hunt went on. The girls were now confirmed and accomplished mediums, and in their tranced state beyond the reach of compunction or discretion. They were accusing people so far out of their orbits that it really did require the hypothesis of second sight to explain how their names come into the case at all.

2

The Nathaniel Carys of Charlestown had, for instance, never to their knowledge met Miss Abigail Williams of Salem Village, nor she them; nevertheless early in May young Abigail began to talk about them a great deal, or at least about Mrs Cary. Her remarks carried to Charlestown and were of a disturbing nature. On the advice of friends the Carys went to Salem Village on 24 May to seek an introduction and clear up what was obviously a misunderstanding.

An examination was being set up as they arrived so that an immediate interview with Abigail was out of the question. Cary, welcoming the chance to get first-hand acquaintance of procedure, found him a "convenient place" in the meeting-house and kept his eyes open. He looked with particular interest at the girls; two were mere children, the rest about eighteen. One, most likely Ann Putnam, was conspicuously gifted "and could discern more than the rest."

The girls were placed between magistrates and prisoner. The latter was guarded by two officers on either side who held her arms and made sure that her glance did not stray to her victim, a safety measure, Cary gathered, designed to alleviate the torture of the girls. At one point, usually after the prisoner had been made to recite the Lord's Prayer—and how wonderfully the devil twisted her tongue when she tried, "hollowed" instead of "hallowed," tricks which the unobservant might not notice but which converted holy litany to hellish parody—the girls were asked to make the test of touch.

"Which of you," gently asked a magistrate, "will go to the prisoner at the bar?"

The girls hung back; they had been through so much, poor things; who could blame them? But eventually, while the officers took a tighter hold on the arms of the captive, to the eyes of Cary a decent matron, but in the eyes of nearly everyone else a thing more deadly than a rattler or a mad dog, one brave girl timidly inched forward. But for all these precautions she gave a shriek of agony and fell to the floor in convulsions. These would not cease until she was picked up and carried to the accused. Then one officer would twist the prisoner's head so that she could not "overlook" her victim and the other would guide her hand to the afflicted girl's, so that her touch might draw her devil back to her. That done, the afflicted one was pronounced officially out of danger; Cary could only admire the discernment of the judges in doing so, for he himself could not always make out any change in her conduct.

During the morning Mrs Cary quietly entered and sat by her husband. She did so deliberately, by way of making a test. Abigail Williams had cried out on her when she was minding her own business in Charlestown; what would the child do now that she was here? She did nothing. She and the other girls were oblivious to her presence. Later, however, in a dull interlude, one or two looked around, and spotting the strangers, came up to inquire their names. The Carys told them and still nothing happened.

They had already had a word with their old friend, John Hale, who had promised them an opportunity to interview Abigail privately at the parsonage after the examination. This arrangement proved, however, to be not immediately feasible. The Carys adjourned, like most of the spectators, to Ingersoll's ordinary, where they ordered cider and made friends with the waiter. This was none other than John Indian, a celebrity now and a kind of official guide to the witchcraft; delighted at a chance to reveal its wonders to strangers, he shared their cider, and in an expansive moment stripped off his shirt to show the scars of witchcraft he bore on his body. Cary inspected these with reserve; they were scars all right, but old scars, too long healed in his opinion to have been produced by any contemporary witch; his scepticism, however, he kept to himself.

This interview was interrupted by a stir at the door. The girls were coming in, not Abigail alone, but all her sorority, and coming in full cry. They tumbled about the floor—"like swine" later commented the irreverent Cary—and even the experienced attentions of three older women could not calm them. The spirit of prophecy was upon them; those present held their breath to see whom they would accuse. They had not long to wait.

"Cary! Cary!" cried the girls.

Mrs Cary thus achieved the distinction of being the only witch on record to go out of her way to present herself at court without waiting for an invitation. To be sure, she had one now; a warrant was produced so abruptly that it was like magic, or like the irrational sequence of events in a dream. In the afternoon she was led before the magistrates and ordered to stand with her arms outstretched. This time there were no officials to support her and when Cary demanded the right to do so, he was snubbed.

"She is strong enough to torment these girls," remarked Hathorne drily. "She should be strong enough to stand."

Cary was not used to being silenced in such a manner. In Charlestown, Captain Cary, a prosperous shipbuilder with considerable political influence, was a figure to be reckoned with. One addressed him deferentially. But Cary was now learning the levelling properties of the witchcraft. When he lashed out at the magistrates, they told him he could hold his tongue or leave the room. To leave, abandoning his wife to such men, was out of the question; dumbly he remained, standing by his wife and sometimes wiping the tears from her eyes and the sweat from her brow, this office not being forbidden him.

When the afflicted were brought in, it was the Carys' late confidant, John Indian, who led all the rest. He gave one look at the trembling woman at the bar, her arms held cruciform, and fell roaring and tumbling to the floor, "like a hog" thought Cary. To him it was incredible that any attention would be paid to so witless a lout except to order him out of the place, but Cary was wrong. The girls crowded around him and studied him with professional interest.

"Cary! Cary!" they shouted at last. It was the witch Cary who possessed him, the new, naïve witch, who had walked straight into the witch-hunt, supposing it best to be straight-forward about such things.

John Indian could not be left in torment. The magistrates ordered the woman to relieve him by touching him. But when Mrs Cary put out her hand, he snatched it and hauled her down to the floor with him, and bellowing like a bull, tumbled her about. Cary might have had his rapier in the Indian but for the celerity with which attendants stepped forward. They caught one of Mrs Cary's hands, guided it properly to John Indian, and the man relaxed his hold, ceased howling, and fell into a stupor.

The evidence was in; Mrs Cary's witchhood had been demonstrated; she would now go to prison to await her trial.

"God will take vengeance!" cried out Cary, unable any longer to contain himself. "God will deliver us out of the hands of unmerciful men!"

But there was nothing he could do for his wife but try to settle her comfortably in prison. This was difficult. In Salem Village he found a room where he could stay with her until the transfer to Boston, but the room had no bed. When she was taken to Boston Prison, Cary managed to get her transferred to Cambridge, which was in his own Middlesex County, but even here he had to watch helplessly while the jailer fastened irons to her legs. It was too much; the woman became hysterical. Yet there was nothing he could do now but watch for the opening of the witch trials. The best minds of Massachusetts would be in charge; impossible to believe that they would permit such a travesty of justice as he had seen in Salem Village.

3

John Alden had never met what he was to call "the Salem wenches"—when nothing stronger—nor they him, but everyone had heard of John Alden. He was the firstborn of the John and Priscilla whose romance had sweetened the early days of the Plymouth Colony; his fame, however, rested less on that romance, which having not yet found its Longfellow was not now spoken of, than on his own attainments as sea captain and soldier; he had been much in the wars against the Indians and had thereby not only a reputation for valour but for a wide and intimate knowledge of Indian life.

He was also a tall man and from Boston. At long last the magistrates had succeeded in decoding that cryptic phrase of Tituba's. Or rather the girls, never allowed for long at a time to forget their duty of identifying this culprit, had at last hit upon a plausible suspect. Now that they had done so, the event was considered so significant that it was Deputy Governor Stoughton himself who had ordered John Alden to report to Salem Village.

Alden strode into the courtroom on 28 May, his hat on his head (or at least so the girls reported), his sword at his side, and like Cary before him, looked about and took stock of the situation.

The girls, the "afflicted children" so called, whose names were on the lips of everyone these days, were already in place and already in possession. Alden looked them over and was not impressed. "Juggling tricks" was the way he later put it; they were falling down "crying out and staring into people's faces." He was glad to note that a good friend of his was sitting on the bench to-day; Bartholomew Gedney had for the occasion joined Hathorne and Corwin, and Gedney, though of Salem, which seemed to have taken leave of its wits, was not one to be taken in by this sort of thing.

The stage was set when Alden entered. The magistrates,

noting where he stood, turned to the girls and asked them
to point out the author of their present woes.

The girls rolled their eyes over the courtroom for some
moments in silence. Their acquaintance with Alden had
been exclusively spectral; they found his physical presence
confusing. Indeed when one at last ventured to point a
tentative finger, she pointed at quite the wrong man, one
Captain Hill, who all blameless of witchcraft either then
or thereafter, stood by the guilty Alden.

A man standing behind her quickly bent over the girl
and whispered to her.

"Alden! Alden!" cried the girl, and redirected her finger.

"How do you know it is Alden?" asked a magistrate.

"The man told me so."

Much as the magistrates longed to clear up their long-
standing account with the "tall man of Boston," they had
to regard this identification as equivocal. Remembering the
case of Nehemiah Abbott, they had the suspect led outside and told the girls to gather around him and get a good
look by daylight. And now, beyond any possibility of
doubt, the girls saw who Alden was.

"There stands Alden!" cried one. "A bold fellow with his
hat on before the judges. He sells powder and shot to the
Indians and French and lies with Indian squaws and has
Indian papooses."

"There is not a word of truth in all they say of me!" exploded Alden, and indeed, these were not the charges on
which he had been summoned. That he had been identified, however, was incontestable. He was put into the hands
of a marshal, and his sword, with which he now heard he
had been nicking the tender flesh of these maids, who had
scars to prove it, was taken away from him. In the afternoon, swordless and hatless he was led into the meeting-
house, stood on a chair, and put through his examination.

The afflicted girls stood all about him, wincing away
from him and whimpering that in spite of all precautions
he was pinching them. Alden, forbidden to so much as look
at them, turned irascibly to the magistrates.

"Just why do your honours suppose I have no better

things to do than to come to Salem to afflict these persons that I never knew or saw before?"

The magistrates silenced him coldly. Facts interested them, not words. It was time for the demonstration. Let him look at the girls.

Alden looked; the girls fell in a heap at his feet.

"Set his hand to theirs," a magistrate called to the officer.

It was done. The girls got up and dusted themselves off. The wizard on the chair had difficulty keeping his face straight. He turned to the magistrates and stared hard at his friend Gedney.

"What's the reason *you* don't fall down when I look at you?" he demanded. "Can you give me one?"

Gedney said nothing. His eyes were hard. He had come to court really anxious to help an old friend. Not for a moment had he believed Alden capable of such conduct until with his own eyes he saw him knock the girls down with a look and raise them again with a touch. Sophistries were of no use against such facts.

"Confess and give glory to God," said Gedney.

"I hope to give glory to God, but not to gratify the devil," retorted Alden. "I wonder at God in suffering these creatures to accuse innocent people."

He could not be permitted to go on. Ponderously the Reverend Nicholas Noyes arose and "stopped his mouth" with a prayer and a long discourse on God's providence. Alden managed just one more outburst before they led him away. Granted that it was a spirit these girls had, "it was a lying spirit!"

His own spirit subsided somewhat in captivity. He was, to be sure, being a personage, given special consideration; he was allowed to await trial under guard in his own home in Boston. Here during fifteen weeks of blistering heat he learned to take his predicament seriously, and was grateful when friends came to pray with him. Cotton Mather came, and Samuel Willard and Samuel Sewall, and they all prayed and wrestled with the spirit together. But when later in the season matters reached their crucial point, John

Alden, used to looking after himself, did not leave his fate to the Lord.

4

Philip English of Salem was finally brought in on 31 May. His wife Mary was already in custody, and he himself had been eluding the constables for some weeks. Now he appeared in court and heard Susanna Sheldon testify that he had spectrally represented himself to her as God.

The English family were almost gentry; at least they gave themselves such airs. They lived in a fine, many-gabled house on Essex Street in Salem, and English was a seafaring man with a finger in any number of the more profitable Salem pies. He owned fourteen buildings, a wharf, twenty-one sailing vessels and shares in many others. But his prosperity had not brought him popularity. He was for one thing an outlander, born not decently in England, but in Guernsey; the very name he bore bred suspicion, being an anglicization of his real name, L'Anglais, which being French, had papist overtones. His carriage on the Sabbath was not irreproachable, and for all his means he resented paying rates to a church not of his choosing. His own leanings were to the Church of England, and he had long fretted at not being allowed to build a church where he could worship in his own manner.

"Where now is your religious toleration?" he had been heard to exclaim. That was loose, improper talk, savouring of radicalism if not atheism in the ears of proper Salem folk of 1692. The new charter, to be sure, was about to commit them to exactly what English demanded, but Salem was as yet by no means won over to the new charter.

So English was committed and went moodily into duress. Like Alden, he and his wife were given privileges suitable to their station; they might on occasion go forth to meeting so long as they were back under guard by candlelight.

At the opposite end of the social scale stood Martha Carrier, who came up for examination the same day as English. Martha was of Andover, but Andover did not claim her gladly. In fact when her family had first arrived in 1690 it had been "warned off"; Martha and her children had not only stayed but proceeded to have smallpox and to spread it "with wicked carelessness" and then to assume that "the care of them belongs to the Salactmen of Andover," an assumption with which the "salactmen" by no means concurred. Now she had brought in a viler distemper, the witchcraft. She had been connected with a proved witch of Billerica, called "Aunt Toothaker" by her children, and any number of Martha's neighbours stood ready to testify that she was no less practised in this art. The young seeresses of Salem Village had recently discovered that she was not only a witch but queen of all Massachusetts witches, Burroughs being the king.

Doubtless it was her consciousness of this eminence that prevented Martha Carrier from keeping a civil tongue in her head when she stood at the bar before her betters.

"What black man did you see?" asked a magistrate.

"I saw no black man but your own presence," answered Martha smartly.

There was more of that sort; then Susanna Sheldon said dreamily from a trance, "I wonder what you could murder thirteen persons for."

The prisoner turned fiercely on the judges. "It is a shameful thing that you should mind these folks that are out of their wits!"

The yelling of the girls became ear-splitting; even so Martha sometimes lifted her voice above theirs.

"You lie! I am wronged! . . . The devil is a liar!"

Visitors watched, listened, and shuddered. The Reverend Henry Gibbs of Watertown, present purely as a spectator, wrote in his diary that there were "remarkable and prodigious passages. Wonders I saw, but how to judge and conclude I am at a loss."

The experienced magistrates had no difficulty in concluding and judging. They had only to ask Martha's pockmarked children. The asking involved some complexities; the two older boys had to be tied head to heels until the blood came from their mouths before they would testify, but when they started they talked freely. They too were witches, they gasped; their mother had made them so. A younger child volunteered some interesting revelation without such persuasion. Her mother was a black cat. How did she know? "The cat said so."

So the "rampant hag," Cotton Mather's phrase, was indicted and put away to await her trial.

5

Of interest among recent arrests in Salem Village was that of John Willard. He had been a deputy constable and as such had in March brought in several of the witches. Then he turned against his own profession and cried out against the whole witch-hunt.

"Hang them, they're all witches!" he had cried.

This is no sane talk from a constable, and his behaviour, the extreme disinclination he now showed to attend any further to his sworn duties, was no better. His own family was aroused against him. When a young cousin fell ill, Willard's grandfather called in Mercy Lewis and Mary Walcott to diagnose the case. It was as he had suspected. The girls could see Willard crushing the boy's throat and chest. Nor could they stop him. The boy died in agony, "bewitched to death," as Parris wrote in his parish book, and the spirits of other victims of his began to appear to the mediumistic Mrs Ann Putnam; Willard had been involved in no less than twelve murders, one of them her own six weeks' daughter Sarah.

Willard knew better than to hang around Salem Village with such talk going on. He fled, but not far enough. On 18 May, ten days after a warrant had been issued, Constable John Putnam, Jun., picked him up in Lancaster and turned him in.

CHAPTER XII

VILLAGE CIRCE

By now every responsible person in Massachusetts was looking to the witch trials as the one measure that could bring the runaway inflation in witchcraft under control.

It was an unhappy providence that had allowed three months to lapse between the taking of the first witch and the trials. Thanks to this prolonged stress and uncertainty, the farmers in the communities most concerned were neglecting their work exactly when it needed their undivided attention; there would be real want if things kept on this way. Worse, the delay was giving the devil's evangelists time to canvass the entire country. It wrung the heart to hear how recently some of the confessors had fallen. "It was lately then—the night before last," poor Deliverance Hobbs had testified. It had not been enough merely to arrest and examine the witches. For one thing, many of them had the spectral agility to slip out of both bars and chains and enjoy their abominations with whetted appetites; for another, they supposed themselves immune to punishment under the devil's protection. Until the legend of the devil's invincibility was shattered by trial and hanging, there would be no real restraining the witches, no deterring of goodwives and goodmen from listening to their lies.

The devil's timing of his assault had been a stroke of genius. He had taken the one moment when the government was powerless to act. A provisional government of dubious legality, headed by a senile and incompetent governor, dared not initiate decisive action in a capital case of such magnitude.

So everyone now longed for the trials, even, oddly enough, many of the witches themselves.

This statement could not have held for all witches, however, particularly the confessors. Many of these were shamed, reluctant creatures, and some were actually nerving themselves to recant their confessions. Besides, though they were now treated considerately, with a mercy denied the unconfessing, none could know for sure what would happen when their cases came to court. All precedents from the old world indicated that a confessing witch would hang with her unregenerate sister. There was a feeling, which grew stronger as time went on, that the Massachusetts justices would be inclined to disregard precedent in this direction, that they would not inflict capital punishment on the repentant. No one, however, could be sure until the matter had been put to the test, and few were eager for such a test. It was only the likes of Abigail Hobbs who looked forward to the notoriety of further court appearances.

On the other hand, witches who had held to their plea of innocence looked forward to the trials as a chance to obtain a fair hearing. To the more intelligent of these it was preposterous to suppose that the trials, conducted by the best minds in Massachusetts, would proceed on the same dreamlike plane as the examinations, that men and women of sound mind and good repute would be condemned on the basis of the fancies of young girls. Massachusetts as they knew it was a saner place than that. Martha Cory still had her faith in her ability to reason with reasonable people; the "Towne girls," Rebecca Nurse, Sarah Cloyce, Mary Esty, brought intimately and how strangely together for the first time since their youth, had been comparing their experiences and discussing how not only hearings but examinations for witchmarks could be more rationally conducted; if the judges would not see these things for themselves when the matter came to a trial, they would point them out. John Procter had been collecting evidence on how "free confessions" were being extracted from the men. His own eldest son, brought in later in the spring, had been chained heel to neck in the form of torture that had wrung "confessions" from the sons of Martha Carrier, a torture almost impossible to withstand. The chances were that the decent men appointed to preside over the trials were ignorant of this aspect of "confession." John Procter would instruct them, and his spirit unbowed by his prison experience, he looked forward to the trials as a fighter in training looks forward to the ring.

And all witches longed for a respite, however brief, from the weight of the chains on their limbs, the foulness of the quarters into which some of them had been packed for months, the indignities and worse to which they were periodically subjected by prison officials, especially by the juries assigned to search them for witchmarks. The only alleviation of their lot was that they were not held *incommunicado;* they could entertain visitors. The daughters of Elizabeth How, one of the recruits brought in from Topsfield in May, took turns in making weekly trips to Boston to bring her country butter, clean linen and comfort; sometimes Elizabeth's blind husband rode with one of them.

But if access was not denied to friends, neither was it denied the idly curious who came to stare at the prisoners as if at a rare kind of zoological exhibit, in spite of the risk of such inquisitiveness. Sarah Good still had her pipe and begged tobacco of every comer. When seventeen-year-old Mercy Short replied by throwing a handful of shavings into her face, saying, "There's tobacco good enough for you!" Sarah, her witch fires unquenched, muttered to such effect that Mercy fell into sore affliction, and being of Boston, became a fruitful subject for one of Cotton Mather's psychoanalytic studies.

Sarah's little daughter Dorcas was in prison all this time, shut out of the sun, cooped up with ageing women in all degrees of piety, intelligence, iniquity and imbecility, listening to them scream out in their nightmares or under the stress of searches for witchmarks, living on meagre fare. She was no longer "hale and well looking." Her face was pinched and sullen, her hair wild and matted. No one looking at the little creature, now furtive and savage as any alley cat, could doubt that here was one of Satan's breed. Treat a child like a witch and you'll have one.

Nearly all of these people craved the release of trial. But they craved it a little nervously. Almost everyone preferred that someone else be the first to try the temper of the judges. On 2 June that honour fell to Bridget Bishop.

2

Of the seven judges originally appointed to the Court of Oyer and Terminer, only one, Bartholomew Gedney, was from Salem. Of the others, four were from Boston, these being Samuel Sewall, John Richards, William Sergeant, and Wait Winthrop. Nathaniel Saltonstall was from Haverhill, and Deputy Governor Stoughton, presiding justice, from Dorchester. Thus not only were the judges all picked men of sound past experience in the Court of Assistants, but they were as free as anyone in Massachusetts could be of entanglement in the web of spite that was the fabric of so many of the accusations. This is not to say that they all came fresh and unprejudiced to their sittings; at least three, Stoughton, Sewall and Gedney, had already played some part in the examinations.

The clerk of court, Stephen Sewall, was not only of Salem but was intimately concerned with the witchcraft through the presence in his household of little Betty Parris. Thomas Newton, "gent," sworn in as King's Attorney, was apparently free of any such connections. Neither of the magistrates most closely connected with the witchcraft, Hathorne and Corwin, was to sit on the court, at least at first; the examinations were still going on; they could ill be spared.

But when this court convened in Salem in early June it dealt a blow to the hopes of those who had supposed that the trials would be conducted on a different basis from the examinations. So far as this court was concerned, the examination was the trial; its records were reviewed not as hypotheses to be tested, but as facts already proved; the only really new business was the hearing of testimony collected since the examination and the deliberations of a jury in whose hands the fate of the prisoner nominally lay. Cotton Mather described court procedure in the case of Bridget Bishop with a kind of naïve accuracy when he remarked "there was little occasion to prove the witchcraft, this being evident and notorious to all beholders."

Yet those who were eventually to follow Bridget on the stand need not lose heart from this one precedent. Bridget was too special a case, too marked a character, for her fate to govern the fate of all the rest. Thanks to her flashy taste in dress, her "smooth and flattering manner" with men, the questionable gaieties that had gone on in her two taverns, she had been gossiped about as a witch as far back as King Philip's War. Even without the question of witchcraft, a Puritan community would be almost certainly bound to investigate the conduct of such a woman sooner or later.

Poor Bridget, denied any counsel but that of the devil whom the girls saw accompany her, got off to a bad start. In the very act of walking with the guards from Salem Prison to the court, she cast a glance at "the great and spacious meeting-house" in passing and at once a great clatter rose within. Investigators looking in to see what the woman's evil eye had done "found a board which was strongly fastened with several nails transported into another quarter of the house." Obviously Bridget had sent her devil inside to make whatever gesture of defiance could be made on short order.

Much of the testimony collected since Bridget's first appearance in April and now read in court stressed the fact that she was one of those women who, though no longer young, had power over the imaginations of men. William Stacy admitted that when he was two and twenty he had admired her, largely because of her kindness in visiting him when he had smallpox. Later he had his doubts of her character and began to listen to gossip: Bridget had expressed her resentment of his joining such discussions "because folks would believe me before anyone else," and it was after that that he began to have some unnerving experiences. Once his wagon wheel sank in a hole, and when he climbed down to free it, the hole itself vanished before his eyes.

Then he, now a decent husband and father, began to be plagued by the Shape of Bridget in his chamber at night.

Nor did she haunt young Stacy alone; she also hovered over the beds of Samuel Gray and Richard Coman and Jack Louder. To the latter she came sometimes in her own form, sometimes as a black pig, and once with the body of a monkey, the feet of a cock, and the face of a man. She was a village Circe, though it was herself she turned to beast—or at least so honest men, unable to keep her scarlets and laces out of their minds, interpreted their night thoughts.

There was worse. Because these good men virtuously repelled her advances, their lawfully begotten children pined and died, Samuel Gray's little boy, Tracy's daughter Priscilla, and Shattuck's epileptic son. She was not enchantress only, but murderess.

That Bridget's own husband (her second; she sometimes still went by the name of Oliver after her first) had suspected her of witchcraft was reported by Elizabeth Balch, who had once seen a quarrel between man and wife. Bridget was riding on the pillion behind her husband when the latter spurred his horse to a pace that nearly threw her. Bridget lost her temper, and they had words. She was a "bad wife," said her husband; "the devil had come bodily to her . . . and she sat up all night with the devil." Shocked at such talk Goody Balch had scolded him, but afterwards, the more she thought over the incident, the more it bothered her. What was particularly odd was that during the entire tirade Bridget had not once opened her mouth to defend herself.

Deliverance Hobbs, almost as indispensable now as the afflicted girls, reported that Bridget had helped administer the sacrament on the witches' sabbath, and that after she herself had confessed, Bridget's Shape had beaten her with iron rods to try to make her retract her confession. The judges found this last statement especially interesting; it answered people like Procter who claimed that confessors confessed under torture. What if it were true? The torments inflicted by the officials were legal and just and at worst

she even suck
ed a snake
VILLAGE CIRCE 155

nothing compared to the secret, invisible tortures that the witches inflicted on the godly.

The afflicted girls gave appropriate demonstration of their anguish, backed up the charges that Bridget had murdered several children, and Susanna Sheldon added that she had seen this witch give suck to her familiar, a snake. This detail was something of a novelty; snakes, common enough in the new world, were comparatively rare in the old, where this folklore originated, and were mentioned in the testimony only on this one occasion. To Bridget fell the honour of nursing a strictly indigenous imp.

Both Bridget's houses, past and present, had been ransacked, and the searchers had found in the cellar of the old house in Salem Village poppets made of rags and "hogs Brussels," stuck with headless pins. Bridget, confronted with these objects, could give no explanation that was "reasonable and tolerable."

She was searched for witchmarks just before her trial and right after. On the first occasion a jury of women, equipped with pins which they stuck into any part of her body that looked at all unusual, discovered a "witch's tet" between "ye pupendum and anus"; on the second, three hours later, this "tet" had withered to dry skin. The witnesses had these observations put in writing and carefully set their marks thereto, signing not with a vulgar X, but each with her own ingenious hieroglyph, distinct from all the others.

What Bridget said and did in court Stephen Sewall took no pains to record, or else the notes were mislaid. The only surviving clue to her defence is a deposition made the day before the trial by her stepson Edward Bishop and his wife Sarah, attacking the credibility of the afflicted girls in the person of Mary Warren, who had in the privacy of Salem Prison frequently contradicted statements she had made to the magistrates. The judges were little likely to give weight to such testimony. They knew all about poor Mary Warren, her brief transgression, her lasting repentance. Mary herself, now safely restored to the ranks of the accusers, was not disposed to risk her reputation again. If she couldn't save her master thus, why should she attempt it for the likes of Bridget Bishop?

The jury, possessed of these facts, had no doubt that the woman was guilty and pronounced her so; the judges condemned her to hang. Then a difficulty arose on a question of the present status of Massachusetts law. Not until after 8 June, when the General Court legalized the sentence by reviving an old colonial law making witchcraft a capital offence, could action be taken. On 10 June, High Sheriff George Corwin took her to the top of Gallows Hill and hanged her all alone from the branches of a great oak tree. Now the honest men of Salem could sleep in peace, sure that the Shape of Bridget would trouble them no more.

3

The dispatch of the judges had been heartening to any law-abiding person. Now, however, came a perilous and dismaying delay. Following the trial of 2 June the judges did not sit again until 28 June. During that time witch after witch was brought in, examined, and crammed into prisons already packed to bursting, and still the judges tarried.

The cause of the delay was carefully veiled from the public, but the fact was that a schism was developing among the judges on questions of procedure, particularly the interpretation of spectral evidence. At least one member of the court had been struck by the fact that were such evidence barred, Bridget Bishop had been convicted for little more than wearing scarlet, countenancing "shovelboard," and getting herself talked about, all offences, perhaps, but hardly capital offences.

An authoritative, unequivocal statement on procedure was indispensable if the court was to function. Governor Phips, in and out of Boston these days, his real attention concentrated on crises along the Canadian border, would not presume to speak with authority on a matter so spectral, so foreign to his practical experience. Writing to England for advice would entail unthinkable delay; one might as well consult Samuel Pepys of the Admiralty on what to do about a fire currently raging among shipping on the waterfront. An unimpeachable authority in New England must be appealed to, and what other authority could there be but the Puritan ministry? The witchcraft was by no means a legal matter only; it involved theological considerations that only the ministers could pass on. Let the ministers, agreed the judges, give guidance in this emergency, and let them give it quickly.

It was done. By 15 June a conference of twelve ministers of the Boston district were ready to put themselves on record, Cotton Mather acting as amanuensis. And some of the details of this document were of a nature calculated to bring joyous relief to many a heartsick prisoner.

"A very critical and exquisite caution" was advised in the trials "lest by too much credulity of things received only upon the devil's authority there be a door opened for a long train of miserable consequences." Proceedings must be "managed with an exceeding tenderness towards those that may be complained of, especially if they have been persons formerly of unblemished reputation"; the ministers hoped for the clearing of many.

Spectral evidence was to be handled with care; in plain words the ministers stated that the "dæmon may assume the shape of the innocent," a suggestion that both Rebecca Nurse and Susanna Martin had made before them. Conviction should therefore be on evidence "certainly more considerable than barely the accused person being represented by a spectre unto the afflicted." Even "touching," which in the experience of the Carys and of John Alden had become the magistrates' prime test of guilt, was discredited as "no infallible evidence" and "frequently liable to be abused by the devil's legerdemain."

Thus far it was by modern standards an enlightened document, reflecting close observation, hard thinking and honest soul-searching on the part of its reverend authors, who included among others Samuel Willard and Increase Mather. It remained, unfortunately, in effect an equivocal document. In spite of the caution against too much reliance on spectral evidence, it went on to laud without reserve "the sedulous and assiduous endeavours" of magistrates and judges who had in practice disregarded nearly all other evidence, and to "humbly recommend the speedy and vigorous prosecution of such as have rendered themselves obnoxious."

It seems also to have been at the time a top secret document. Its effect released to the public at large might have been one thing; its effect as a confidential memorandum presented to the judges and juries alone, and to be used at their own discretion, was simply to confirm the former at least in the way the magistrates had already chosen. William Stoughton, presiding justice, probably played the decisive role in its interpretation. He himself, who had received at Harvard and Oxford as sound a theological training as any minister in Massachusetts, had no misgivings at all about the validity of spectral evidence. In his eyes the notion that the devil could take the shape of an innocent person was close to sacrilegious, a questioning of the omnipotence and benevolence of God Himself.

When the trials were resumed on 28 June not the closest observer could detect any deviation in procedure. Presently, however, there was one. Saltonstall, whose Haverhill home was far removed from the storm centre of witchcraft, could not bring himself to believe the pretensions of the afflicted girls or the evidence on which convictions were being obtained; nor on the other hand could he single-handed reform such proceedings. Accordingly he resigned from the bench and the experienced Corwin of Salem took his place.

Saltonstall did not retreat from such a battle unscathed. His nerves must have been sorely tried, for in Haverhill he took to drinking heavily, so heavily that Sewall, himself no teetotaller, felt obliged to write and reprove him. In the same letter he assured him that he still trusted him in spite of recent reports. For although Saltonstall had withdrawn so quietly that the general public probably supposed that he had no other reason than the necessity of giving his full attention to renewed raids on Haverhill by the Indians, his defection had not escaped the attention of the afflicted girls and their counsellors. Some of them were now crying out on him; they had plainly seen his Shape under incriminating circumstances.

CHAPTER XIII

DAMNED FOR THE GLORY OF GOD

One of the first cases tried by the court when it resumed its sittings late in June was that of Rebecca Nurse. A jury headed by Thomas Fisk heard the evidence, retired to Corwin's house to deliberate and returned to court with the verdict: not guilty.

Obviously these good men and true had read every word of the ministers' advice to the judges and had taken it to heart. In court, for instance, the Putnams had testified that Rebecca had murdered six children, and Sarah Holton that she had killed her husband for letting his hogs get into her garden. But all this was spectral evidence. The jury read over again the ministers' recommendations of "exquisite caution" and of convicting on something "more considerable than the accused persons being represented by a spectre unto the afflicted" and decided that all this testimony could be disregarded.

The ministers had urged "an exceeding tenderness" towards "persons formerly of an unblemished reputation." What was Rebecca's reputation? The jury had before it a petition signed by more than a score of respectable citizens of Salem Village attesting to Rebecca's upright and unwitchlike character, to her piety, to the extraordinary care she had lavished on the Christian upbringing of her children. In addition they had the evidence of their own eyes; they had watched Rebecca on the stand and could well believe that this gentle woman, so patient in her adversity, so steadfast in her protestations of innocence, had indeed "never afflicted no child, no never" in her life.

There was one other significant testimony. As many of Rebecca's children as could manage it attended court and there kept a vigilant eye on the conduct of the accusers. Sarah Nurse, greatly daring to save her mother, came forward with a deposition: "I saw Goody Bibber pull pins out of her close and held them between her fingers and claspt her hands round her knees and then she cried out and said Goody Nurse pinched her. This I can testify."

Having deliberated on all these matters, the jury had no great difficulty in coming to an agreement; they filed back into court and gave their verdict: not guilty.

They were at this stage an inexperienced jury, at least as regards the witchcraft. The trials were held in Salem Town instead of in the village, and probably few of these men had seen the tumult that had attended some of the examinations; though the girls had "cried out" during the trial of Bridget Bishop, nothing very sensational had happened then. There had been nothing in their experience to prepare them for what happened now.

Before their eyes the courtroom became a madhouse. Out of the throats of the girls issued a howling and roaring that was both more and less than human. Their bodies jerked and snapped in the unearthly choreography of their convulsions.

Some of the newer judges, as inexperienced as the jury in the ways of bedlam, stared about them and at each other. To all of them, with one probable exception, since Saltonstall was still of the court at this trial, the verdict was as unexpected and improper as it seemed to the girls. Through the tumult one was heard to express his displeasure and another, getting up to leave the bench, to say that he would have the prisoner indicted anew.

Only Chief Justice Stoughton, man of granite, was untouched by this disorder. He sat a fine figure of composure, his hair silver under his black skull cap, and fixed his dark eyes on the spokesman, Thomas Fisk.

"I will not impose on the jury," said Stoughton, and at his calm, judicial tone the din subsided somewhat, "but I must ask you if you considered one statement made by the prisoner. When Deliverance Hobbs was brought into court to testify, the prisoner, turning her head to her said, 'What, do you bring her? She is one of us.' Has the jury weighed the implications of this statement?"

Fisk, faltering before the steady eye of the chief justice, troubled by the clamour of the girls which was rising again like an ill wind, found that for the life of him he could not remember. Neither, when he returned to it for consultation, could the jury. Some members had not even heard the original statement; others could not agree on just what form the words had taken, much less what they meant. There was nothing to do but send Fisk back to court to ask Rebecca to repeat and explain herself.

Rebecca had been left in peace for some time now. Relaxing her anxious straining to hear, she was at rest, staring fixedly ahead of her. In some ways deafness was a blessed providence; the racket of the girls was to her only a confused buzzing. In her abstraction she did not mark the man who stopped before her—so many came and went—and "something hard of hearing and full of grief" as she explained afterward, she did not know that he had spoken to her.

Fisk waited in embarrassed uncertainty. No one came to his assistance; no court official intervened to call Rebecca from her brown study, probably because, given the disorder of the courtroom, no one grasped the situation. At close range Fisk was discovering that there was indeed something unearthly, something witchlike about this woman. The glassy stare of her eyes passed over him unseeing; her mouth worked as if in prayer, but to whom? He returned at last to the jury his question unanswered.

The jury weighed the implications of the incident. There were two incriminating factors, one of them the renewed affliction of the girls. Long ago Hathorne and Corwin had discovered as a kind of unwritten rule of evidence that the girls could be used as a kind of judiciary barometer; let any degree of false pity creep into the administration of justice and the girls were tormented. What havoc their verdict had wrought the jurymen could see for themselves.

Then there was Rebecca's silence at such a moment on such a point. They bowed before the acuity of Justice Stoughton, so much more learned than any poor juryman. Obviously Rebecca's "one of us" in reference to Goody Hobbs had been an involuntary admission of guilt. It was an allusion to the witches' sabbaths in which Deliverance had participated with her before she repented; Rebecca had seen her there, and now dared not deny it.

When the jury came back into court they brought the verdict expected of them: guilty.

2

Rebecca had no less than three pastors who should have known her piety, her charity—and her deafness. How often had not Parris seen the old woman leaning forward in meeting, cupping her ear to catch the word of God?

Technically, of course, Parris was not really her pastor, since though she regularly attended his services, she had never had her dismission from the First Church of Salem. The responsibility for her soul's welfare accordingly lay with John Higginson and Nicholas Noyes. The former should have remembered Rebecca, but he was far gone in years and infirmities and had of late left pastoral details to his second in command, Noyes. The latter, called to Salem Town three years after the Nurses had moved to the village, hardly knew the woman; in fact his acquaintance with her was almost wholly based on his sedulous attendance at examinations and trials. He must have asked Parris for further detail, but if he expected thereby to hear extenuating circumstances, he was expecting bread from stone. Not once had Parris questioned the guilt of any member of his parish, no matter what his past record, once the girls had accused him.

How then did these shepherds of souls minister to this lost sheep in her affliction? They haled her into meeting and had her publicly excommunicated.

Noyes lost no time in carrying out this wholesome measure; the ceremony took place on the first Sabbath after the

trial, at the afternoon meeting on 3 July. The fact that the
prisoner had collapsed after the trial was not allowed to
make any difference. Rebecca, unable to walk, was carried
from Salem Prison in a chair, and that chair set down in
the broad aisle of "the great and spacious meeting-house"
so lately desecrated by the demon of Bridget Bishop. Then
not only Noyes but his senior pastor, old John Higginson,
mounted the pulpit, and two deacons and ruling elders took
their seats before them. The auditorium was full; the congregation sat in deathly hush, for this was a deathly occasion.

The reading of the sentence was left to Noyes, and the
congregation shuddered under its impact. There was something unearthly, something intolerable in the scene. It was
as if Michael Wigglesworth's day of doom were being enacted not in the next world, but here in this plain and decent meeting-house. Before their eyes one of them was being judged, and not merely to the gallows, but to eternal
damnation. God was relieved of any necessity for passing
on the case in a later judgment; the visible congregation
of God had respectfully taken over His function; the woman
was damned here and now.

Rebecca alone heard nothing; again her deafness was
merciful. Her trembling hands clutched at the arms of her
chair, and before her strength had altogether given way,
silent men carried her back to prison.

But though the church had renounced her, her children
had not. They would not accept her sentence, either temporal or spiritual. Sons and sons-in-law dropped their work
on the farm and made for Boston, where Phips was briefly
in residence, and though they were simple folk, without
friends of great estate to help them, they gained an audience. Before him they laid the dossier they had been collecting: the testimony of her character that the neighbours
had signed; Fisk's explanation of why the jury had revised
its original verdict; Rebecca's explanation of why she had
not answered the unheard question and of what her remark
had meant (knowing Deliverance Hobbs as a fellow prisoner, she had challenged her right to testify). They brought

also an appeal from Rebecca herself. A jury of women had found a "witchmark" on her; Rebecca asked that qualified midwives be allowed to examine the mark on the grounds that it was an injury of childbirth such as any woman might bear and any midwife would recognize.

For all his eminence, Phips was as simple at heart as most Salem Villagers. Gladly would he have kept himself clear of the whole affair; what did a plain ship's carpenter with no pretensions to learning know of such things as these? But he could not deny himself to people so honest and so distressed, and when he heard the story and saw the evidence they bore with them, he could not deny the plausibility of their claims. So he signed a reprieve for Rebecca Nurse.

But if Phips could not deny himself to the friends of the prisoner, neither could he deny himself to her enemies, who were also honest, distressed, and who brought evidence with them, and who, moreover, had the backing of some of the great ones of Massachusetts. They also brought frightening news. At the very moment the governor's hand had been put to the reprieve, Rebecca's devils had been unleashed and had gone into the girls again; some of them were dying. Was it really the will of the Governor that an old proved criminal be kept alive at the cost of the lives of young and innocent girls?

It was not; Governor Phips recalled his reprieve and fled again to the peace of the Indian wars in the north.

3

It was at this time that Parris began to note an unseemly falling away in attendance at meeting on the part of the Nurse family. The closer the day of the execution, the more conspicuous the absence of the sons and daughters of Rebecca, who had never stood in greater need of the church and its consolations. He spoke rather sharply on the subject from the pulpit, but even this did little good. If the children of Rebecca came at all they did not sit at his feet quite as they had of old. There was an indefinable difference, something in their eyes that even this insensitive man found difficult to meet.

To the members of the Nurse clan was being revealed in these days a new concept of the strategy of the devil. Those who said that his assault was directed against the churches had told only half the truth; they now knew that the devil had not merely attacked the meeting-houses: he had taken them. It was he who looked out from the hard eyes of these black-coated ministers, who forgetful of every Biblical injunction toward charity preached only the doctrine of vengeance to their lost and desolate flock. They would never forgive the likes of Noyes and Parris; the Bible, which counsels forgiveness for men, does not suggest it for devils; a devil can only be cast out.

The kinsmen of Rebecca did not talk this way of course, not publicly, perhaps not yet even privately. There was nothing they could do now but bide their time and give what comfort they were permitted to give to that poor saint, their matriarch. As for Rebecca, a Puritan born and bred, unshakable in her faith, for the glory of God she would even suffer damnation. But ever again as she prayed, as she bent over psaltery and testament, that look of strained, listening puzzlement came over her soft crumpled face. What was her sin, still unrepented of, that in her old age God had sent her such affliction as this?

CHAPTER XIV

BLOOD TO DRINK

Fortunately for the future of the Church in New England, not all ministers showed themselves as hard of heart to the defendants in the witchcraft as did Noyes and Parris. There were more compassionate men. One of these was the Reverend Samuel Willard of the Old South Church of Boston. A member of the conference of ministers consulted by the judges, he had been one of those most responsible for the recommendation of "exquisite caution" in handling the whole programme, and would indeed, left to himself, have ruled out spectral evidence altogether.

Whether or not he attended the trial of Rebecca Nurse and heard the abortive acquittal, whether or not he made any public remarks on that occasion, he drew himself somehow to the attention of the afflicted girls, for one of these created a scandal by crying out on him.

To many the accusation must have seemed not implausible. Willard had not always been popular with his fellow ministers in Boston. Strict as he professed himself in doctrinal matters, he had sometimes given offence by admitting to his church applicants rejected by other congregations. In the present crisis his attitude seemed perilously close to that of what Cotton Mather called a "Sadducee." True, he had never gone so far as to deny the existence of witches, but he carried his distrust of spectral evidence to a point where it amounted to almost the same thing. Were his ideas put in practice there would and could be no successful prosecution.

Back in 1671 he had been instrumental in preventing

prosecution on that charge when sixteen-year-old Elizabeth Knapp of his parish in Groton had severe hysterical fits in which she accused not only a "very sincere and holy woman" but reviled her own pastor, Mr Willard. Owing to his intervention, the accused woman had never come to examination before the magistrates; instead he had brought her to the girl herself, and had allowed her to reason and pray with her accuser. Under these circumstances the latter began to contradict herself, and finally, coming out of her possession, withdrew her accusations.

Other pastors had done something similar from time to time, notably John Hale of Beverly. But where the latter now implied that his early lenience had been a dangerous error, Willard did not. In spite of the evidence of his own eyes, in spite of the virtual engulfing of Massachusetts by the uncontrolled forces of diabolism, Willard believed that his way had been the right way.

Now witchcraft had invaded his parish again, John Alden being of his congregation, and Willard was giving close and critical attention to the manner of the trials. Had he been in charge he would not for a moment have stood such a one as Rebecca Nurse before the bar to answer questions which were in their very nature unanswerable. In effect it was as if the judges were saying to the prisoner, "What was your spectral Shape doing on the night of Wednesday last?" It did not lie within human power to reply to such a question, for the frame of reference was beyond and above the world of demonstrable facts. Instead of so bedevilling a gentle old woman, he would have taken her aside with her principal accuser, Ann Putnam, and would have let accused and accuser talk it over. To a realistic eye, the most arresting quality of young Ann was her impressionability. Withdrawn from the atmosphere of malignant spite and of hysterical devotion to lost causes that prevailed in her home to the lovingkindness and understanding of a good old woman, who knew from large experience how the storms of oncoming puberty may beset and torment a little girl, who knew what miraculous cure God might not have wrought?

This approach had been tried recently with another who stood trial with Rebecca Nurse, Elizabeth How of Topsfield. Goody How's chief accusers were members of the Perley family of Ipswich, who claimed a ten-year-old daughter was being afflicted by her. One day the Reverend Samuel Phillips and a colleague named Payson of Rowley, undertook a test in the manner prescribed by Willard. They brought Goody How to the child just as she was coming out of a fit and remained on hand during the interview.

"Did I hurt you?" asked Goody How, taking the child's hand.

"No, never!" said the girl, and reflecting she added, "If I did complain of you in my fits I knew not that I did so."

The interview took place out of doors. A young brother listened from the window.

"Say Goody How is a witch!" he called. "Say she's a witch!"

But the child, her hand in Elizabeth's, smiled up at her confidently and said nothing. The ministers, convinced that the "witchcraft" was no more than name-calling incidental to an ordinary neighbourhood unpleasantness, made a formal deposition of their observations to present as testimony for Elizabeth How.

So and not otherwise would Willard have worked with witches. His views were well known and were a thorn in the side of some of the afflicted and their advisers; they multiplied the difficulty of convicting such a criminal as Rebecca Nurse. So one of the girls cried out on him in court, and common people quivered and thrilled at the audacity of the accusation. Now indeed were the mountains laid low.

But not this mountain. Willard was no obscure country parson like Burroughs; one of the most distinguished figures in Boston, he had been acting president of Harvard in the absence of Increase Mather. Every judge on the bench knew that the charge was preposterous and indecent, and unlike the friends of Rebecca Nurse and Elizabeth How, they were in a position to enforce their conviction.

"There will be no more of that; you are mistaken," one of them said in effect, and another kindly added that the girl had doubtless confused the minister with his namesake, Constable Willard, who lay in jail awaiting trial. This semantic explanation satisfied everyone, and the girl subsided. The other girls did not, however, subside for long. Their demons, heady with success, were acquiring a taste for bandying the names of the great. The judges had not heard the last of improbable accusations, and since they came up unexpectedly the public could not be prevented from hearing them too. They were to become a source of serious embarrassment.

2

On trial with Rebecca Nurse on 29 June and the days following were Elizabeth How, Sarah Good, Sarah Wild and Susanna Martin. Goody How, like Bridget Bishop, was a victim of long-standing gossip connecting her with witchcraft. Because of such talk she had been denied membership in the Ipswich church, and even a friend who had defended her as a "precious saint," saying that "though she be condemned before men she is justified before God," recanted after a revelatory dream and proclaimed her a witch as loudly as any.

Aside from such talk there was nothing remarkable about the reported conduct of Goody How. Her two daughters and her blind husband were devoted to her, and she had many friends, among them the venerated Deacon Ingersoll of Salem Village, who were willing now to testify to her good character. To such testimony was added that of the ministers of Rowley who had gone out of their way to trace and expose the source of the gossip about her.

Such testimony, based on the conduct of the accused in the visible world, could not in the nature of things be of any relevance to what was the real crux of the matter, her activities in the invisible world. As usual, the friends of the witch were defeated by the fact that accusation and defence were conducted on two planes with no possible point of contact. They were, in the phrase of a latter-day philosopher, trying to set the polar bear against the whale; it couldn't be done. Elizabeth How was convicted and sentenced.

No one seemed likely to come to the defence of Sarah Good, yet unexpectedly someone did. During the trial, one of the girls accused her of attacking her with a knife and produced a fragment of the blade as proof. Most of the spectators clucked their tongues with sympathy for the girl, but one young man straightened up and looked hard at the evidence. He recognized the blade; it had broken off his own knife the day before, and the accuser had been present at the time.

He got right up in meeting, asked to see the blade, and pulling out his own knife demonstrated that it was an exact fit. The girl, shrinking from the cold eyes of Stoughton, dared not deny his story.

She was, however, allowed to go on with hers. The judge merely told her to confine herself to the facts and let her go on. The vigilance of the young man did not save Sarah Good. She too was sentenced.

She went back to her prison, sucked on her pipe and mumbled to herself until the day should come. "It was my commandments. I may say my commandments, I hope."

Sarah Wild was a farmer's wife with a strong sense of property rights; if people borrowed a scythe without her approval she was capable of flying out at them and then sending a demon to plague them by overturning their haywagons. Or at least, some of her neighbours so reported. Others testified in quite a contrary direction. The reports of the first harmonized better with the visions of the girls and the present party line of theocracy, and the jury in any case was taking no more chances with acquittals. Sarah Wild too was condemned to death.

3

Susanna Martin was every inch a witch, bright of eye, salty of tongue, and the central figure of every marvellous event that had happened in Amesbury for going on three decades. She had established herself as community witch as far back as 1669 when she had been presented at court for bewitching a neighbour, though not, as it happened, put on trial. Since then the wistful folk spirit of Essex County, denied its natural outlet in Robin Goodfellows and in fiddling and dancing around the maypole, had focused itself on the neat, birdlike figure of Susanna Martin, and made her something of a Paula Bunyan among witches.

She had set the tone for her prosecution in early May when she came for her examination. An active body, she came in fresh and invigorated from the long ride up from Amesbury, and matrons looking over her dress could not see a pin out of place. No flashy dresser like Bridget Bishop, there was a trimness about Susanna which was somehow even more arresting. She wore her simple hood and scarf with an air, and carried herself pertly. She had emerged unscathed from this situation once before; she had been called a witch for so long that she had come to relish the distinction. So it happened that when the bewitched girls were brought in and went into their angular antics before her, she emitted a sound seldom heard in this grave court. She laughed out loud.

"Well may I laugh at such folly!" she said when the magistrates reproved her.

"What do you think ails them?" they asked.

Susanna shrugged.

"I don't desire to spend my judgment on it."

"Don't you think they are bewitched?"

"No, I do not think they are!" and being pressed further the woman insinuated, "If they be dealing with the black arts, you may know as well as I."

She let her hand be guided to the girls that her devil might be plucked from them, but was more diverted than impressed by the results of this exercise. Listening to the recital of her spectral misdeeds, however, she did make one serious comment.

"He that appeared in the shape of Samuel, a glorified saint, may appear in anyone's shape."

No good Puritan, searching the Bible for light on the witchcraft, had missed the episode of the Witch of Endor, who had lawlessly caused the shape of Samuel to appear before the lawlessly inquiring Saul. The implications of the episode were far from clear; some claimed that it was here that the Bible set its seal of approval on spectral evidence; others that it demonstrated the opposite. Susanna's remark was disregarded in court, but her reasoning would not be forgotten.

At the trial the judges knew better than to give rein to the tart tongue and irreverent wit of this witch. Instead they heard what her neighbours had to say of her, heard a recital, in short, of the wonder tales of Amesbury, Massachusetts.

There was the tale of the Enchanted Oxen of Salisbury Beach. Fourteen head that John Allen had put out to fatten on the salt grass had one day been goaded by the devil into swimming to Plum Island. When Allen traced them there and tried to round them up, the oxen ran from him "with a violence . . . wholly diabolic" and plunging into the water swam straight out to sea. Only one of the infatuated beasts came to its senses in time to turn back, and even he, reaching shore, crashed past his pursuers and galloped through the marshes to Newbury Town. This one alone, captured in the woods a day or so later, was saved, though soon the tides began to wash the bodies of the others upon the shore.

Faced with so ruinous a disaster a good Puritan searches his conscience to see "what sin unrepented of" God is punishing him for. Allen may have started such a search, but he was interrupted by a memory ringing in his ears like a spiteful echo of the shrill voice of Susanna Martin.

"Your oxen will never do you much service!"

It came back to him now. Just before he turned his oxen out to grass he had refused to hitch his oxcart to haul her some staves, and in those words had Susanna mocked him.

"Dost thou threaten me, thou old witch? I'll throw thee into the brook!" he had shouted, but Susanna had nimbly run across the bridge out of his way. Who but Susanna had sent the devil into his cattle?

There was the tale of the Phantom Puppies.

Susanna owned these puppies. At first they existed on the physical level; her bitch had produced a likely litter, and John Kembal had contracted to buy one. But when he came, Susanna would not let him have his choice and was wroth when he then refused to buy at all.

"I'll give you puppies enough!" she cried after him. And indeed she did.

It began towards sundown with a little black cloud in the north-west. Kembal saw it when he came out of his wood-lot with his axe over his shoulder, and at the same moment found himself in the grip of a power that made his feet unsteady. Though a broad straight cartway lay before him, he began to weave from side to side, lurching into stumps, tripping and sometimes falling headlong, axe and all.

When finally he came out to the road near the meeting-house he found a puppy waiting for him. At least it was a Thing like a puppy, small, dark, and devilish playful. It nipped at his heels, ran back and forth between his feet. Kembal took it for a real enough puppy until he swung his axe at it. Then the queer thing happened; the Thing leaped aside and vanished into the ground.

Kembal stared about him, rubbed his eyes, and stumbled on. Uncanny or not, at least he was rid of puppies. But he was not. Up the shadowy road waited another Thing, a larger puppy, black as coal and vicious. It sprang for his throat, his belly, and darting behind him made for his shoulders. Swinging his axe made no impression on it at all.

"In the name of Jesus Christ avoid!" cried Kembal at last, and lo, the Thing was gone.

He was panting when he got to his kitchen, but took care to say no word to his wife. It might scare her; besides, there is no knowing what a woman's inconsequence will suggest; it is common enough for maids to bring beer by the pailful to men working in field or wood-lot; his wife might say that he had refreshed himself once too often.

His reticence made it the more remarkable that the story was all over town next day. People grinned at him knowingly and asked for the puppies. How, he demanded, did they know? And he traced the gossip to Susanna Martin, who could have had only one way of knowing. She herself had sent her devils in the form of puppies to torment him.

There was the legend of Susanna walking dryshod over watery ways. In wicked weather she had once taken a notion to call on Sarah Atkinson in Newbury, going on foot all the way. She entered the kitchen neat as ever; even the soles of her feet were dry.

"I'd be wet to my knees if I'd come so far," said Sarah.

"I scorn to have a drabbled tail," said Susanna tartly, and the retort, which sounded somehow like a comment on Sarah's general appearance and her housekeeping, had rankled. It rankled so much that when Susanna was taken in the witchcraft, Sarah Atkinson went to a magistrate to enter the incident in the records.

Other wonder tales concerned the Shapes assumed by the protean Susanna. Once she showed as "a marvellous light about the bigness of a half bushel" to John Pressy in an open field at night. Once a goodwife saw her melt into empty space and then materialize again in the form of birds who "pecked and pinched." Once she came at night to Robert Downs as a cat and was like to kill him before he had the presence of mind to exorcize her by saying, "Avoid, thou she-devil! In the name of God, the Father, the Son and the Holy Ghost, avoid!"

Like Bridget Bishop she was fond of molesting honest men in their bedchambers. At night would come "a scrabbling at the window" and there was Susanna, hopping down from the sill and boldly getting into bed. One man, Joseph Ring, she had enslaved. She and her fellows used to snatch him through the air and drag him to witch meetings. For more than two years they had struck him dumb so that when he returned from "feasting and dancing" in unknown places, he could report his adventures only by signs. Now his voice had by grace of God returned; he used it to make a damnifying deposition on Susanna's secret social life.

An attentive listener might note that in the bulk of Susanna's exploits there was no great harm done; her familiar could have ranked no higher than a common poltergeist, a

prankish fellow, related no doubt to Robin Goodfellow, but
no murderer. In all of three decades no death had been
laid to her door except for John Allen's oxen. There could
be no doubt, however, that she was an unpleasant neighbour, a dangerous person to cross, and besides she had
lately practised her arts on the girls of Salem Village. The
judges condemned her with the rest, and if there were any
in Amesbury who deplored the loss of their most picturesque character, they did not put their sentiments on
record.

4

Now on Tuesday, 19 July, came the decisive event for
which so many in Massachusetts had been praying, a mass
execution of the witches. Five were hanged on Gallows Hill,
all women, the five whose trials had begun late in June:
Rebecca Nurse, Goody Good, Elizabeth How, Sarah Wild,
Susanna Martin.

The ceremony was carried out decently with only one
discordant note. That was the snubbing Sarah Good gave
the good Noyes when he made one last appeal to her to
save her immortal soul by confessing; he reminded her that
she well knew she was a witch.

"You're a liar!" said Sarah. "I am no more a witch than
you are a wizard! If you take my life away, God will give
you blood to drink."

They took away her life and Noyes did have blood to
drink, years later, when he lay dying of a hæmorrhage,
though not so many years later that Sarah's words were not
thought of.

The bodies of the witches were thrust into a shallow grave
in a crevice of Gallows Hill's outcropping of felsite. But the
body of Rebecca did not remain there. Her children bided
their time—or so the story goes—and at night when the
crowds and the executioners had gone home again, they
gathered up the body of their mother and took it home.
Just where they laid it none can know, for this was a secret
thing and not even Parris, whose parsonage was not a quar-

ter of a mile up the road past the grove where the Nurses buried their dead, must see that a new grave had been opened and prayers said. This was the hour and the power of darkness when a son could not say where he had buried his mother. Yet the hour would pass. Under the trees a granite shaft would one day be raised to Rebecca, and beside it another honouring the names of the neighbours who spoke up for her in a day when it was dangerous to speak.

But now in July 1692 there were no shafts, there was only a secret grave, and across the fertile, but this year half-neglected, fields there were the children of Rebecca, silently going their way. Not even yet was their cup of sorrow full; their mother's sisters, Mary Esty and Sarah Cloyce, still lay in the hands of what Cary had called "unmerciful men." Yet the whole story had not been told; not for nothing had Elizabeth Procter said to little Abigail, "There is another judgment, dear child."

CHAPTER XV

THE DEVIL IN ANDOVER

The executions of 19 July had a profound effect upon the other witches awaiting their turn at trial. The earlier hanging of Bridget Bishop had made less impact because, guilty or not, she was too isolated and individual a case to set a precedent. But of these others, three were respectable women; their neighbours had attested to their decency; yet they had been hanged just as dead as that indubitable witch, Sarah Good.

Most frightening was the fate of Rebecca Nurse. Thanks to the devotion of her family and to her own intelligence and courage, her case had been defended with a skill that even more highly connected witches could not hope to surpass. But it had all been in vain; whatever was accomplished with the jury was immediately undone by the implacability of the judges; even when she was reprieved, the reprieve was revoked. What hope was there for any of them if all this that had been achieved for one had been brought to nothing by the steely purpose of William Stoughton and the clamours of the afflicted?

It was no accident that it was the day after the hanging that a day of fasting and prayer was held in the home of the now thoroughly unhappy John Alden. Not only were prayers offered by Willard and Cotton Mather, but one of the judges participated, Samuel Sewall. His contribution was the reading of a sermon, Dr Preston's "First and Second Uses of God's Allsufficiency," and the recording of the event in his diary. During the prayer the drought broke, at least momentarily, "in a brave shower of rain," but whether this

was a sign of God's providence in regard to the witchcraft
none ventured to prophesy.

Some of the witches, especially those who had means,
now began to lay plans which had no reference to the
court of Oyer and Terminer. Nathaniel Cary's matured first,
although this man, who had of his own accord brought his
wife to court, abandoned the legal process with reluctance.
After he had followed the Salem trials and had found them
a "cruel mockery," he at first tried to have his wife brought
to trial not in Salem but in Suffolk County. Only when that
plan failed did he sound out the chances of breaking jail.
On 30 July he succeeded in smuggling her out of prison
and getting her to Rhode Island, and that proving a precarious sanctuary, with pursuers hot on the trail, to New
York.

Edward Bishop and his wife Sarah, aware that little
mercy was likely to be shown any connection of the notorious Bridget, made a break somewhat later, and managed to lie low until the storm had passed.

Philip and Mary English waited in Boston almost until
the eve of their trial, and if tradition can be believed, then
had to be coaxed into flight. Being people of influence,
friends of Sir William and Lady Mary Phips, they were
privileged characters even under restraint, and had to some
extent the liberty of the town during the day; at least they
were allowed to go to meeting and hear the Reverend
Joshua Moody preach.

Moody had interested himself in witchcraft when Cotton
Mather was still a stammering stripling; long experience had
given him an outlook somewhat like that of Samuel Willard. At the very least, whatever his opinions on the common sort of witches, like Sarah Good and Susanna Martin,
he had no patience with people who preferred such charges
against people like Philip English. But he was also aware
that the judges were little likely to encourage the acquittal
of one who was not merely a suspected wizard but an outspoken critic of the children of the Covenant. His very eminence made it the more imperative to prosecute him, for
some people were murmuring about their failure to prose-

cute other eminent suspects, for instance ex-Judge Salton-stall.

With all this in mind, Moody, selected his text with care one Sunday when he saw the Englishes taking their places before him. "If they persecute you in one city, flee to an-other." This he followed with a sermon which in Salem would have sounded like treason, its proposition being the wisdom of flying from injustice.

After the sermon Moody and his associate Willard visited the Englishes in prison and explicitly urged flight.

English demurred; he preferred to face the judges, not out of heroism—he had spent much of the spring dodging arrest—but because he knew that flight would be the legal equivalent of conviction and that his property would be forfeit. And Philip English had great possessions.

"God will not permit them to touch me," accordingly said Philip.

But his wife had endured several more weeks of prison than he, and had so many more weeks' experience of the magistrates' minds and of the character of those whom the magistrates had been hanging.

"Do you not think the sufferers innocent?" she asked. "Why may not we suffer also?"

Philip still hesitated. The ministers told him that if he could not carry his wife away, they would; she was ill, hav-ing fallen into a consumption during her months in prison.

So the Englishes fled, and it was a flight *de luxe*—again if tradition can be believed, for all this story about them except the mere fact of flight was recorded a generation or so after the event. The merchants in New York are sup-posed to have sent a carriage for them; Sir William is sup-posed to have smoothed their way; he who had thus far lacked the courage to interfere decisively and openly with his subordinate Stoughton's prosecution, was willing in pri-vate to lend a helping hand to friends. He arranged for them to leave prison at midnight and gave them letters of introduction to his colleague, Governor Benjamin Fletcher of New York. The latter was already showing Mrs Cary every courtesy and stood ready to protect many more. New

York, a colony where, thanks to the influence of the rational
Dutch, witchcraft was not taken very seriously, was in the
way of acquiring a distinguished little colony of refugees.

John Alden held out until September. It was of a midnight that friends in Duxbury were wakened by a pounding on the door and the bursting in of a "tall man from
Boston."

"The devil is after me!" cried John Alden, and his friends
saw to it that the devil did not lay hands on him again.

All these escaped and in time many more; nor, so far
as plain people could discover, did the judges make any
serious attempt to pursue the fugitives if they were of the
"better class" and got as far as New York. After a while this
observation created a scandal. There was no democracy
among witches after all. If you were poor and could run no
farther than Lancaster, the law would overtake and hang
you; if you were rich and well connected and were thus
able to flee New England altogether, the judges would ignore the fact that extradition in capital cases is possible between colonies.

2

It was in this season, that is some time between the June
trials and the hanging of 19 July, that the devil took over
Andover.

He got in by the selfsame doors through which he had
entered Salem Village, medicine and the ministry. But from
the latter he did not get so warm a welcome as he had
from the ministers of Salem, village and town. There were
two ministers in Andover; it was apparently the younger,
Thomas Bernard, who opened the door; the elder, Francis
Dane, applied all his might to closing it, at least when he
saw who was coming through. Dane was indeed to fight
the plague with a heroism unequalled by any who had
choice in the matter, risking not only his own life and reputation, but what must have come harder, the lives of nearly
all the womenfolk in his family. And in this fight he was at
first alone, deserted by his own deacons who regarded him

at best as an old and failing man, too far behind the times to appreciate the methods of modern science.

It began with the illness of the wife of Joseph Ballard. It had been going on for a long time and there was little satisfaction to be got from the doctor who attended her. About the time that the Queen of Hell, Martha Carrier, was uncovered in Andover, Ballard was making up his mind where the real difficulty lay and looking about him for a more expert diagnostician to confirm his belief. Such a one could not be found in Andover; it was not that the town lacked for people who dreamed dreams and saw visions, but the local mediumistic talent had never impressed anyone very much. To be sure of the facts, to avoid any suspicion of unfairness, it was necessary to import one of the young seeresses of Salem.

Once Ballard made up his mind to undertake the experiment, he won the support of many of the leading citizens who regarded his plan as a civic project of great virtue. Goody Ballard was by no means the only invalid in town. Any number of people had sickness in the family, and even when the doctor found a plain physical cause, it was foolhardy to deny that witchcraft might not have originated and aggravated it. Ballard's neighbours stood ready to share the expense. Accordingly man and horse were sent to Salem to fetch back the likeliest accusers that could be spared.

That was how the younger Ann Putnam found herself one summer's day riding up to Andover for an outing. Puny though she was, the little girl sat well on a horse, for all the Putnams, male or female, were famous riders, and on the rare occasions when Ann was thrown, she had always been able to spot the witch responsible. She did not on this occasion ride alone. Mary Walcott had been persuaded to come with her.

It was a quite wonderful experience for the simple village maids who until now had hardly been farther from home than Salem Town. They were received with utmost respect, even something like reverence. It had not always been so in Salem Village. For all their fame they had always been plagued by the knowledge that there were sceptics about. Though magistrates and judges hung on Ann's every word, her Uncle Joseph Putnam did not; even that decent woman Sarah Ingersoll had never let her forget that for all her powers of divination she was only a little girl, as subject to discipline as any.

But here in Andover it was different. There were no sceptics—at least they did not meet any—and the deference accorded them could not have been greater had they been princesses.

What awaited them was touching. It was not only superstition but love and need that had summoned the girls. In a score of homes, sickrooms had been readied with pious care and the visitation was being awaited in the same prayerful faith that the lame, the halt and the blind had once waited on Christ and his disciples. Such faith should have made them whole, and indeed in some instances it did, but there was tragedy for Andover in that the healers were not themselves whole, but full of corruption, and that it was the corruption they imparted.

The girls, led from house to house, focused their tranced glare on the sickbed and almost always saw a variant of the same vision: one witch at the patient's head, the other at his feet. When they reported these things, very often young people in the house broke into howls, fell into convulsions, and had their own eyes opened to the horror. Ann and Mary could hardly enter a house without giving the gift of second sight to some of those within.

They had not gone far, however, before a serious difficulty arose. The girls were in a strange town where they were ill acquainted with names and knew almost nothing of the gossip which attaches itself to the witchlike, though in this they were probably receiving instruction. They could see a witch spectrally ply her trade but they could seldom positively identify her.

In justice to all it was necessary to conduct a scientific experiment. A conclave of public-spirited citizens, among them Bernard, most of the deacons of the church, and Justice of Peace Dudley Bradstreet, son of the venerable ex-

governor, arranged the details and appointed the meeting-
house for the purpose. If the senior pastor, Francis Dane,
disapproved at this stage, he did not succeed in making his
disapproval effective against such impressive opposition.
And anyway, the whole thing was an experiment which
might come to nothing. At the meeting, however, he remained observantly in the background, leaving the public
prayers to his eager colleague.

The experiment took the form of a kind of ghostly police
line-up. The gifted girls were brought into the house in the
throes of full possession, and one by one various men and
women were led up blindfolded to touch them. Possibly not
all of these so led had been originally suspected; in the interest of complete impartiality some people who should
have been above suspicion were included with the others.
But this impartiality produced unforeseen consequences.
The test was that of touch. The hands of the suspects were
guided to the hands of the girls, and if the latter then drew
a sobbing breath and relaxed her struggles, the entire assembly was witness to the fact that yet another witch had
been made to call off her devils.

What was unforeseen and horrible was that this phenomenon occurred nearly as often as the test was made. No one
had supposed that more than half a dozen witches would be
picked up in Andover. But before this business was done,
Justice Bradstreet found he had made out forty warrants.
Even that was not the end. Bradstreet quit at that figure not
because Andover had run out of witches, but because he
personally had declared himself done with signing any more
warrants on such evidence.

3

On no one was the effect of the disaster more electric
than on the men and women who so unexpectedly found
themselves exposed as witches and wizards. "We were all
exceedingly astonished and amazed and consternated and
affrighted, even out of reason," testified six women in a joint
deposition made much later. It was not uncommon for some

of them to agree after so dramatic a demonstration that they must indeed have been practising witchcraft; the difficulty was to remember how or when. Mary Osgood, whose husband was deacon, searching her conscience remembered a time twelve years back after the birth of her last child, a time when she had been ill and unhappy. Most likely the devil had got at her then. On further thought she connected this period somehow with a cat, a cat that must have had diabolical powers though at the time she "no whit suspected the cat to be the devil."

Samuel Wardwell, diligently searching out his memories under the psycho-analytic probing of the magistrates, remembered that he had sometimes said "the devil take it" when a creature got into his field; perhaps that had given the devil his opening. Then he recalled that at the time of his unrequited love for the "maid Barker" he had seen an assemblage of cats. Cross-examination induced him to remember that the Prince of the Air had been with the cats and had made him promises, had sworn him to a covenant for sixty years and had baptized him in the Shaw Shin River.

The most remarkable confession either at this time or at any other came from William Barker, probable kin of the "maid Barker," vainly beloved by Wardwell. Subtracting from his account the compulsory fantasy without which no confession could pass as *bona fide*, one finds a significant element of sincerity. That he had wearied of the Puritan's endless preoccupation with damnation was indicated by the fact that the devil seduced him by promising an end to resurrection and judgment, to punishment and shame. That he chafed at class restrictions was suggested by the fact that he found appealing the devil's promise that all men under his rule should be equal and "live bravely." Barker was plainly a homespun philosopher with advanced ideas. In the cold eyes of the judges, however, his admissions were only proof of a damning heterodoxy and dissatisfaction with God's providence.

It was Barker who described the business-like, go-getting nature of the witches' sabbaths and explained why Salem

Village had been chosen for attack; it was "by reason of the people being divided and their differing with ye minister." He also could and did give the exact number of witches now operating in Essex County, a dismaying figure far exceeding the present arrests—307, and this without counting some Connecticut witches who had ridden up during the spring to help start the campaign.

If one Andover witch faltered in his confession, a companion urged him on. The tormentors of Goody Ballard were early identified as Ann Foster, her daughter Mary Lacy, and her granddaughter, who bore her mother's name. The senior Mary Lacy sharply reproached her mother for pleading not guilty.

"Oh mother, how do you do? We have left Christ and the devil hath got hold of us. How shall I get rid of this evil one? I desire God to break my rocky heart that I may get the victory this time."

The younger Mary confessed glibly. "Where is my mother that made me a witch and I knew it not?" declaimed the girl, and went on with her disordered thoughts. She had not always obeyed her parents, had once run away for two days, a flight which in retrospect seemed virtuous. To her the devil had come in the shape of a horse. She had not been a witch long, not over a week, well—hardly over a year.

Accused women who refused to confess were relentlessly pressed to do so by their next-of-kin. Sometimes this was because their husbands, to quote Thomas Brattle, "did break charity with their dear wives," aghast to find themselves mated with monsters. Other kinsmen insisted on confession true or false as the only hope of escaping the gallows.

Goodwife Mary Tyler had made the dismal journey to Salem with her brother and Schoolmaster John Emerson riding on either side, each demanding that she confess until she "wished herself in a dungeon than to be so treated."

Emerson, having made a shadow play of beating the devil away from her eyes, finally washed his hands of her. "Well, I see you will not confess. I will now leave you, and then you are undone, body and soul together."

Her brother persisted, saying that in confessing she "could not lye."

"Good brother, do not say so," wailed Mary Tyler. "For I shall lye if I confess and who shall answer to God for my lye?"

That she might be innocent was a preposterous notion to her brother. "God would not suffer so many good men to be in error about it." He talked of hanging and continued his demands so "long and violent . . . that she thought verily her life would have gone away from her and became so terrified in her mind that she answered at length almost anything they propounded her, but had wronged her conscience in so doing. She was guilty of a great sin in belying herself and desired to mourn for it as long as she lived."

Mary Tyler was not the only one who after confessing in the first panic, repented after sober reflection in prison. Samuel Wardwell, exposed there to the reasoning of the tougher-minded, including probably John Procter, renounced all his admissions of acquaintance with the Prince of Air, of baptism in the Shaw Shin River, and if he had seen an assemblage of cats, what of it? Who had not?

There were some stout enough to forbear any confession at all. Abigail Faulkner had a father who would not ask his kin to save their necks by inventing fantasies; he was Francis Dane, who was now trying to arouse the town against the insane course of action to which it had committed itself. The most that Francis Dane's daughter would admit to was to say that when the accusing girls irritated her she had struck her hands together, and for all she knew the devil might take advantage, but "it was the devil not I who afflicted them."

4

At its height the terror in Andover was worse than that in Salem Village. It came on so suddenly and on such a scale as to cause uncontrolled panic. No one was safe. When a dog was discovered to have been bewitched by John Bradstreet of Andover, another son of the ex-governor,

Bradstreet did not stand on ceremony; he moved out to New Hampshire. When his brother, the Justice of Peace, refused to sign any more warrants, he too was cried out on. Afflicted girls produced spectral evidence that he and his wife had committed nine murders. They too went into hiding.

But the gale that blew so high the more quickly spent its course. An accusing circle which had formed in Andover, sometimes crying out on the dogs in the street, sometimes on their rulers and elders, finally met their match. They cried out on a gentleman in Boston, possibly though not probably the sceptical merchant, Robert Calef, and the latter took novel action; he sent a "writ to arrest these accusers in one thousand pound action of defamation" and entrusted local friends to put the accusers under observation. So coldly legal an act, which no one in Massachusetts had thought to perform before, had a chastening effect. Adolescents tough enough to watch a hanging without a qualm blenched at the idea of someone's having to pay a thousand pounds. Their voices became discreet and then fell silent altogether.

And now that the clamour was subsiding people began to listen to the voice of reason and to the voice of Francis Dane. It was as if they had been in a dream; only under the spell of a dream could they have believed so much evil of wife or sister. But if they were awake now where formerly they slept, they were still faced with the results of their somnambulism. At least fifty of their own, fifty decent people, not tramps or scoundrels, now lay in prison awaiting trial before a court that had never acquitted a suspect. What was Andover going to do about it?

CHAPTER XVI

ON GALLOWS HILL

Nathaniel Cary had called the officials in the witchcraft "unmerciful men." The epithet was unfair. Necessarily they might seem unmerciful to the unregenerate, but let a witch repent and confess and she found the bar of justice a veritable mercy seat. Surely it was goodness and mercy that had caused the judges, up to this point at least, to ignore in behalf of the confessors the blunt Old Testament command, "Thou shalt not suffer a witch to live." Given the number of confessing witches now in their hands, they could have met popular demand for action by ordering a really impressive series of mass hangings of avowed witches. That they did not was a demonstration of the quality of mercy inherent in the Calvinistic concept of sin. All men are sinners; salvation lies therefore not in innocence, but in renunciation and repentance. Each token of repentance in this dark matter was accordingly to be received tenderly, and the sinner cherished even as was the lost sheep returned to the ninety and nine.

So for the time being there was no talk of hanging the confessors; possibly it would be arranged later, but no one really knew. Whatever their eventual fate the confessors would in the meantime be given full opportunity to repent and prove their repentance by informing on their fellow witches. Their willingness to do this provided a very utilitarian reason for keeping them alive. By means of the confessions, round every witch on the roster was woven a web of spectral evidence which in the end became more damaging than the original charges. People who complained that condemnations were being made on the say-so of ignorant young girls ignored the terrible admissions that the witches made about each other.

Meanwhile no matter how many confessed—the outpouring from Andover added page upon page of incontrovertible evidence to the already bulging dossier on witchcraft—there always remained an irreducible minority who would not seek mercy at this price, who would not confess, who in the face of testimony sworn to by half a hundred witnesses still insisted on their innocence.

Some of these, had the judges known it, represented the truest expression of the indomitable Puritan spirit; that spirit which a few decades earlier had refused to bow before a misguided king, now, at the risk of life, would not bow before misguided magistrates. It was wonderful how such men as John Procter and such women as Rebecca Nurse and her sisters managed to keep unshaken their hold on reality in the face of the impregnable if mad logic of the judges and afflicted girls, and how, firm in their knowledge of their innocence, in their faith in God, they would not belie themselves, even though lying was sometimes made so easy that a mere "Yes," whispered on cue, would be accepted as full and free confession.

Puritan was ranged against Puritan in these courts. If the judges were Puritan, so were their victims, and though the latter were doomed, the future was theirs. Were the Puritans given to canonizing their saints, such a one as Rebecca Nurse would surely in time have been beatified. Her faith in the Covenant was as deep as Cotton Mather's, deeper indeed in that his was never put to such a test. Thanks to the rooting of that faith, frail as she was, she had faced the dreadful reality unflinching without once taking flight into fantasy. What is more remarkable, her children never urged her to do so. They would move heaven and earth to save their mother, but one thing they would not do, ask her to belie herself.

Six more defendants were coming up for trial in early August, and most of these were in their several ways no less worthy of veneration than Rebecca herself.

2

John Procter was one of the six and he came up fighting. There was nothing of the martyr's will-to-die in John Procter. In his fierce will-to-live he did not wait for the trial to make his voice heard, but two weeks earlier, on 23 July, addressed to five ministers of Boston a petition in behalf of himself "and others."

The substance of this petition was an appeal to the ministers to exert their influence to transfer the trials from Salem to Boston, or if that were not possible, at least to substitute other judges, the present incumbents "having condemned us already before our trials."

The force of the petition lay in the detailed account, already described, of how "full and free confessions" were being wrung from the male suspects by torture. "These actions," concluded Procter, never one to mince words, "are very like the Papish cruelties." The last was an unthinkable phrase to apply to any enterprise conducted under Puritan auspices; it gave such affront that Procter's kinsmen in Lynn were immediately cried out on and arrested.

The petition went to Moody and Willard, no doubt chosen because of their notorious sympathy with certain defendants; to James Allen, from whom the Nurses were buying their estate in Salem Village; to John Bailey, who had once been Willard's associate and was now Allen's; to the elder Mather.

None of these took any decisive action on the petition. Those most sympathetic to its reasoning were in the poorest position to do anything; though Willard's courage had not abated, his influence had, thanks to his known deviation from the party line on witchcraft. Increase Mather's interest was awakened, but he too was at a low ebb of public influence because of the storm of criticism aroused by his championship of the new charter. Besides, he had returned from England too late to observe the inception of the witchcraft and had since then been largely preoccupied by defending the charter and catching up with his arrears of duties as president of Harvard and senior pastor of the meeting-house in the North End. He was in general content to follow the reasoning of his son Cotton, who had done so brilliant a piece of laboratory work on demonolgy at the time of the possession of the Goodwin children.

Nevertheless Procter's thesis apparently did serve to focus his attention anew on the prosecution. Soon after receiving the petition he called a conference of seven ministers in Cambridge to discuss, not explicitly the question of confessions, but rather the perennially troublesome matter of spectral evidence. His proposition was "Whether the devil may not sometimes have permission to represent an innocent person as tormenting such as are under diabolic manifestation." This time there was unanimous agreement that it could happen, with, however, the reservation "that such things are rare and extraordinary especially when such matters come before Civil Juridicature."

After obtaining this decision Mather took the trouble to go to Salem to see for himself how the trials were conducted when they reopened in August. Here, however, his interest was less in the inconsequential Procter than in Burroughs, and the trial of the latter seemed fair to him. "Had I been one of his judges," he later wrote, "I could not have acquitted him." Even so, whether because of Procter's appeal or his own observation, questions continued to arise in his mind. At long last, far too late to help poor Procter, he did undertake a personal investigation of the methods under which confessions were being secured. It was thanks to him that Mary Tyler's account of the ordeal of the Andover witches was put on record.

3

On 5 August and the days following the judges tried John and Elizabeth Procter, John Willard, old George Jacobs, Martha Carrier, and their most notorious captive, George Burroughs; and they condemned them all.

Procter did not come unbefriended to court. Thirty-one friends in Ipswich and twenty-one neighbours in Salem Village had risked the sensitive responses of the afflicted girls by putting their names to petitions which attested to their faith in Procter's good conduct. "His breeding hath been among us," said the Ipswich petitioners in reinforcement of this statement, and added that he "was of religious parents in our place and by reason of relations . . . with our town hath had constant intercourse with us."

This Ipswich petition was especially interesting. One of its signatories was its probable author, the Reverend John Wise. During Andros's regime this stiff-necked parson had gone to jail for twenty-one days for encouraging his congregation to resist a tax they judged illegal. In this petition he now undertook to instruct the judges, William Stoughton and all, in Scripture; he called their attention to the Book of Job.

Puritans were in this crisis turning more and more to the Book of Job as more "Christian" in its philosophy than the Book of Revelation, a terrifying document which many people were guilty of using as a kind of august manual of fortunetelling. Through Job's experience it was plain that contrary to the usual Calvinistic interpretation, affliction was not necessarily punishment of sin but might on occasion be God's method of testing a man's integrity. God who had once delivered the guiltless Job into the hands of Satan for this purpose might even now be undertaking a similar experiment. Boldly the petition asserted that God "sometimes may permit Sathan to personate, dissemble and thereby abuse innocents and such as in the fear of God defie the Devil and all his works."

Procter at least had more loyal comforters than Job in these friends who pleaded for him on so sublime a basis. But they were as helpless to save him as Mary Warren had been in her brief flash of sanity. If Mary came to court at all to watch the trial of her once beloved master, it was only to sit in sick apathy and to lend her voice to the meaningless mouthings of the other girls.

Procter did, however, accomplish one thing. He had originally become involved in the prosecution through his attempt to save his wife Elizabeth. Well, he had saved her.

She was pregnant, and these judges would not condemn to death an unborn child even though it was begotten by a wizard on the body of a witch. Elizabeth, condemned with the others, was given a stay of execution until the baby came, and Procter, who could hardly believe that insanity could reign so long as this in Massachusetts, from March into August, must have had faith that the light of reason would shine again before his wife's months were fulfilled.

At the trial the defendants heard themselves accused of the usual malefic wonders. John Willard, the village constable whose stomach had turned against the necessity of arresting good neighbours, heard that his Shape had been giving suck to a black pig, that he had knelt in prayer to a "black man with a long crowned hat" and that four apparitions haunted him crying, "You have murdered us." These marvels had been revealed to the clairvoyant Susanna Sheldon, to whom had also appeared a "shining man," who, having first taken the precaution of making a pass with his hands to cause the eavesdropping Shape of Willard to vanish, had ordered her to report her discoveries direct to Magistrate Hathorne.

Burroughs came to the bar in dignity. He had grown in spiritual stature since that May day when he, bewildered by so swift a transition from privacy and peace to the bedlamite court in Salem, had quailed before the yelling maidens. On that occasion he had been close to believing that what he saw was the work of witchcraft. Now he knew it was nothing of the sort. For two months he had been living in the society of "proved" witches and wizards, and he knew them to be as innocent as himself. Girls, magistrates, judges, and most of all the general public of Massachusetts, had fallen prey to delusion. If there were to be health and sanity again, that delusion must be exposed and destroyed. Perhaps God had brought him here expressly that he might do it.

Accordingly Burroughs had spent little time elaborating on his plea of not guilty; he was too far from his friends, too despised by most ministers of Massachusetts because of the discredit he had brought upon their profession, to hope for such support as Procter had. Instead he attacked the concept of witchcraft itself. He composed a written address to the jury, the tenor of which was that "there neither are nor ever were witches that having made a compact with the devil can send a devil to torment other people at a distance."

It was unfortunate that having so written he succumbed to the temptation to bite his accusers. On the very eve of the trial he sent his Shape to them so that they came to court next morning with toothmarks all over their arms. Scrupulously just, the judges declined to take their unsupported word for this; they had Burroughs's mouth prised open and his teeth compared not only with the bites but with the teeth of others in the courtroom. It was thereby established beyond doubt that Burroughs and Burroughs alone had bitten the girls.

After such a demonstration the poor man's defence was merely laughable. When Cotton Mather got a look at it he found wry amusement in the discovery that the devil hadn't even managed an original document. Burroughs had cribbed and garbled his entire paper from *A Candle in the Dark*, written in England in the godless days of the Restoration by a notorious sceptic, Thomas Ady. It might well have been the "new fashion" book that Mercy Lewis had seen in his study.

No fair-minded man could doubt the story of the girls that Burroughs, in trying to seduce them to witchcraft by offering them "fine cloathes," had revealed to them his plan to pervert the whole of Salem Village, a plan in which, it must be admitted, he had made no little headway.

4

Martha Carrier, so passionately maligned that even now it is difficult to see beyond the strong language used by Cotton Mather, had a defender in Francis Dane; he reported that she had been the victim of malicious gossip. The judges must have raised their eyebrows at such a defence from such a source; by now at least three of Dane's kinswomen had been arrested; one might have supposed that he would have found something better to do than speak out for the Queen of Hell.

The case of George Jacobs, the last of the six, brought up some rather special complications.

Jacobs, as master of the afflicted Sarah Churchill, had had the opportunity to study the nature of demoniac possession at close range and had viewed it as irreverently as had John Procter. His word for Sarah and her colleagues was "witch bitch." The epithet was afflicting; on 10 May Jacobs had been summoned before the magistrates to answer charges of abusing the girls by spectral methods.

Jacobs, toothless, grey, and so lame that he was able to get about only with the help of two canes, remained nevertheless a giant in stature and vigour. He swung himself into the courtroom and faced the judges in businesslike fashion.

"Here are them that accuse you of acts of witchcraft," the magistrates had begun.

"Well," said Jacobs briskly, "let us hear who they are and what they are."

He was attentive while the afflicted ran through their repertory. New talent made its debut on this occasion in the person of an "afflicted boy," one sixteen-year-old John Doritch. He had wistfully attached himself to the dynamic girls and was occasionally permitted to report a vision in court; he never, however, succeeded in attracting more than casual attention to himself; the detection of witches was apparently women's work.

"Who did it?" demanded the magistrates when the recital was complete.

"Don't ask me!"

Later his manner became momentarily less brusque. There was after all something unnerving about the capers of the wenches and the seriousness with which the magistrates regarded them.

"Pray do not accuse me. I am as clear as your worships," said Jacobs almost plaintively; then he reverted to normal. "You tax me for a wizard; you may as well tax me for a buzzard!"

What, the magistrates asked severely, was all this about

his not regularly holding family prayers? To Jacobs's reply
that he couldn't because he couldn't read, they said that
the Lord's Prayer, as any Christian knew, was good enough
for anyone. Let him repeat it before the court. Jacobs tried,
and fatally he stumbled over it.

"Well burn me or hang me!" exploded the patriarch. "I'll
stand in the truth of Christ. I know nothing of it."

But one piece of news gravely disturbed him. The constables had undertaken to round up the entire family; a
son and daughter-in-law had escaped, but the granddaughter, Margaret, had been seized and in prison had confessed.
Jacobs correctly surmised that the girl had been tricked into
it, but her surrender bothered him. "If she were innocent
and yet confessed, she would be accessory to her own
death." But even more was she an accessory to his and to
that of Burroughs, since the magistrates had not let her rest
until she had incriminated both. Also Margaret had the
privilege of confessors; there was for the present no talk of
putting her to death.

But Margaret was by nature an upright girl and her privileges, and the company she kept, that of the other confessors lodged with her in Salem Prison, gave her small joy.
The trial and condemnation of Burroughs and of her grandfather were too much for her. She sent for the magistrates
to recant her confession. She had, she now said, confessed
only under pressure of fright when she had seen the accusing girls tumble down before her, and out of her terror of
hanging. Her confession had been "altogether false and untrue. . . . What I said was altogether false against my
grandfather and Mr Burroughs, which I did to save my
life and liberty." Now she preferred "death with a quiet
conscience than to live in such horror."

This document was produced in court. It had no effect
on the judges, but the girl was allowed to visit Burroughs
the day before his death and receive his forgiveness, and to
write a letter to her father, presumably to be delivered
when he came out of hiding. "Let me beg your prayer to
the Lord in my behalf and send us a joyful and happy
meeting in heaven." Old Jacobs was allowed to hear of

Margaret's act of courage; before he died he had a new
provision in her favour inserted in his will, as if a proved
witch still had the right to dispose of his earthly property,
or as if the property itself would be of any use to a confessor
who failed to abide by her confession.

5

Five witches, four men and one woman, were placed in a
cart and ridden through the streets of Salem to Gallows
Hill on 19 August. Procter, his courage sinking at the last,
had tried to postpone the date, pleading that he was not
ready to die. But the convenience of a wizard is not consulted in making such arrangements. Nor would Noyes heed
Procter's plea that he pray with him; prayers are only for
the repentant. Cotton Mather, however, who had been visiting the condemned in prison, responded to the appeals of
both Willard and Procter by riding out from Boston for the
occasion; what spiritual help he could offer under the circumstances was questionable, but at least he came.

When the cart set out, jolting through streets lined with
spectators, Procter found his will was steady again. His
calm and Willard's made a deep impression.

But at the scaffold all eyes were on Burroughs. He was
allowed to speak from the ladder, and he spoke so simply
and so well that "unthinking people"—Sewall's phrase, he
being there—wept to hear him. At the end, slowly, gravely,
faultlessly, he repeated the Lord's Prayer.

When he had done a murmuring went through the
crowd. Was not this the supreme test? According to all the
books, all the goodwives and all the ministers, no servant
of Satan is capable of doing what Burroughs had just done.
One of the girls shrilled out that she had seen the black man
at his shoulder giving him his cues, but this was no explanation at all. The devil can't do it either.

The muttering grew as Burroughs mounted the ladder,
and with it came a surging forward, almost as if there were
some in the crowd who proposed to snatch him away from
the sheriff. Then a young man dressed all in black swung

upon his horse, stood high in his stirrups and addressed the crowd.

It was Cotton Mather, an old hand at hangings and not without valour. Solemnly he reminded them of Lawson's warning that the devil is never more subtly himself than when he most appears like an angel of light. Burroughs was not what he appeared to be; he was not even an ordained minister.

That last was a technicality which must have struck some as an anticlimactic irrelevance. Nevertheless Mather's words served their purpose; the mutterings diminished and the sheriff was allowed to finish his work. But Mather's explanation did not have the effect of obliterating the impression made by Burroughs. It haunted the spectators long after the man's body, bereft of its good trousers, was ignominiously thrust into its shallow grave; and presently it haunted Cotton Mather too in that people he met wouldn't stop talking about it. In time, as he was later to remark in print, he came to wish that he had never heard "the first letters of his name."

but it stayed
w/ them that
Burroughs could
say it faultlessly

CHAPTER XVII

EIGHT FIREBRANDS OF HELL

The wheels of justice now turned at full speed. On 9 September the judges tried and condemned six witches, and on 17 September nine more. Of the total of fifteen, eight were hanged on 22 September.

All but one of the seven who escaped hanging could be judicially accounted for. Five were confessing witches, Rebecca Eames of Boxford, Abigail Hobbs of Topsfield, Mary Lacy and Ann Foster of Andover, Dorcas Hoar of Beverly; these were condemned but reprieved. The sixth, Francis Dane's daughter, Abigail Faulkner, got a stay of execution by pleading pregnancy. Only with the seventh was there any irregularity. Mary Bradbury of Salisbury "escaped," or if escaped is too strong a word, she being too feeble to do anything for herself, at least her friends had in some obscure way managed to hide her from authority; and authority, it was suspected, was taking no very positive action to assert itself.

Mary Bradbury was one of the best-loved members of her community. Ninety-three neighbours had signed a statement that in half a century they had never known her to make trouble. Robert Pike and the Reverend James Allen testified to her charity and piety. Her husband Thomas, to whom she had been married fifty years and had borne eleven children, said that she was "of a cheerful spirit, liberal and charitable," but now that she was old, "weak and grieved under her affliction, may not be able to speak much for herself, not being so free of speech as others may be."

Such testimony came from the circle of Mrs Bradbury's

affectionate acquaintance. Not everyone in Salisbury belonged to it; at its outer edges were people who took the view that her seeming goodness was a false front behind which she concealed abominations. The elder Ann Putnam, having lived in Salisbury in youth, and not having moved in Mrs Bradbury's social set, knew all about the abominations. Her kinsman Richard Carr had as good as seen the woman turn herself into a blue boar; anyway he saw the boar rush out of a gate which Mrs Bradbury had just entered and dash at the feet of his father's horse. Neither he nor another witness doubted that the boar was Mrs Bradbury, and apparently neither did judges or jury when the story was duly relayed to them.

The woman even haunted ships at sea; Samuel Endicott had caught her at it. By bad luck his captain had bought two firkins of butter from her, and these had spoiled, not too surprisingly since the ship was bound for the Barbados and ill equipped with refrigeration. The spoiling of the butter was, however, only the beginning of Mrs Bradbury's display of malefic powers. Soon after the Barbados, the ship ran into a storm, lost a mainmast, and sprang a leak which ruined several tons of salt. At this point Mrs Bradbury, gloating over her accomplishment, could not resist the temptation to show off. On a bright moonlight night Endicott looked up and there she sat on the windlass, neat and composed in her white cap and neckcloth as she had ever been at meeting in Salisbury.

There could be no plainer evidence than that. Mrs Bradbury was sentenced to hang—yet did not. Her friends found means of spiriting her away and concealing her. The success of the concealment and the probably not ungrounded suspicion that local magistrates did not over-exert themselves to track her down gave rise in some quarters to discontent. It did not reassure common folk to feel that special privilege existed even among witches.

2

The other kind of special privilege was involved in the case of Dorcas Hoar, the privilege accorded confessing witches.

Goody Hoar, the same who had once shouted at the girls, "God will stop the mouths of liars!" had been a last-minute confessor. She had been tried, sentenced, and her hanging was imminent before she confessed at all, and it was then so late that she would have gone to the gallows regardless had not influential friends got up a petition for her. Now she was safe. At least she was reprieved, being given, as the petition put it, "a little time of life to realize and perfect her repentance for ye salvation of her soul."

All this was very well, and of course very merciful of the judges; just the same some people wondered whether so dramatic an eleventh-hour repentance had been based on the woman's desire to save her soul or just to save her neck.

Such doubts occurred sometimes even to John Hale, who had helped initiate the petition. There were moments when the woman's reckless defiance in court seemed to him in retrospect more convincing than her present eager acknowledgment of extravagant sins. To be sure, the woman had undoubtedly served an apprenticeship for witchcraft; two decades ago she had admitted to borrowing a book of palmistry, and six years later she apparently still had it. Hale's servants kept sneaking over to her house on dubious errands, bearing gifts pilfered from their master, and his little daughter Rebecca had followed them and seen a book "with many streakes and pictures in it." Not at all improbable that Goody Hoar had gone on from such minor sorceries to the real thing. Even so, how probable was it that she would have confessed had she known that they would hang her anyway?

There was nothing bloodthirsty about the kind, long-suffering John Hale, yet sometimes he secretly wished that the justices would get around to hanging some of these confessors. A murderer was not spared because he confessed; why then spare a confessing witch? How could the sincerity of all these confessions be tested but by the hangman's rope?

The fact was that until now the rope had been reserved not for those who pleaded guilty, but for those who professed innocence. How could it be that so many whose souls were burdened with such a crime had gone to death without seeking the solace of confession? Had the devil so hardened their hearts that none was capable of repentance? Or was it possible that they had nothing to confess?

Hale shuddered away from the thought, but it kept recurring, and not to him alone. Nor was it made easier by the fact that two of the former confessors had renounced their confessions. Margaret Jacobs escaped condemnation in the September trials only because she was too ill to be brought into court. Samuel Wardwell of Andover stood his trial, heard his sentence, and suffered it without once going back to his former story, his confession, though his wife and daughter clung to theirs for dear life. What was it that guided Wardwell now? Was it the devil, or was it perhaps an angel of God, and if the latter, who were the sinners, who the murderers?

3

Samuel Wardwell was the only male involved in the September trials. The women sentenced on 9 September were Martha Cory of Salem Village, Alice Parker and Ann Pudeator of Salem Town, and Mary Esty of Topsfield. Added to the roster on 17 September were Margaret Scott of Rowley, Mary Parker of Andover, and Wilmot Redd of Marblehead.

All Marbelehead had known for a lifetime that "Mammy" Redd, ageing wife of a fisherman, was a witch, but until the girls had come along, Marblehead had not been disposed to do anything about it. God had suffered the woman's generally harmless sorceries, expressed mainly in the curdling of milk and spoiling of butter, why not Marblehead? But Wilmot Redd was cried out on and taken, and being a poor thing, unable to do more than mutter, "I know nothing of it," at the trial, had been condemned.

Ann Pudeator had struck out at her accusers. She had petitioned that the testimony sworn against her by Sarah Churchill, Mary Warren, John Best be stricken from the record as "altogether false and untrue," and that "my life not be taken away by such false evidence." But though she reminded the judges that Best had formerly suffered public whipping as a proved "lyar," her defence availed her nothing.

Long imprisonment had not quelled the militant self-righteousness of Martha Cory. When on 14 September Parris and a delegation from the Village church called on her to tell her that she now lay under the sentence of excommunication, Martha expressed herself very forcefully. Parris did not dignify her words by recording them; he entered in the parish book only the observation that she was "very obdurate, justifying herself and condemning all that had done anything to her just discovery and condemnation." Nor did Parris record his own words, except to intimate that they had been few, "for her imperiousness would not suffer much." He did manage a prayer, but not at the invitation of Martha; she had had enough of the prayers of men like him.

It was well that they had not risked bringing her to church to be excommunicated publicly as Nicholas Noyes had done with Rebecca Nurse. Martha Cory was not the sort of martyr who suffers in silence.

Rebecca Nurse's sister Mary Esty had been fighting for her life all summer. As early as June, when there was hope of saving Rebecca's life as well, she and her third sister, the door-slamming Sarah Cloyce, had pleaded that fairer conditions should prevail at their trials than at their examinations. Since they were allowed no counsel they asked "that you who are our judges would please to counsel to us, to direct us wherein we may stand in need." They asked that the testimony of ministers, friends, and their children be admitted, and that the testimony of witches or of "such as are afflicted as is supposed by witches may not be improved to condemn us without other legal evidence."

The petition asked for nothing that the council of ministers had not already recommended, yet it had no effect at all. The judges, determined to get on with their work, could not afford to be guided by such considerations as these proposed, and which if adopted would have caused the collapse of the whole prosecution. What "other legal evidence" can you get against a criminal whose malefaction is by definition spectral but the reports of his victims and of criminals who have turned king's evidence?

After her condemnation Mary Esty made one last appeal, not now for herself, but in behalf of all the others who might come to trial as innocent as she.

"I petition to your Honours, not for my own life, for I know I must die, and my appointed time is set, but . . . that no more Innocent Blood be shed, which undoubtedly cannot be avoided in the way and course you go in. I question not but your Honours do to the utmost of your pains in the discovery and detection of witchcraft and witches, and would not be guilty of Innocent Blood for the world; but by my own Innocency I know you are in the wrong way. . . .

"I would humbly beg of you that your Honours would be pleased to examine some of the confessing witches, I being confident there are several of them have belyed themselves and others. . . . They say myself and others have made a League with the devil. . . . I know and the Lord he knows . . . they belye me, and so I question not but they do others; and the Lord alone who is the Searcher of hearts knows that, as I shall answer to at the Tribunal Seat, I know not the least thing of witchcraft; therefore I cannot, I durst not belye my soul."

4

The executions were set for Thursday, 22 September. Before they could take place, they were preceded on Monday of that week by an unscheduled execution. Giles Cory, hus-

band of the unrepentant Martha, had been pressed to death
by the sheriff on 19 September in an open field beside the
jail.

Death was probably not the explicit objective of the sheriff's attentions. He was merely applying the English procedure of the "peine forte et dure" to a criminal so stubborn
that he had "stood mute," thereby refusing to place himself
formally on trial under the "common law of the land." In
the whole history of English law very few people placed
on trial for felony had had the fortitude to "stand mute"
and endure a penalty expressly designed to discourage such
obstinacy. It must have been supposed when the ordeal
began that after a certain number of rocks had been placed
on Cory's chest he would break down and consent to giving
testimony. But Giles Cory had endured, his only recorded
utterance—and it is tradition which records it—being an occasional gasp, "More weight."

Giles had come a long way since that day in March when
he had offered his fumbling testimony against his wife. To
the magistrates his testimony had seemed mere stupidity,
being little more than an expression of wonder that his
wife should linger by the fire to pray long after he expected
her in bed. It appeared stupid, however, only in contrast
to the livelier offerings of the girls. The old man, credulous
as he was as to the cause of their affliction, had stubbornly
kept to the facts as he knew them, and a fact will often
show poor and plain in contrast to the leapings of imagination.

At his own examination he had still been credulous and
humble. "I am a poor man and cannot help it." But the
examination and the long months in prison that followed it
had slowly opened his eyes. He knew himself to be innocent,
and yet the girls had accused him of just such pranks as he
had believed against his wife. Now he saw that he had
"broken charity" with Martha in believing the word of a
pack of lying girls against hers. By his own innocence—his
reasoning paralleled that of Mary Esty—he knew that his
wife was innocent as well.

While he lay in jail turning over these things in his slow

mind, the trials went on, and it was borne upon Giles as upon every witch accused that there was hope of nothing from a trial but of further injury to one's good name. When his turn came, he stood speechless before the judges. He would not plead, he would not testify before such a court. Better the breaking of his bones one by one than the mockery that the she-brats would heap on him if he opened his mouth.

Sent back to prison to await execution of judgment, he undertook an experiment. Except in cases of treason, conviction could not be obtained on a prisoner who stood mute, and without conviction his property could not be confiscated. Accordingly Giles deeded his land to those of his sons-in-law who had refused to believe the charges of witchcraft against Martha even when he himself had done so. So it was that though the sheriff slowly crushed the last breath out of the massive body, he could not make a condemned wizard out of old Giles or lift a finger to prevent the property from going to his heirs. For the deeds held.

His death in an open field did not go unwitnessed. Though there were some who indulged their blood-lust in the sight, others who found reassurance in the righteous severity of the judgment, there were still others who wondered if this were justice at all. There had been a kind of sublime obstinacy in the old man. There was a meaning in his death, a symbolism which they could not define and by the same token could not stop talking about.

It was a relief to Samuel Sewall, most conscientious of judges and not at all immune by nature to considerations of mercy, to get a letter on the subject from Thomas Putnam, father of the gifted Ann.

Giles, he thereby learned, had not been the only sufferer. During the whole Monday while so many in town had given way to false pity for the deserved fate of a foul old man, an innocent maid had lain in torture just as painful. Exactly as the rocks had been laid on Giles's chest, a whole convocation of witches had closed in on poor Ann to crush her chest, choke the breath out of her body, and mock her, saying that she should be pressed to death before Giles.

But by God's grace there came release. Ann was saved by an apparition in his winding-sheet who, having driven off the witches, explained to her why Giles had to be pressed to death, a fate concerning which Ann herself seems to have had some barely conscious compunctions. Giles, she now learned, had once pressed a man to death with his feet, the very man whose ghost was now with her. Giles had also at the time of his covenant with the devil driven a special bargain; the devil had promised that he should not hang. So it was, and God had expressly hardened his heart against the advice of the court, which would have arranged an easier death, because, as the apparition said, "It must be done to him as he has done to me."

Putnam, hearing this testimony, recalled an incident which had been forgotten during the prosecution of Giles. Seventeen years ago, long before Ann had been born, Giles had been haled into court to account for the death of a man living in his house who had been found "bruised to death and having cloddens of blood around his heart." Giles had somehow got clear of the charge of murder, by enchantment Putnam now realized. By God's providence he had now undergone the punishment he had inflicted on an innocent man, and the truth had been revealed out of the mouths of babes and sucklings, or anyway of young Ann, who could not possibly have known of the event except by spectral revelation.

So reasoned the father, so reasoned Judge Samuel Sewall, and so Cotton Mather, to whom Sewall presently turned over this bit of evidence. All of them thereby displayed a certain naïveté as to the depth of the ancient lore of sickly young Ann, who had sucked in with her mother's milk all the slanders of the neighbourhood.

5

On 22 September seven witches and one lone wizard were packed into a cart and hauled the long mile to Gallows Hill. The sheriff had not chosen the most convenient spot for his hangings, but he had chosen a conspicuous one.

The hangings were made a spectacle by intention. The Puritans never denied themselves this sort of show; it was considered a sound deterrent to immoral impulses, especially now when the devil was proselytizing the country. Besides, it was always interesting to watch. People who could not follow the spectacle at close range spied on it at a distance from their upper windows.

From Gallows Hill the witches in their turn could take one last look at the distant waters of the bay, grey to-day, for the sky was overcast and rain threatening, at the brightness of the low rugged hills that rolled down to the shore, alight with goldenrod, rich with the smoky blue of the asters and the first turning of the leaves, for winter was coming, a winter for which they need cut and carry no wood.

At the steep ascent to the hill the cart stuck in the road. The accusers, riding close behind, plainly saw the devil hold it back. At the gallows Wardwell tried to address the people of Salem, protesting his innocence, but the waiting sheriff was smoking a pipe by his head and the smoke blowing into his face choked him off. The girls said that too was the devil's work, though it seems somewhat inconsistent of him.

Then it was over.

"What a sad thing," remarked Noyes, looking up at the oak tree with its heavy fruit, "to see eight firebrands of hell hanging there."

There was, had he looked, a sadder sight beside him, the no longer quite human faces of the afflicted girls. Seven months of carefully cultivated hysteria had not improved these flowers of Puritan maidenhood. They had coarsened and toughened and become nearly as insensible to normal feeling as so many automata. People who shrank from the cruelty of their jests at the dying misjudged them, for they were no more capable of conscious cruelty than of any other really human feeling. The very violence of their apparent emotion disguised a sick inner apathy. Given over so long to a world of dark fantasy, they were no longer capable of response to the electric shock of reality.

Almost any of those who hung on the gallows had been

happier than they. Mary Esty had the love of her children who did not cast her off because she was despised. Martha Cory had, besides her honest, blazing moral indignation at the folly of men, the satisfaction of having at last been allowed to pray in public; she had ascended the ladder with "an eminent prayer on her lips."

All these were happier than the girls, for they had pulsated with warm life to the end, and it was doubtful if the girls would ever again know what life was. They were famous; they were powerful; no one in Massachusetts had such power over life and death as they. But they were also alone. They created a little lifeless vacuum about them wherever they moved. Few but their own kin, and some of these reluctantly, dared come close to them. They were nubile, and some were comely, and yet most youths, barring the likes of John Doritch, did not willingly come nigher than the yonder side of the road.

They did not mind, for they lived in a dream, their senses so spellbound that they did not know how bad a dream it was, how stale with repetitions, without the interpolation of a fresh idea since they had fallen into it. They went on and on in the old bad dream, responding to suggestion as insensately as a machine responds to the touch of a hand.

Though some day some of them might awaken, it now seemed impossible. Mary Warren and Sarah Churchill had already had brief respites into humanity, and their awakening had been so painful that they had fled thankfully back into joyless fantasy.

But their outward state could not last for ever. They would not always be eminent. Now, on 22 September 1692, the spell over Massachusetts was lifting. There would not again be a hanging on Gallows Hill for this cause.

CHAPTER XVIII

THE GHOST OF MARY ESTY

In Wenham, a town which though close to Salem had by
God's providence largely escaped the witchcraft, lived a
seventeen-year-old girl named Mary Herrick. On 22 September this young woman received an uninvited guest, the
Shape of Mary Esty.

"I am going upon the ladder to be hanged for a witch,"
Goody Esty told her, "but I am innocent and before a
twelfth-month be past you shall believe it."

Then she vanished. The girl stared incredulously after
her. She knew this Witch Esty, at least by reputation, and
did not doubt at all that she and the others with her were
getting on the gallows exactly what they deserved. She decided to keep her mouth shut about this incident; she would
not lower herself by reporting the words of a lying witch;
there was enough wild talk going on without her adding to
it. She was a sensible girl, Mary Herrick, quite without
precedent in the ranks of the afflicted.

But Mary Esty, so gentle in life that the magistrates
themselves were with difficulty convinced of her witchhood,
and her very jailers pleaded for her, nevertheless had the
will of a Cromwell. Even when she knew that there was no
hope of establishing her own innocence, she had continued
her contest with the judges in the hope of saving others.
Now, instead of accepting failure, she rose from the dead
to bring her fight to a conclusion.

And this was an unthought-of providence. That a witch
once hanged would have the power to return to haunt the
living was a possiblity which had never entered the calcula-

tions of the judges; were it to happen the entire legal process would be robbed of its therapeutic value. And now it happened.

It was shortly after 22 September that Mary Herrick became aware of mysterious pains. At first they had no visible cause; then gradually during her affliction a Shape materialized before her, but a Shape of which she could not bring herself to speak, for it was none other than that of the pious wife of John Hale of Beverly.

Yet there could be no doubt that Mrs Hale was the tormentor. She appeared regularly, and it was her hand that pinched and choked. To be sure, after a while she did not come unattended. Mary Esty came too, but only to look on thoughtfully, her hands at her sides. Occasionally Mary "made as if to speak and did not."

At length it was the Shape of Mrs Hale who spoke.

"Do you think I am a witch?" she asked.

"No! You be the devil!" shouted the girl.

Now Mary Esty knew her plan had worked. For the first time she spoke. She told the girl "that she had been put to death wrongfully and was innocent of the witchcraft and she came to vindicate her cause." Then she cried "Vengeance! Vengeance!" or at least that was what the girl thought she said—it seems not in character for just this ghost—and gave her instructions. She "bid her to reveal this to Mr Hale and Mr Gerrish and then she would rise no more, nor should Mrs Hale afflict her."

Mary dare not disobey; she went to her pastor, the Reverend Joseph Gerrish of Wenham, and told him of what she called the "delusion of the devil." The pastor, having cross-examined her and found her at least as sincerely convinced as the Salem mediums, made a business-like record of the incident and then summoned Hale to hear from the girl's own lips this quite wonderful parable of the nature of delusion.

Hale, however impassive his ministerial demeanour, felt the ground rock under him when he heard the story. What man would not feel so on getting evidence that his wife has committed a capital crime? Yet that was not the point.

Hale knew that his wife had done nothing of the sort; she was flesh of his flesh, and had she been practising witchcraft he would have known it. But he now knew, and the revelation came to him with the force of a physical blow, that just so must John Procter have felt when his own wife was cried out on, and so a hundred others when wife or child or mother was taken. If his present feeling was justified, why not theirs?

Suddenly Hale knew with a conviction beyond logic that spectral evidence was madness. God had permitted the devil to use the shape of the innocent to delude. And this being so, how many of the innocent had been hanged in Salem?

He went home to brood among his books and papers; when he had thought the thing through he would not keep silent about his conclusions. He was a humble and courageous man; it takes courage twice to reverse one's position publicly in a matter of such moment.

Mary Esty for her part haunted the girl no more; her mission was accomplished. What further need of childish spectral shows when her courage and faith had at last made their impact, were winning to her own point of view the mind of one who had not before consciously doubted a witch's witchhood?

2

In the meantime a number of other people had reached the same conclusion as John Hale if for less dramatic reasons, and were making themselves heard. Though the judges had adjourned their sittings in September with every intention of resuming them on schedule in October, so many people were now converted to Mary Esty's opinion that they were "in the wrong way" that it was a question if the Court of Oyer and Terminer would be allowed to sit again.

Opposition to this manner of investigating witchcraft was of course no new thing. It had begun exactly where the witchcraft had, in Salem Village. An impressive number of simple country folk in and about the community had from the first faced the crisis far more realistically than had their sophisticated and learned betters in Boston and Salem Town. Moreover, in spite of the fact that death or exile had usually been the penalty for coming out in opposition to the official view, an extraordinarily large portion of the community had at one time or another consented to take the dangerous risk of protesting the innocence not indeed of witches in general, but of some special witch, long known and respected among them.

For all the conspicuous and ruthless part that the ministry in Salem itself had played in the prosecution, ministers at large in the Bay Colony had not done any such thing. Indeed, had they done so, the panic would never have been localized as it was, roughly to the limits of Essex County, or put in another way, within the approximate range of Mrs Ann Putnam's acquaintance. Plymouth, for instance, though it must have had its share of hysterical girls, managed to get along without cultivating an "accusing circle"; Andover had one, but only after deliberately exposing itself to the contagion of Salem, and as Thomas Brattle was now saying, poor Andover did "now rue the day."

Far more ministers were making a stand against prosecution than were lending themselves to it. Francis Dane was now successfully rallying Andover to his viewpoint. Willard of Boston had been working on the judges, three of whom were in his congregation, and though as a friend reported he had "met with little but unkindness and abuse" and had indeed been cried out on by the accusers, he did not desist.

Indeed he is believed to have gone so far as to have published anonymously a *Dialogue Between S and B*, in which it was suggested that the accusers were "scandalous persons, liars, and loose in their conversation," and even at best disqualified as "humane witnesses" by the very fact of their affliction. Spectral evidence he renounced utterly. "If the fact may be done and yet the persons doing it be innocent of the crime, the verdict is merely conjectural," said his "B," presumably Boston, "and the man dyes by will and doom; whereas God hath not granted to man such a power over another's lives."

"You are an admirable advocate of witches," finally said "S" scathingly; it was a retort which Willard must have often heard.

In Salem the Quaker, Thomas Maule, took the attitude that the whole witchcraft had been fabricated from the petty hates and envies of the community and could be destroyed if people would obey the injunction, "Love your enemies." Who, he asked, could count himself wholly guiltless? It was like the story of the woman taken in adultery. "He that is wholly clear of every degree of witchcraft may cast a stone at witches."

Any number of country preachers had come to the defence of accused parishioners: the two ministers of Rowley who investigated and defended Elizabeth How; Wise of Ipswich, who had cited the eloquent example of Job in behalf of John Procter; Mrs Bradbury's pastor. The credulity and pitiless zeal of Nicholas Noyes and Samuel Parris, far from being characteristic of the ministers of Massachusetts, seem to have been the conspicuous exception.

Increase Mather himself, who had earlier been disposed to keep aloof from the witchcraft except when his opinion was solicited, had gradually been drawn into the controversy.

"Is there not a God in Boston," he had demanded of a parishioner who had carried a sick child to the accusing circle for diagnosis, "that you should go to the devil in Salem?"

On 3 October he read before a conference of ministers in Cambridge a long scholarly paper called *Cases of Conscience*, in which he set forth his matured reasoning on the nature of the evidence on which conviction could be obtained in witch trials. In his warning against placing too great reliance on spectral evidence, in his denunciation of the use of the test of touch and such superstitious devices as the making of witch cakes, he did little but repeat what he and his colleagues had said before. But his language was so forceful as to suggest a new urgency of conviction. "It is better that ten suspected witches should escape than one innocent person should be condemned."

Mather's text contained no direct criticism of the conduct of the trials, and a preface signed by fourteen ministers, among them Gerrish, Wise and Willard, went no further than to hint discreetly at the dangers of "over-hasty suspecting or too precipitant judging." Mather, however, was still investigating. On 19 October he at last acted on the petition of John Procter; he went to Salem and made personal—and revealing—investigation of the conditions under which "confessions" were being obtained.

3

Up until late summer, however, no one in a position of authority had come out openly against the conduct of the trials. The granite will and fierce conviction of Stoughton had set the pattern; none of his associates, not even his superior, Sir William Phips, had so far taken issue with him, or at least taken it to any effect. There was an exception in Nathaniel Saltonstall, but his controversy had been carried on behind closed doors and ended with his resignation and, at least so far as the general public was concerned, with his silence. Silence may have an eloquence of its own, but only in the long run. Opposition can hardly rally around a man who merely withdraws and shuts his mouth.

There may have been an occasional misgiving in Judge Samuel Sewall, at least so far as the accusation of his friend John Alden was concerned; he was willing to pray with the latter. But his diary, punctually continued during all this period, is no secret history of the witchcraft. He who wrote so freely of his dreams, of his struggles to train his children, of his searchings of God's providence, wrote of the witchcraft as drily and impersonally as if it were a subejct on which he did not trust himself to have any feelings or opinions at all. Essentially a kind and honourable man, capable of generosity in recognizing and confessing a wrong, it may be that Sewall got through his inhuman duties as judge only by a kind of self-hypnosis. He no less than the girls had become something of an automaton.

But while Sewall and the other judges clung to the party line, scepticism was making inroads among other representatives of the magisterial mind. Judge Bradstreet of Andover had flatly declined to arrest any more witches. Judge Jonathan Corwin of Salem was in correspondence with an outspoken heretic of Salisbury.

Corwin's whole contribution to the witchcraft had been oddly passive. Sometimes he had acted as scribe at the examinations, but he had almost never played any real part in questioning the accused. That role had usually fallen to Hathorne, while Corwin listened and made record of his observations; possibly from that vantage he got points of view to which his more active associate was blind. If he fell a prey to misgivings, however, he was loath to give them voice; had it been otherwise he would hardly have been asked to replace Saltonstall on the Court of Oyer and Terminer, where to all appearances he obediently followed the leader.

Yet had there not been some stubborn demon of doubt at work in him, it seems unlikely that he would in August have incurred the letter that he got from the Salisbury magistrate, Richard Pike.

Being of Salisbury, well removed from the storm centre, Pike had at first small occasion to give close attention to the witchcraft. When, however, Saltonstall of nearby Haverhill resigned from the bench, he quite likely rode over to get some first-hand impressions, and at the same time he became involved to an extent in the accusations against Mary Bradbury and Susanna Martin. Though the latter was not of his town, she was known there, and people came to him to make formal deposition of her witcheries. Sometimes during these labours Pike looked up at an informer drily.

"It's a pity you didn't tell that story four and twenty years ago," he remarked once, "when it happened."

To Corwin on 9 August, shortly after the trial of Burroughs, Pike wrote a letter to which he signed only his initials, in which he expressed his opinion that the present handling of the trials left the lives of innocent people "to the pleasure and passion of those that are minded to take them away. . . . The witnesses were not only informers . . . but sole judges of the crime."

How, he asked, was witchcraft to be proved? By reports of spectral journeys to Parris's pasture as so often made by the accusing girls, by confessors, and by such erratic witnesses as Susanna Martin's accuser, John Ring? Why the devil had once carried Christ himself from place to place in order to tempt him "and yet left him innocent." By a witchmark? But how often might there not be found "a superfluity of nature . . . as the piles"? No, proof was dark and uncertain, confession often "necessitated." Under these circumstances it was safer "to leave a guilty person alive until further discovery than to put an innocent person to death."

Who was it who told these Salem girls "things that they do not see, but the devil, especially when some things that they tell are false and mistaken? . . . Is the devil a competent witness in such a case?" And how reliable was the "touch test" on which the judges were setting such store? Was it not against nature that the accused, in the very act of denying their guilt, would publicly practise witchcraft, sending their Shapes to pinch and throttle in the very faces of the judges? On what grounds did the latter suppose that the devil "is now become a reformer to purge . . . witches out of the world"?

That the reticent Corwin did not keep altogether silent about the doubts such a plea stirred in him is suggested by one expressive fact. His mother-in-law, Margaret Thacher of Boston, was accused; she was accused repeatedly. Somehow she was not arrested. One just doesn't swear out a warrant for the kinswoman of a judge. This was another judicial oversight that did not fail to attract attention.

4

"I am sensible that it is irksome and disagreeable to go back when a man's doing so is an implication that he has been walking in the wrong path; however, nothing is more honourable than, upon due conviction, to retract and undo (so far as may be) what has been amiss and irregular."

Yet another notable was expressing himself about the prosecution of the witchcraft. This time it was the Bostonian, Thomas Brattle, a merchant, somewhat as the princes of the Renaissance were merchants. He was much more besides—mathematician, astronomer, experienced traveller, and he was about to become treasurer of Harvard (and a thorn in the flesh of President Increase Mather) and shortly to help found a new church which would be a thorn in the flesh of any Mathers at all.

His recommendation came at the end of a long, reasoned analysis of the course of the trials. He agreed with Pike's denunciation of spectral evidence and went beyond him. In Brattle's eyes it was disgraceful that the magistrates had based their judgments on such evidence as common gossip, irresponsible "confessions," and above all on the pretensions of the afflicted girls. These last seemed to him to be so many liars and mountebanks. He heaped scorn on the mentality of what he called the "Salem gentlemen," carefully defining the term to exclude those Salem citizens who did not participate in the prosecution and to include Boston men who did. "But in Salem this sort of gentleman does most abound."

Brattle signed his full name to this document, which took the form of a letter, but began it only "Dear Sir," addressing no one in particular. He probably intended it for a circular letter to be passed from hand to hand in lieu of publication. Its timing was canny. Brattle had obviously been mulling over its contents for months, but he did not risk even so discreet a publication as this until he was fairly sure of immunity from reprisal. Now in October his point of view was sufficiently supported in other quarters for him to be reasonably sure that the crisis had passed its peak. At least there was a fair chance of exorcizing the demoniac possession of Massachusetts if enough men of goodwill had the courage to speak in the name of reason.

5

More than protest was causing the collapse of prosecution. The voice of reason had after all been lifted long before, but until now it had been a voice crying in the wilderness. That it was heeded at last was due to the fact that the devil had now progressed to the stage of total war. Literally no one was safe. No degree of eminence insured one against accusation. Recently the girls had cried out on the spirited Lady Phips, who in the absence of her husband had the daring to sign a release for one prisoner personally known to her. All very well for the judges to tell the girls that they had made a mistake, as they had done when Willard was accused, but when they had done this just so many times, the line between mistaken and true accusation became obliterated.

Indeed the multiplication of the accusations was now bringing not only embarrassment but confusion upon the judges. As Hale said, "It cannot be imagined that in a place of so much knowledge so many in so small compass of land should abominably leap into the devil's lap at once." In adjourning their sitting to late October the judges had it in mind that by then Phips would have returned and would have an opportunity to express himself on policy.

The governor, who had counted on the affair's being disposed of without him, returned in October to find the colony an aroused and angry hornets' nest. Those to whom he had entrusted the task of weeding out the witches and restoring order seemed rather to have multiplied confusion. Nevertheless he could not at this stage blame them. In the report he got off to England on 11 October, describing what had been done and urgently asking counsel from the Crown, he defended the judges. Indeed in his haste he made copious use of a history of the witchcraft which Cotton Mather had been drafting from some documents furnished by Stephen Sewall. Mather, in spite of his professed distrust of spectral evidence, had found no fault with its actual use,

and some of this credulity had crept over into Phips's
account.

On the other hand Phips did report some positive action
on his own part. Finding that "the devil had taken upon
him to assume the shape of several persons who were doubtless innocent and to my certain knowledge of good reputation"—Lady Phips for one—he had forbidden further com-
mitments; also he had prevented the printing of discourses
—here he may have been thinking of Brattle—that might
kindle "an inextinguishable flame." Plaintively the driven
man added that some people "are seeking to turn it all on
me."

The uproar continued. Andover was now mobilized for
an attempt to undo the results of its folly. First on 12 October came a petition from seven of its citizens asking that
their wives and children be released to their care on bond,
and describing their distress in prison, the poor food, the
cold coming on, and the unhappy company of "poor distressed creatures as full of inward grief and trouble as they
are able to bear up in life withal." The petition was to be
the forerunner of many, and not from Andover only; people in Topsfield, Gloucester, Haverhill, Chelmsford joined
the plea for the release of their kin.

A second more vigorous step was taken on 24 October,
when twenty-four Andover citizens presented a paper de-
nouncing the accusing girls as "distempered persons" and
protesting their position of authority in court. "We know
no one who can think himself safe if the accusations of children and others who are under diabolical influence shall
be received against persons of good fame."

On 26 October the General Court took at last decisive
action. It called for a fast "and convocation of ministers
that may be led in the right way as to the witchcraft."
Sewall added dispassionately in his diary, "The season and
manner of doing it is such that the Court of Oyer and
Terminer count themselves dismissed."

The court was officially dismissed three days later by
Phips. Stoughton, who still held to his original position as
firm as a rock, and had come up from Dorchester the day

before to be ready for court, had wet his clothes in the
storm and high tide for nothing.

Postponement of the trials did not in itself solve anything.
At least 150 witches had been legally arrested and must
be tried, no matter by what means. The devising of more
realistic methods would take time, and meanwhile it was a
question if with winter coming on all the witches would
live long enough to stand trial. The prisons of Massachusetts had not been planned with such a crime wave in mind.
Most of them were shoddy structures at best, and over-
crowding had produced inhuman conditions. At least two
witches, one of them the confessing Ann Foster of Andover,
had recently died there.

Accordingly Phips now turned his attention to the petitions for release. The tender age of some of the witches
must have moved him. Dorothy and Abigail Faulkner, for
whom Nathaniel Dane and John Osgood were willing to go
£500 bond, were ten and eight respectively; Stephen and
Abigail Johnson were thirteen and eleven; Sarah Carrier
was eight. The detention of adult witches was causing difficulty to their families; the children of Martha Sparkes had
become a burden on Chelmsford neighbours because while
she tarried in prison her husband Henry was "a soulder in
their majesties service at the Eastern parts." The petitioners
identified themselves as weavers, husbandmen, and signed
with ingenious marks; the favourite in Andover was a heart;
Francis Faulkner encircled his and pierced it with a broken
arrow.

Governor Phips inspected the evidence against these
prisoners, and when he found it to be spectral only, accepted the responsibility of releasing them on bond into the
custody of their families. Such witches as must remain in
jail he made the charge of the judges; they must keep an
eye on their welfare and not let them suffer want.

Thus winter began in Massachusetts more hopefully than
had the spring. And yet the spectral peril had by no means
ended; people at large were not enjoying an intellectual
awakening where so recently they had succumbed to superstitious panic. Even the vote of the General Court which

led to the suppression of the court had been close: thirty-three to twenty-nine. A law enacted on 14 December hardly offered indulgence to practising witches; it confirmed the death penalty for those who used charms to kill or hurt, for "any invocation or conjuration of any evil spirit," or for taking up "any dead man, woman or child" out of their graves. The law did, however, differentiate between degrees of witchcraft; only a prison sentence and the pillory were prescribed for persons who used charms to find secret treasure or stolen property, to destroy cattle, or "to the intent to provoke any person to unlawful love."

Meanwhile, even while the governor laboured to release the congestion in the prisons, new prisoners came in. For neighbour still bore spite against neighbour, and the spirit of prophecy still lay on the girls whose vision had first set off this long train of events.

In October, Gloucester, undeterred by the example of Andover, sent for the girls. Gloucester had reason to believe that witches were about because during July it had fought off an invasion by devils. These swarmed out of the swamps upon lonely garrisons and looked at first like French and Indians; some of them wore blue shirts and had bushy black hair. By the token that bullets had no effect on them the garrison knew that the invasion was spectral. They called for reinforcements and in town good people cast about to identify the witches who had called the devils in. This panic had subsided before October; nevertheless the girls were sent for, and thanks to their ministrations, four women were taken. They had a melancholy time finding lodgings; Salem, to which they were taken first, had no room for them; eventually they wound up in Ipswich.

In November, even after the suspension of the court, a Gloucester citizen summoned the girls again. But this time there was a difference. It happened that on Ipswich Bridge they met with an old woman, and veteran automata that they were, they fell at once into their fits. But it was not Ipswich that had summoned them; such Ipswich people as were about had had their bellyful of such as they. For all Ipswich proposed to do about it, the girls could lie on the bridge and bellow until Doomsday.

Being ignored was a therapy that had rarely been tried upon these girls. Fits under such circumstances left them confused. The familiar cues were lacking. Although eventually they got back on their nags and rode on to Gloucester, their performance there lacked its usual conviction and led to no arrests.

Winter came on without further recorded incident so far as the witchcraft was concerned. But about Salem and Salem Village, where fields had been neglected during the frantic uncertainties of spring and summer, there was want.

CHAPTER XIX

JAIL DELIVERY

Those Massachusetts men who openly opposed the manner of prosecuting the witchcraft had in late October a powerful reinforcement from outside. It is probable that what precipitated the new decision displayed by Governor Phips was an impartial opinion on the witchcraft drawn up by a group of Dutch and French ministers in New York. Until then Phips had played a womanish part, yielding first to one pity then another, or dodging the issue entirely. That, however, had been less from want of character than from the fact that like an earlier administrator, he did not know what was truth. Once he knew, there had been no more vacillating; he had no hesitation now in substituting his own common sense and humanity for the learned sophistries of William Stoughton.

The opinion in question had been solicited by Joseph Dudley, deputy governor of Massachusetts under Andros. Since the revolution of 1689, Dudley had been a kind of exile; imprisoned for a time with Andros, he remained so unpopular after his release that he left Boston and took an appointment in New York. He remained a Bostonian at heart, however, hoped now that the issue of the charter had been settled to make an early return, and in the meantime took a lively interest in anything that went on at home.

The most burning issue in Massachusetts was now the witchcraft, and of this Dudley could not have failed to get a report not only from correspondence but from the presence in New York of such refugees as the Carys and Englishes. Having bent his judicial mind to the facts in the case, he compiled a list of eight questions and sent them to some leading ministers of the colony. Their reply, which reached him on 11 October, he had immediately copied and forwarded to Phips.

The correspondence with the ministers had been carried on in noble Latin, the Esperanto of the age, a language in which Sir William, literate only since the age of twenty-one, was unversed. But when it was translated to him he was profoundly, not to say painfully impressed. That outsiders and outlanders, bearing names like Henry Selijns and Peter Peirilus, completely detached from the uproar in Massachusetts, could reason thus, made it impossible for him to ignore the almost identical views of men like Brattle, Pike, and Willard.

New York, though now an English colony, still lived in the climate of opinion created by the Dutch patroons. There was among its leaders more of a certain kind of realism than could be easily found in Massachusetts; it carried over into the art of their painters, who still borrowed from the wonderful Dutch School of Van Dyck and Rembrandt; it carried over into their thinking. Long ago Dutch philosophers and theologians had taken the lead in denying, like poor Burroughs, that there either were or could be witches.

The ministers had not, to be sure, gone so far. To Dudley's explicit question they replied that there were witches, "the exact and formal nature" of whose wrongdoing lay in allying themselves with the devil and "throwing off the yoke of God." But that witches could be detected and proved by any simple rule of the thumb they forcefully denied; indeed they condemned nearly every device on which the Massachusetts prosecutors had relied for the purpose.

Could spectral evidence be trusted, Dudley had asked. "By no means!" said the ministers, and referred him to the Book of Job for evidence of how much latitude the Lord could sometimes allow the devil. What of evidence of previous malice, Dudley had inquired further. They answered that it was no evidence at all in proving witchcraft; honest men could have their fallings out, and the devil, subtle as he was, would take pains to avoid performing under such

obvious circumstances. On the other hand it was not probable that a person whose whole life had been outwardly
virtuous would be guilty of witchcraft; it could happen,
given the devil's duplicity, but it would be rare.

The divines were kind to the afflicted girls. Brattle had
called them mountebanks, largely on the grounds that their
agonies had never marked them with lasting physical injury. The Dutch ministers, shrewd observers of their own
hysterical parishioners, knew that an "affliction" could be
real enough and yet not physical at all. But in the act of
defending the girls, they undermined belief in their com-
petence as witnesses. The girls, they said, deluded by the
devil, were in the worst possible position to identify the
cause of their affliction.

This report probably reached Phips during the third
week in October, and he did not keep it from the judges.
Some of them must have looked at it bleakly. Theirs had
been a thankless task. Their critics had had little to say
about their selfless devotion to duty, the hours they had
put in searching the books on witchcraft for the exact legal
precedent, the long rides to Salem, and the sultry days
spent in court while their own affairs languished without
them. Yet exactly because they were good and faithful
servants, some of them had not been able altogether to
close their ears to the storm of criticism, or having listened,
to keep themselves wholly free of doubt. On such as they
the effect of the opinion of the New York ministers was
crucial. They now heard from reasonable men who had no
conceivable personal stake in the case that the entire basis
of their judgment had been false. They could not deny that
every conviction had been made on spectral evidence, or
that such secondary evidence as had been called into account was exactly of the kind rejected by the New Yorkers,
testimony of old quarrels between neighbours.

If this view were just, what they had done did not for
the present bear thinking about. Mary Esty with her brave
appeal to reason might send her ghost to walk in other
places than Wenham. Yet the past could not be undone;
the dead, even those unjustly condemned, could not be re-

called to life. To look back was as futile as it was dismaying; what was necessary now was not to undo the irrevocable, but to look forward, to devise a sounder method of trial for the witches still on the docket.

"Some of them," wrote Sir William of the judges in a later report to England, "were convinced and acknowledged their former proceedings were too violent and not grounded upon a right foundation, but if they might sit again, they would proceed after another method."

2

new court

By acts of the General Court of 23 November and 16 December, special sessions of the Superior Court of Judicature were appointed to complete the trials. The composition of this court must have dismayed the witches, for it was substantially that of the old, discredited Court of Oyer and Terminer. Stoughton would still preside in spite of the fact that he and Phips were now close to a break on principle; Samuel Sewall, John Richards, Wait Winthrop had all served on the old court; and though the fifth member, Thomas Danforth, had not, he had sometimes sat with Hathorne and Corwin on the examinations.

There were, however, some innovations. Salem of fatal memory would no longer be the only seat of the trials; the court would circulate from Essex County to Middlesex and Suffolk, according to the origin of the defendant. The jurors impanelled in these several localities were also new, and in more ways than one; thanks to the new charter they were no longer drawn exclusively from members of the Covenant.

The most important difference was in procedure. Everyone—even, necessarily, William Stoughton—had agreed to eliminate spectral evidence as a basis of conviction. This fact was made plain early in the day when some of the "jewry" specifically asked what weight they should give such testimony; "as much as of Chips in Wort" was the answer they got from the judges.

Deprived of such evidence, however, there seemed to be little point in trying a witch at all. Of the fifty-two witches whose trials were opened in Salem on 3 January, the cases against forty-nine melted like moonshine at daybreak once the new touchstone was applied. Rule out the visions of the girls and their friends, the tales of airy travels, of meetings behind Parris's orchard, the testimony of being pinched and choked and being presented the book—and there was nothing left, nothing tangible, nothing provable. The only straw that judges and jury had to clutch at was statements by the witches themselves. On this basis three were finally convicted and condemned. These were the wife of Samuel Wardwell, still clinging to her confession; one Mary Post, called "senseless and ignorant," and Elizabeth Johnson, whom her grandfather, Francis Dane, called "simplish at best."

Besides condemning these three, Stoughton signed the death warrants for five of those who had been condemned in September but for various causes reprieved. Probably Elizabeth Procter, now delivered of John's posthumous child, was one of these; the rest were confessing witches. Under the new system there seemed to be no further reason for sparing the life of a confessor. Their testimony on others, being spectral, was of no further use; there was no need to prove their guilt since they had admitted it. The judges were able to move on to Charlestown, heartened by the knowledge that though they had cleared the innocent, they had not dealt timorously with the guilty.

But in signing the death warrants, Stoughton had reckoned without the aroused and now thoroughly sceptical conscience of Sir William. The latter would not pass on these cases without personal investigation; when he heard from the King's Attorney that the evidence against the eight condemned differed in no substantial way from that against those who had been cleared, he signed reprieves for all of them. It was not in him again to risk the shedding of innocent blood.

His action was a direct rebuke to his deputy governor, with whom his relations had for some time been strained. Phips was even now composing a second report to England in which he complained of Stoughton's having "hurried on

these matters with great precipitancy" and seizing "the es-
tates, goods, and chattels of the executed . . . without my
knowledge and consent."

Stoughton was sitting on the bench at Charlestown when
news of the reprieve came, and he took it ill.

"We were in a way to have cleared the land of the
witches!" he exclaimed. "Who it is that obstructs the course
of justice I know not. The Lord be merciful to the country!"

And so, in the words of his enemy, Robert Calef, the
redoubtable judge "went off the bench and came no more
that court." That is, not in its Charlestown sitting. By 25
April when the court moved to Boston as the seat of Suffolk County, Stoughton was back in his place.

During the interim, however, both court and jury had
made a complete break with the Stoughton viewpoint. Re-
jecting every testimony that smelled of the spectral, they
had cleared the witches almost as fast as they could be
brought before them. Even in Boston, with the benefit of
Stoughton's presence, they cleared the eighty-year-old
Sarah Daston, though one of the judges later admitted that
there was more evidence against her than there had been
against any who had been hanged. She was a most unsavoury old woman, far gone in age and malice.

"Woman, woman, repent!" Judge Danforth had admon-
ished her. "There are shrewd things come against thee."
But condemn her he could not, for all the evidence that
was not spectral was of that other type denounced by the
Dutch divines, testimony derived from ancient garboils.

Even one "confessor" was cleared at this Boston sitting.
This was Mary Watkins, an intermittently deranged indentured servant, who on being caught trying to strangle herself, had volunteered the information that she was a witch.
In this case, however, the acquittal did not have the approval of the judges. When the jury first returned with the
verdict of "*ignoramus*," the judges repeated their manœu-
vre in the Rebecca Nurse case and sent them out to re-
consider. This time the jury stuck to its guns; the verdict
stood.

The good name of John Alden was cleared "by proclamation," and in May Governor Phips, anxious to clean up the matter, discharged all remaining witches and made it safe for refugees to return by issuing a proclamation of general pardon. "Such a jail delivery," wrote Hutchinson, "has never been known in New England."

3

Mere pardon, however, did not guarantee jail delivery; the prison fees must first be paid. Criminals were not coddled in these days, nor were those on whom the merest shadow of suspicion had ever rested. You did not in prison become the guest of the state; you paid your way. Even if you were wholly innocent, if it were proved that you had been wrongfully deprived of your liberty, you still could not leave until you had reimbursed the jailer for his expenditures in your behalf, the food he had fed you, the shackles he had placed on your wrists and ankles.

Prices varied slightly at the various prisons, but in general board averaged at about two shillings and sixpence a week. Some of the witches had been running up a bill at this rate for more than a year; their people were plain farmfolk who seldom had cash to spare and had already spent all that they had in buying comforts for the prisoners and making long journeys to visit and consult with them. Farms had to be mortgaged to raise the ransom, and they were often farms already impoverished by the half-hearted attention they had had while the trials monopolized everyone's time and attention.

Nor did every witch have kinsmen willing to mortgage a farm. No one was interested in restoring Sarah Daston to circulation; innocent or guilty, the old woman remained in prison until she died. The same fate might have befallen Mary Watkins had she not had the wit to ask the jailer to find her a new master; she was then bound out to a gentleman of Virginia who got him an indentured servant for the price of a witch's prison fees. Tituba was eventually released on a similar arrangement, except that for Tituba the servitude was for life.

Poor Margaret Jacobs thought for a while to spend the rest of her life in prison. She who had shown courage second to none, who would have forfeited her life but for a timely illness when she recanted her confession on the eve of her grandfather's execution, had none to help her. Old George Jacobs had remembered her generously in his will, but the testament of a wizard condemned and hanged was not yet worth the paper it was written on. Her parents had fled accusation and had not as yet ventured back to the community that had used them ill, nor, their goods being seized, could they have helped her if they had.

There was compassion, however, even in hag-ridden Massachusetts. The plight of Margaret Jacobs was talked about and a stranger heard of it. One day he came to the jailer and paid her fees, and Margaret went free at last. She was an upright girl and in time managed to repay her debt.

Even release did not solve the most serious problems of some of the accused. When at last the elder Abigail Faulkner and Elizabeth Procter left prison, their jail-born babies in their arms, the shadow of their conviction still hung over them. Each had been condemned to death and reprieved only until her child could be born. Hence, though the sentence had never been carried out, both were in the eyes of the law dead women. Elizabeth could claim none of John Procter's property, some of which had now been salvaged for the family, not even her own dower, because she had no legal existence. It would take more than a decade and a far profounder change of heart on the part of the people of Massachusetts before even a fraction of such legal complications could be straightened out.

CHAPTER XX

THE DEVIL AND COTTON MATHER

What had actually been accomplished on the spiritual plane by the wholesale jail delivery of 1693 was a point which at the time could only be described as moot. In spite of the relief which many communities felt at the lifting of the nightmare, the eagerness with which husbands welcomed back their witches, repenting that they had ever distrusted them, people further removed from the scene could look on the whole process as a monstrous miscarriage of justice, boding no good to the future of Massachusetts. These agreed with Stoughton, "We were in a way to have cleared the land of the witches. . . . Who it is that obstructs the course of justice I know not."

It was true that some of the most obvious symptoms of witchcraft were disappearing. Little was heard from the afflicted girls once the jail delivery got under way. Though logically the return of so many witches to civilian life should have afflicted them even unto death, none of the girls did die; they remained well enough. A few, notably Mary Walcott and Elizabeth Booth, presently settled down and got married. Some of the others, still manless, and apparently at a loss how to put in their time in these duller, flatter days, turned, it was rumoured, to coarser pleasures; certain of them, never explicitly named in history, went unmistakably bad.

In Salem Village where this development could be watched at close range, there was said to be a general revulsion against them. It was not good to watch a wench at her harlotries and remember that on that harlot's word the good and chaste had been hanged. But at a further remove other interpretations were possible. The girls were being slandered, and the judges with them; would the likes of William Stoughton have been taken in by harlots? Also it was by no means certain that the girls had come out of their fits; it was more probable that these were being callously ignored when they fell into them. Look what had happened in the fall of 1692 when the girls had tried in vain to warn Ipswich of a malefactor. God was punishing an unworthy, half-hearted people by so hardening their hearts that they were incapable of receiving further revelation.

The plain truth was for those who had eyes to see that the devil was by no means bound up, had not lost his battle against New England, but was well on his way to bringing the entire community under his power. Of this there were unmistakable signs.

2

What was the devil? To the Puritan the question was no less important than the question, what is God. A surprising variety of answers were possible. Some in Massachusetts were still reading an English best-seller two decades old, John Milton's *Paradise Lost,* in which the poet in defeat and blindness had all unconsciously created Satan in his own image, doomed, but not without his grandeur. Such a being could be abhorred but not despised; one might pity, even respect the enemy of mankind. In his contest with Omnipotence he showed a perverse nobility of spirit; there was something almost Promethean in the tragic Satan who from hell defied the lightning of heaven and reached out to make mankind his own.

Yet how far was such a concept understood in provincial Massachusetts whose own tastes were represented not by the organ music of Milton's blank verse but by the jigging and jingling of Wigglesworth's *Day of Doom?* Certainly

Cotton Mather, who had his own copy of *Paradise Lost*, did not associate Satan with the grandeur of lost but not ignoble causes. His Satan had more the spirit of the poltergeist, or of the comic devil of the early miracle plays. The fellow was ubiquitous, and as such damnably dangerous and eternally a nuisance, but as little dignified as the worm that eats up the garden.

Still a third concept was possible, the strange Adversary who presented himself before God in the time of Job and was received with courteous attention. What manner of devil was this who did not stoop to laying petty ambush for his enemy, but came openly into God's presence to challenge him; and what meaning could be read into God's acceptance of a challenge from such a source? Could it be that such was the omnipotence of God that the very devil worked for him to examine the hearts of men and test the limits of their faith? Was it even possible that God made use of the devil to bring a new thing on earth, that out of ill good would come?

Yet what good would come out of what the devil had done in Massachusetts? The phase of the colony's martyrdom had been not single but multiple. Not the witchcraft only but the new charter had delivered the faithful into the devil's hand. Now that people outside the faith could vote and shape the course of government, the power of theocracy had been for ever broken. No longer would it be possible to get rid of perversely creative minds—the Ann Hutchinsons and Roger Williamses—by exile or death. Demoniac energies had been loosed now, and God alone could foresee the outcome. Was it possible that what the devil had promised William Barker of Andover would come to pass under God's providence, that there would be no more sin or shame or judgment, "that all men should be equal and live bravely"?

Well, it was God's will. God had delivered them if not to the devil, at least to an adversary. God save the Commonwealth of Massachusetts.

If symptoms of diabolism had faded at last in Salem Vil-lage—so odd a site for God to choose as the battleground between hell and heaven—there was deviltry aplenty in Boston. Even while the judges were dismissing the witches, Cotton Mather's own wife, she who had once had to smother a laugh at the sight of diabolic manifestation as observed in the person of little Martha Goodwin, had been affrighted on her porch by a diabolic vision and had in consequence given birth to a malformed, short-lived child.

And as if that were not enough, Mather himself, because of his charitable interest in certain afflicted maids of Boston, was about to be given to drink of the vinegar of mockery by what he called "the witlings of the coffee-houses." The devil had lately discovered to Boston a new brew which sharpened the wit and incited it to scepticism. Here in the waning days of the witchcraft were wont to sit several of the devil's own who made it their business to keep a derisive eye on the current activities of Cotton Mather and to publish them to the town.

Until lately there had been little occasion to connect the younger Mather with the witchcraft. He who had been so active in the Glover affair, and whose record of the case had helped prepare Massachusetts for the new outbreak, had nevertheless remained surprisingly aloof from the latter. Not that the aloofness had been by intention; it was simply a matter of living far from Salem and having much to detain him in Boston.

Early in the day he had written the Salem authorities offering to receive any six girls into his home for observation and treatment; had the magistrates responded it is probable that they would have exchanged a major calamity for yet another quaint, archaic monograph. The segregation of the girls would have served to localize the psychic infection, and the girls themselves, exposed to the wayward streak of poetry in Mather's composition, would almost certainly

have found their fantasies deflected to the more normal pre-
occupations of adolescence. They would, in short, like a
large proportion of the female members of his congregation
at any given time, have fallen in love with him. Infatuation
is not any guarantee against hysteria; quite the contrary.
But in this case such a development might have diverted
the antics of the girls to less malignant forms. Young Ann
Putnam might, like Martha Goodwin, have ridden an airy
horse up and down the stairs and into the pastor's study,
to find her catharsis there rather than before the gallows.

It had not been given Mather thus to experiment; he
had watched the case from afar and had only thrice taken
positive action. One of these occasions had been his drafting of the advice of the ministers to the judges, cautioning
them against too great reliance on spectral evidence, though
praising their zeal. Even before then Mather had unoffi-
cially written in the same vein to Judge John Richards, not
only warning him against spectral evidence but against uncritical acceptance of such confessions as might come from
a "delirious brain or a discontented heart." He specifically
denounced torture as a means of getting confessions.

His only dramatic intervention in the witchcraft had been
the speech he had made to the crowd at the hanging of
Burroughs. This speech was the only real complaint that his
enemies could make against him. There were some who
thought that Mather had shown small charity to a fellow
minister in his hour of need. Yet not much could be fairly
made of the incident. Had not Mather spoken another
must, for the crowd before the gallows was fast deteriorat-
ing into a mob. Mather who had seen mobs in Boston in
1689 had acted instinctively and without premeditation to
do what was necessary to quiet this one. Control of the
crowd and not slander of Burroughs had been his purpose.

In any case the incident was now well in the past. It
would not have been held a serious count against Mather,
nor could his name have been fairly connected with the
witchcraft but for what happened after it was all over.

4

On 22 September 1692, a kind of council of war had been called at Samuel Sewall's house in Boston. Present were Samuel's brother Stephen of Salem, Captain John Higginson, John Hathorne, William Stoughton and Cotton Mather. The subject under discussion was the propriety of making public some of the evidence in the witch trials. Not since Lawson's *Brief and True Narrative* of last spring had there been any authoritative published statement, and the latter had been written months in advance of the sitting of the Court of Oyer and Terminer. Now, with so much irresponsible talk going on, it seemed clear that the time had come for an official report on what the judges had accomplished for Massachusetts. It would be an interim report. At this date the judges expected to go forward with the trials in October. In spite of the rising tide of protest none could know that the seven women and one man who that day hung on the gallows in Salem would be the very last witches to hang in Massachusetts.

Mather stood ready to take on this assignment, and had been anticipating it for some time. To this end he had been accumulating some of his own sermons, notably his "Hortatory and Necessary Address" with its charge upon the conscience of New England. "'Tis our Worldliness, our Formality, our Sensuality and our Iniquity that has helped this letting of the Devils in." In addition he had been after Stephen Sewall to copy out such of the documents in Salem as could be used in a history of the witchcraft. Some of this material—not quite so much as he had hoped—was now available. If it was the will of his colleagues he would gladly do his best with a subject which had been, he modestly reminded them, "sometimes counted not unworthy the pen, even of a king."

Whatever the faults of the younger Mather, procrastination was not one of them. By early October when Phips returned, the manuscript was not only complete, awaiting the latter's approval, but had already had some circulation among dignitaries of the colony. That he had also done his work well, had achieved what could be regarded as the authoritative version of the affair, was indicated not only by a laudatory preface by Stoughton, but by the fact that Sir William borrowed whole paragraphs for incorporation into his first report to England.

Phips did not, however, encourage publication. Brattle's letter, which denounced the entire premisses of the trials, was circulating as far and as fast as Mather's defence. At a time of such diversity of opinion so hotly expressed the governor found it wise to suppress any publicity whatsoever. It was not until 1693 when the trials had been resumed on a new basis and the "general jail delivery" begun that he judged it wise to let Mather publish his *Wonders of the Invisible World.*

Mather's narrative was the nearest equivalent Massachusetts was to get to a full newspaper report of the mysterious events in court. The public fell on it with avidity and got their money's worth. Mingled in with sermons and philosophizings, Mather had presented a full and accurate account of the examination and trials of five representative witches, George Burroughs, Bridget Bishop, Susanna Martin, Elizabeth How, and Martha Carrier. He had followed the records in painstaking detail, summarizing competently when he did not quote in full. Not even his worst enemies were ever to find fault with his court reporting, and compared with the chapbooks of such cases put out to entertain the English public, it was a journalistic masterpiece.

Yet this document, so well planned and executed, so invaluable to the historian, was to serve the reputation of Mather ill. It had two conspicuous defects: its omissions and its tone. Those who really knew the trials read a significance into the fact that Mather had carefully avoided several of their most embarrassing aspects, Rebecca Nurse's brief acquittal, the powerful reasoning of John Procter and Mary Esty. The avoidance, to be sure, was by no means necessarily Mather's doing; what to include and what to omit had certainly been one of the subjects of discussion at the editorial meeting at Sewall's house. These circumstances could not, however, negate the fact that Mather had lent his hand to fabricating that most dangerous of falsehoods, the half truth.

The tone of the book was another thing again, and wholly Mather's. It suggested that the Dutch divines had spoken against spectral evidence in vain, and that Mather himself in recommending caution in this direction had not meant it. For he had written throughout in a spirit of child-like, marvelling credulity.

Yet how could Mather, given his temperament, have written otherwise of his witches? As well ask Shakespeare to revise *Macbeth* without mentioning the Weird Sisters, or Milton to erase all reference to Satan in *Paradise Lost* as to ask Mather to do other than what he had done. There was in him much of the artist, and artistry in his austere position in theocratic Massachusetts found only such wayward expression as this. To such a temperament—and some of the afflicted girls probably resembled him in this—the details of the witchcraft, of horns that sounded across Essex County at midnight, the airborne excursions to Parris's pasture, the folklore that gaudily embroidered the life of Susanna Martin, were less a horror and an abomination than part of the suppressed colour and drama of life. Mather's righteous indignation that such things could be was unconsciously submerged in the thrill of having been present as spectator at a collision between heaven and hell. The witchcraft was one experience that Mather would not willingly have forgone; it was the scarlet thread drawn through the drab of New England homespun.

But men who had been painfully involved in the crisis were little likely to respond to so artless and unconsciously poetic a viewpoint. What impressed them was that in his zeal for discovering witches an eminent Boston divine had stultified his capacity to see human beings and their very real agonies, that in short, to judge by the tone of his record, he had learned nothing at all from experience. So far as he was concerned, the delirium might begin again full force to-morrow.

5

Indeed the delusion had by no means spent itself. While the afflicted of Andover and Salem were falling one by one into silence, dampened by the lack of a responsive audience, new voices were being heard in Boston. To two of these Mather was giving all the attention he could spare from his parochial duties. He was, in fact, launched on a whole new cycle of psychic research.

The first case to come to his attention was that of Mercy Short, seventeen-year-old servant-maid of Boston, recently back from captivity among the Indians, who, as natural creatures of the devil, had probably had not too wholesome an influence on the girl. It was Mercy who in the course of a call on the Boston Prison in the summer of 1692 had mocked Sarah Good's plea for tobacco and had been afflicted since.

One would have supposed that the hanging of Sarah would have released Mercy, but not at all. Sarah must have delegated the torture of the girl to her surviving confederates, for it went right on through the summer and fall and became a favourite subject of speculation among the frequenters of the coffee-houses. On 4 December Mercy achieved the attention of Cotton Mather by falling into such convulsions during a sermon that she had to be carried out. Naturally Mather looked her up afterwards, both he and a "little company of praying neighbours." He had long been itching to study at close range the type of case responsible for the Salem outbreak; now at last he had one in his own precinct.

From his interviews with this medium he got a first-hand description of the devil, "a short and black man—a Wretch no taller than an ordinary Walking Staff; he was not a Negro but of a Tawney or an Indian colour; he wore a high crowned hat with straight hair; and he had one Cloven Foot." The eyes of this creature flamed unbearably, resembling, according to Mercy, the glass ball of the lantern

Mather took with him through the dim streets of Boston on his nocturnal rambles.

Sometimes Mercy's affliction took the form of long fasts, during which she could force herself to take nothing but hard cider. Sometimes she was seared by flames, and her visitors could smell the brimstone and see the burns on Mercy's flesh, though, "as 'tis the strange property of many witch marks," these were "cured in perhaps less than a minute." Sometimes the devil forced white liquid down her throat. Sometimes she had fits of wild frolic when she was deaf to all prayers.

It was not for want of name-calling on Mercy's part that these investigations did not result in arrests. She cried out against all sorts of people, especially some with whom she had recently quarrelled. But Mather, acting with a discretion for which he was not to be thanked, decided that most of these were devil's delusions and charged his "praying company" not to report them. Among Mercy's more oblique accusations was Mather himself; this fact gave him more gratification than otherwise, for he gathered from the context that the devil feared and hated him more than any other minister in New England, a very pretty compliment.

Mercy, responding to fasting, prayer, and the invisible ministrations of an angel who sometimes fended the devils off, finally came out of her trance in March 1693, and Mather wrote up his observations under the title of *A Brand Pluck'd out of the Burning*. Somehow he did not publish it. The jail delivery was in progress, and friends and relatives of released witches would not appreciate yet another starry-eyed report of this sort, especially so soon after the *Wonders*, from whose philosophies some of them were cringing. Or perhaps it was the development of Mercy herself which restrained him. The sad truth was that when the devil was cast out of her, seven others took its place, these being devils of the more common and carnal sort. Martyrs are impressive in the long run only when they are also saints; since Mercy was plainly nothing of the sort, Mather's pious account of her sufferings would be oddly received in Boston's coffee-houses, places much more productive of scepticism than the alehouses had ever been. Mather did not risk it.

6

Mather was, however, by no means done with the devil. In September 1693 he made a trip to Salem to get "furniture" for the completion of the work now nearest to his heart, his *Magnalia Christi Americana*. This was to be his epic in somewhat the same way that *Paradise Lost* was Milton's. His purpose was cognate, though whereas Milton had undertaken to justify the ways of God to man, Mather would seek to justify the ways of man to God, particularly man as represented by the leaders of Puritan theocracy. He would eschew the sonorities of blank verse for the plainer sense of English prose, albeit richly embellished by latinisms, and the sombre glory of such characters as Beelzebub and Lucifer for the more unassuming personnel to be found in New England parsonages; the *Magnalia* was indeed to be primarily a history of the churches in New England. Lucifer, however, would not be ignored in Mather's work; he would again give himself the luxury of describing the Fiend's descent on Salem Village.

To such an end he came to Salem. He delivered two sermons and between them pursued his inquiries. He was much interested in a Mrs Carver and her viewpoint on late events. This lady was in direct communication with "shining spirits" who told her that "a new storm of witchcraft would fall upon the country and chastise the iniquity that was used in the wilful smothering and covering of the last."

This news Mather received about as a general might receive intelligence that he would soon be called upon to march again. There had indeed been something abrupt, something questionable about the end of the witchcraft. The case had not been so much disposed of as allowed to collapse. It was as if an army of occupation had been called home without awaiting the signing of a peace treaty. It would be little wonder if the devil were to begin a new assault against a people so little capable of sustained effort.

These reflections were reinforced by evidence that the devil was interfering directly in his own affairs. He had prepared two sermons to deliver in Salem and the devil stole them both. Luckily he was able to give them from memory "so the devil got nothing." The story did not end there. When he got home to Boston he found that affliction had started again in his own neighbourhood in the person of another seventeen-year-old, one Margaret Rule. From Margaret's lips he learned what had happened in Salem. The eight spectral shapes that tormented her had stolen his sermons and were bragging about it. Yet it was not given to creatures covenanted to the devil to keep a hold on a thing so holy as a sermon by Cotton Mather. In October the spirits relaxed their grip and dropped the missing manuscripts leaf by leaf about the streets of Lynn. Every page was recovered in a perfect state of preservation.

After such portents Mather could not deny his time and prayers to the new victim of the invisible world. Margaret was indeed a pitiful case. Her present physical tortures had been preceded by a spiritual phase in which she was prey to a belief that she was damned. Now she was the victim of witches who desired her to sign the Book. She was resisting heroically and before a cloud of witnesses. For Margaret was yet another who had had to be carried shrieking from meeting; since that had first happened on 10 September, she had become the major theatrical attraction in Boston. If Mather wanted to minister to her privately he must first clear the room of a company—by no means a praying company—of thirty or forty spectators. Frequently he did not take this precaution, with the result that a fraction of the population of Boston was entertained not only by the antics of Margaret but by the measures taken by Mather to exorcize her demons.

Margaret's affliction had begun with an involuntary fast. For nine days her teeth had set against food, though occasionally it was possible to get her mouth open just wide enough to admit a sip of rum. ("That's the devil all over," commented a seaman.) Sometimes it was the devil who forced open her mouth in order to pour scalding brimstone down her throat so that people in the room could hardly bear the smell of the stuff or the sound of the girl's screams.

Marvels happened right under the eyes of the beholders. Some of them saw the woman stuck full of pins. Six men signed affidavits that they had seen her pulled to the ceiling by invisible hands and that it took their concerted might to pull her back to bed again. Mather himself once made a grab for something stirring on her pillow and felt an imp in his hand, tangible and yet invisible, and so startling in that combination that he let it get away.

She dreamed dreams and saw visions. She forecast the drowning of a young man and exactly as she spoke it happened—almost; that is, by God's providence the man wasn't actually drowned but was fished out of the water into which sundry devils had impelled him to leap. She saw the thieving of an old man's will. She saw the faces of her tormenters, or anyway of some of them, particularly that of an evil old woman who had been taken in the recent witchcraft and incontinently released again when the judges lost their heart for proper prosecution. Some witches she could not identify because they, having learned a thing or two, now went about their business veiled. Veiled or no, when Mather got to her, he prevailed on her to "forbear blazing their names lest any good person come to suffer any blast of reputation." He was willing that she name them to him privately and was reassured, for they were "the sort of wretches who for these many years have given over as violent presumption of witchcraft as perhaps any creatures yet living on this earth." Even so he did not report them.

He got small thanks for his self-sacrificing labours on behalf of Margaret Rule. His efforts had been observed by a motley company come off the streets of Boston to see the show, merchants, seamen, scholars, goodwives, everybody. These behaved decorously enough in his presence and on the whole he thought it well that a variety of observers witness the agonies of the girl the better to combat the scepticism of the coffee-houses. What he did not know was that one of these "coffee-house witlings" had not only got in with the rest but was taking copious notes of the séances and preparing to publish.

This observer was Robert Calef, an obscure merchant of Boston. He was a friend of Thomas Brattle and agreed with the sceptical viewpoint expressed in Brattle's letter, and had therefore come to watch Mather in none too reverent a frame of mind. What his cold eye noted in the afflicted Margaret was her craving for the attentions of men. She visibly liked being stroked across face and naked breast and belly by the Mathers, father and son, this being a kind of laying on of hands by which they tried to relieve her, but let a woman touch her and she cried out sharply, "Don't you meddle with me!"

When the ministers withdrew, Margaret told the women to clear out altogether, saying "that the company of men was not offensive to her, and having hold of the hand of a young man said to have been her sweetheart . . . she pulled him again into his seat saying he should not go to-night."

Six days later Calef found her enjoying what Mather had explained to observers as "her laughing time; she must laugh now." Mather having already gone for the evening, she was free to make eyes at yet another young man and to fuss with her attendants because they "did not put her on a clean cap but let her lie so like a beast, saying she would lose her fellows."

There was talk, to be sure, about her frightful affliction earlier in the day, and there were symptoms of a recurrence when one or two of the women got a whiff of brimstone. Everyone sniffed with them, but Calef and the others couldn't pick up the scent and said so. The women became less sure of themselves; they could smell something, they said; they were not sure what.

Calef, in short, was less than impressed with the martyred Margaret. Even less had he been impressed in the still recent past by what he called a "Bigoted Zeal stirring up a Blind and most Bloody Rage" against innocent people by such media as these. He resented the credulous interest of the Mathers, particularly Cotton; this sort of thing had led to public disaster only two years earlier. Calef did not propose to stand by and watch the engineering of a second outbreak. Accordingly he copied out his notes and let them circulate from hand to hand.

Never in his life had Mather been so rudely handled or so affronted as he was by the talk to which these notes gave rise. He was enraged by the description of his stroking the half-naked Margaret so as "to make people believe a Smutty thing of me." His first impulse was to bring suit for "scandalous libel"; his second not to risk so public an appearance on so delicate an issue. The warrant was issued against Calef, but when the latter appeared before court, none came against him and the case was dismissed.

The larger case was not at all dismissed, however. The controversy between minister and merchant went on for years and culminated at the turn of the century in a book called *More Wonders of the Invisible World,* a work by Calef with the involuntary collaboration of Mather and a probable but disguised contribution by Brattle. Its core was the later witch writings of Mather, including his unpublished account of Margaret Rule. To this Calef added his own appendix to Mather's *Wonders,* furnishing full details on cases which Mather had neglected, notably that of Rebecca Nurse, and adding reports by such survivors as the Carys and John Alden.

Its publication was one of the most afflicting things that had ever happened to Mather, his sorrow's crown of sorrow. And indeed, though Calef's work was a valuable addition to the history of witchcraft, it did inflict an injustice on Mather in connecting his name inseparably with a tragedy with which he actually had had little to do.

Increase Mather, who himself had drawn Calef's fire, owing to his proposal to New England ministers in 1695 that they continue to collect "Remarkables," among them evidence of the agency of the invisible world, stood loyally by his son and made a spectacle of the infamy of the book —or so the story goes—by having it burned in the Harvard Yard. This fine symbolic gesture had oddly little effect in preventing its circulation.

7

Margaret Rule had in the meantime come out of her fits long since. It was well that Calef never heard of her last séance with Mather, for during it she dreamily named the wizard whose Shape was currently afflicting her, and it was none other than Cotton's.

Mather was terrified. Superstition played little part in his fright, nor did he anticipate taking a place by Burroughs on the gallows. What unmanned him was the derision of the coffee-houses if this accusation ever got around.

Heroic measures were necessary, heights of prayer to which he had never won before. He won them now. Finally, after Mather had spent several hours in the dust before his God, the "shining spirit" that had intermittently appeared to Margaret came again and informed her that Mather was now her father in Christ and that through God's providence he had saved her. The angel also opened her eyes to the actual demons crowded around her. They were rather pitiful; the devil himself stood over them lashing them to further effort, for all the world like an overseer whipping his slaves. Indeed the demons were fainting under the punishment and under the strain of their hopeless endeavour. At last they cried out to Margaret, "Go and the devil go with you. We can do no more." Then they fled the place. Nor did they come again, at least in that guise. Margaret's affliction and Boston's best show were both a thing of the past; hereafter Margaret had no more difficulty in getting privacy for her interviews with her "fellows."

Mather for his part learned to keep strictly away from her. His "spiritual daughter" did not turn out to be a very nice girl.

CHAPTER XXI

VILLAGE PURGE

While Cotton Mather was fighting off the devil in Boston, Salem Village was pulling itself together after its ordeal.

It was not altogether unlike returning to a community which has been sacked by Indians and trying to pick up life again, except that it was in some ways more difficult. The moral effect of a purely physical disaster may be cleansing; when men unite against nature or a common enemy they may keep their dignity even in ruin.

But though this thing which had passed had left the houses standing and the fields untouched, it had brought division and a sore sickness of spirit on the people. Husband had "broken charity" with wife and wife with husband, mother with child and child with mother. Even worse had been the tattling of neighbour against neighbour. Relationships in so small a community are organic; no matter what the petty jars of day-to-day collisions, there must be in a crisis a community of sympathy and understanding else there is no health. And here was little health; not in a generation would it be forgotten how neighbour had responded with spite to a neighbour's need.

Even the many who had kept their integrity, who had spoken out for a friend in danger, had little peace of mind. What they had seen had been corrosive of their faith; malice had been exalted above charity, and the idle words of a pack of undisciplined girls allowed to outweigh whole lifetimes of decency and good faith. If such were the will of God, what wonder that so many had turned to the devil?

If so blasphemous a thought was not openly expressed,

at least its corollary was. God could not have willed such a thing. Not God but the devil had been in command here. Their leaders had suffered the devil to guide them. They were turning from such leaders; in particular they were turning from the leadership of the Reverend Samuel Parris.

2

The January trials of 1693 were hardly over when a meeting was held in Salem Village to "make void" their pastor's salary. Not even the late George Burroughs had been during his ministry so directly attacked; the congregation had not voided his salary, but had simply neglected to pay it. What was remarkable about this act was that it took place only five months after Parris had been able to get "unanimous approval from his congregation to excommunicate Martha Cory. Either this had been the sort of "unanimity" that would not bear close scrutiny, or the vote merely demonstrated the personal unpopularity of Martha who was, after all, an opinionated woman, besides being married to the trouble-making Giles.

The disinclination to pay Parris was not necessarily born of enmity alone. Money was hard to come by now. The witch-hunt, coinciding with the season of planting and harvesting, had cast an economic blight over the community. Everyone suffered, even the officials. Handsome Marshal George Herrick was complaining to Governor Phips that in nine months of almost incessant labour in connection with the witch-hunt, he had been unable to do for his "poor farm" and was now literally in want of enough provision to get through the winter. "I am become despicable in these hard times."

If even in Boston business had almost come to a standstill during the peak of the excitement—Governor Phips had reported to England the urgency of getting the matter settled if the legislators were ever again to attend to anything but the witchcraft—how much more was this true of Salem Village where there was hardly a family but had a personal stake in the affair?

Besides, there had been the drought. And now, as if the yield were not lean enough, came the demand for hard cash to pay the jail fees as one after another of the witches was discharged. Given so great a need and so little to do with, the village could hardly support a church. The pastor had his own field and orchard; let him live off them as the rest were trying to do.

But one cannot dismiss a responsibility so lightly; nor was that sharp bargainer Parris one to forgive his salary while his parishioners recouped their losses. By December he had secured a court order to the effect that people refusing to pay their rates would have to stand suit.

Before that order came, however, other troubles, evidence of irreconcilable differences between pastor and flock, had come out into the open. There were some for whom non-payment of rates was the least of the matter; they simply would not set foot in the church so long as it was Parris who occupied the pulpit.

"The said Parris," reported these in a plea to court in April 1693, had been "teaching such dangerous errors and preached such scandalous immoralities as ought to discharge him (though ever so gifted otherwise) from the work of the minister." His claim that prisoners had knocked down "those pretended sufferers" with a look they charged was "swearing to more than he was certain of" and hence "he was equally guilty of perjury with them that swear to what is false. . . . His believing the devil's accusations and readily departing from all charity to persecute the blameless and godly lives are just causes for our refusal. . . . Mr Parris . . . has been the beginner and procurer of the sorest affliction not to the village only but to the whole country." Was it just, they asked, that they should "honour, respect and support such an instrument to our miseries"?

The court did not honour the petition; its signers, Joseph Putnam and three kinsmen of Rebecca Nurse, were too obviously partisan. Yet these were plainly gaining an ascendancy over the congregation; so strong was the feeling against Parris that ministers from the neighbouring towns were alarmed and urged Parris and his flock to hold a council to settle their differences.

Parris himself was not impervious to the change of moral climate. In an attempt to placate his enemies he humbled himself before his congregation and read a document about the "late horrid calamity" which he called "Meditations for Peace." It was, he said, "a sore rebuke" that the witchcraft had come first to his own family, that unlawful means had not been taken there to raise spirits "though totally unknown to me or mine till after. . . . I desire to lie low under this reproach and to lay my hand to my mouth."

Now at last he acknowledged that God might suffer the devil to take the shape of the innocent and that hence it was wrong to ask the afflicted who afflicted another. He offered his sympathy to those who had suffered "through the clouds of human weakness and Satan's wiles and sophistry." He asked pardon of God and prayed that all might "be covered with the mantle of love and we may . . . forgive each other heartily."

"If half so much had been said formerly," drily commented Rebecca Nurse's son-in-law John Tarbell when this document was read to him, "it would never have come to this."

Parris, however, was trying to placate the implacable, and he had begun too late; it had been for ever too late ever since the hangman had supported Rebecca Nurse up the gallows. "We know not how to express the loss of such a mother in such a way," said one of Rebecca's sons. Those who had not hesitated to risk their lives to save her in a time when to say one kind word for a witch was almost certain to draw the accusations of the girls were unlikely to "forgive heartily" the man who had taken the word of delinquents against the word of a good woman. Etched in bitter acid on their memories was their mother, trembling and yet steadfast before the magistrates; even the magistrates had wavered when she was brought before them, but not this man, and they would not waver now. Not all the courts in Massachusetts could force them to worship with the false shepherd who had misled his sheep.

In November 1694 Samuel Nurse and Thomas Wilkins produced yet another analysis of their motives. Their reluctance to attend Parris's church had begun in the day of the afflicted girls when the "distractions and disturbing tumults and noises made by the persons under diabolical power and delusion" prevented "sometimes our hearing and understanding and profiting of the word preached." They had been afraid to stay in such society, having heard persons "better than ourselves" accused. Besides they found Parris's preaching "dark and dismal," his dwelling on "mysteries of iniquity . . . offensive." They could not "in conscience" join in his prayers, and above all they had found no charity in him, that quality without which a preacher's eloquence is as a sounding brass and tinkling cymbal.

The quarrel went on year after year. Once Parris offered the recalcitrants dismission to another parish. "Ay," said one, "if we could find a way to remove our livings too."

In April 1695 a council of churches of the North Shore met in Salem to arbitrate the case. The assembled ministers agreed with the dissidents that "unwarranted and uncomfortable steps" had been taken by Parris during the "dark time of confusion." Yet now that he had been "brought into a better sense of things . . . Christian charity might and should receive satisfaction therefore." The church must treat the dissenters "with bowels of much compassion for the infirmities discovered . . . on such an heartbreaking day." But it was for the latter to reconcile themselves; if they could not, let them leave and stir up trouble in Salem Village no more.

They would not be reconciled and by now a majority in the parish stood with them. Time had worked for the children of Rebecca. The sceptical talk in the Boston coffeehouses was getting more attention than the voices of the Mrs Carvers who spoke darkly of the "wilful smothering of the witchcraft." If there were any here who still believed that Rebecca Nurse had been done justly to death—or John Procter or Mary Esty—few of them now dared say so. It was at last Parris who consented to remove, on the provision that the congregation pay him arrears of £79 9s 6d; the sum was raised with cheerful alacrity.

So Parris went and took with him the least guilty and most pitiable of the afflicted, little Betty, and his young son Noyes. It is to be hoped that Betty came elsewhere into sunnier days and escaped the shadow that the devil cast over her brother, for this child, born in an evil time and named for the witch-hunting parson of Salem, grew to manhood only to die insane.

3

The successor to Parris, one Joseph Green, was an unexpected choice. He was only twenty-two and had only within the year achieved a state of grace.

Though Green had graduated from Harvard in 1695, he had not prepared for the ministry. He had been exactly the sort of student that Cotton Mather in his own undergraduate days had shrunk from; he had played cards, danced, cursed, and had often profaned the Sabbath by striking off into the country with fishing-rod or fowling-piece.

Light did not come to him until he was out of Harvard and teaching in the Roxbury Grammar School. There he came upon one of Cotton Mather's sermons, and never did Mather make a more electric effect. The young man became overnight not only a convert but an evangelist, speaking of God and His Kingdom in and out of season, to his students, his mother, his brothers at sea, and soon to whole congregations. A city which is set on a hill is not hid; presently Green was being invited to preach, and the reputation of his sermons reached to Salem Village; the village called him and he came.

If he, given his youth, was a surprising choice, he was a wholesome one. Perhaps it is an advantage not to spend one's youth agonizing over damnation and the certainty of death. Green certainly had not, and whatever his present convictions on these subjects, they did not impair his outgoing cheerfulness. He was a pastor who got around. One found him over a mug of ale at Deacon Ingersoll's ordinary, or at a house-raising setting his shoulders to the timber, or off with his gun to track down a bobcat or to shoot wild pigeons. One found him in Wenham, where he courted the Reverend Mr Gerrish's daughter Elizabeth and took her home with him to bear him a brood of lively little boys. "They were a lovely, loving pair," wrote Noyes, who had his sentimental side and sometimes let it overflow into verse. He laboured his fields and jotted down the results in a brief, extrovert diary, "Very hot. Thunder and rain. *Bugs.*" He badgered his congregation to set up a school and build a new meeting-house; he trained with the troop of horse, and when Indian trouble threatened, as it was bound to periodically in those days, he shouldered his musket and rode out smartly with the best of them.

These zestful activities did not take place at any sacrifice of his parochial duties; such neglect Salem Village would not have forgiven him. Young Green grasped the essentials of the situation with a wisdom and compassion beyond his years. Like Quaker Maule he identified the true devils as the small spites that had so long embroiled the village in petty squabbles; he saw deeper dissension in the future if the understandable bitterness of such people as the Nurses could not somehow be assuaged.

To this end he undertook a bold plan of reconciliation which an older man might have judged impossible. He re-worked the seating plan of his church on a symbolic arrangement of lions and lambs. He put Samuel Nurse in the pew of Thomas Putnam, father of Ann; Rebecca Nurse's daughter, the Widow Preston, in the pew of the Widow Walcott, mother of Mary. And what was remarkable, the dissidents, late so unyielding with Parris, accepted this arrangement. It may well be that Samuel Nurse sat many a Sunday stiff and silent beside Thomas Putnam, unwilling to acknowledge his presence by so much as a glance; but no child of Rebecca had grown up unacquainted with the heavenly wisdom of charity and forgiveness. If Rebecca, like Mary Esty, sent forth her ghost, she sent it to underline the message of young Joseph Green: forgive, make your peace, forget. So in time the cold seal of hatred was melted from the hearts of her sons, a great burden was lifted from them and they sat beside their late enemies not with averted eyes but with pity. In truth these had not known what they did.

Green's most ambitious project for reconciliation did not succeed for a long time. As early as 1702 the young man had the temerity to ask the congregation to revoke the excommunication of Martha Cory and restore her name to the church rolls. In 1703 he got a motion to that effect passed in church, but encountered such bitterness in town meeting that for a while he swore never to attend that function again. It was not until 1707, soon after another triumph over the forces of spite, which will be recounted, that he finally won. The spirit of Martha Cory could now sit unchallenged in meeting.

In spite of these reconciliations it would be long before Salem Village would regain the prosperity it had known before calamity came. There were farms cleared and tilled and set about with stone walls with back-breaking labour that were reverting to wilderness, for their owners had fled in the panic and cursed the place and would not come again. Peter Cloyce had tarried only until Rebecca's sister Sarah was released; then he shook the dust of the place from his feet and never looked back. For a century or more some places would be shunned. It was as if people feared to break the devil from the ground. Yet many stayed, and for them at last there was peace.

4

While in the village the children of Rebecca had been closing in on Parris, Philip English in Salem Town was avenging himself on Sheriff George Corwin. But if the children of Rebecca had borne themselves with dignity, the same could not be said of English.

He had, of course, suffered much in the persecution. His pious wife, ailing in prison, did not long survive her return from exile. Added to this sorrow was the heavy loss to his pocketbook; indeed malicious tongues said that this pinched sharpest. When he had finally consented to flee, Sheriff Corwin had fallen upon his wharves, his warehouses, his many-gabled house, and had seized property valued at £1,500, none of which English had recovered.

In doing so, Corwin had acted strictly according to the law and not, provably at least, from personal animus. When the returned English made trouble about the seizure in 1694, the Superior Court absolved Corwin of blame for this act and others and declared that no claim could be made against him for such cause.

But the sheriff died in 1697 and English had his revenge, not a pretty revenge. He seized the body of Corwin for non-payment of debt. He couldn't in the nature of things hold it indefinitely, but he held it long enough to complicate the funeral arrangements, create a scandal, and impel Corwin's executors to pay him £60 3s.

The spirit of Christian forgiveness did not predominate in the character of Philip English. Once he got himself sued for calling Noyes a murderer; he went no more to Noyes's church or to any other infested by the breed of Puritans. At long last he was able to contribute to the founding of a church of his own faith, St Peter's; but this was so late in the day, so near his death—and the poor man died deranged—that his only profit thereby was to get burial in the church-yard, safe from the hands of the Puritans.

Magistrate John Hathorne he hated to his dying day. Only on his deathbed did he forgive him the humiliations he had inflicted during the witchcraft, and then not heartily. "If I get well, I'll be damned if *I* forgive him!"

Fortunately he died without suspecting that his line was fated to merge with the line of the hated Hathorne and to bear its name. His only legitimate son had died before him; but he did leave daughters, and one of these, deprived of her father's choleric guidance, knew no better than to marry a son of Magistrate Hathorne and so found a dynasty which added a W to its name and presently produced that remote pale flowering of the witchcraft, the haunted Nathaniel Hawthorne. And Nathaniel in his turn would walk the ways

of Salem, town and village, and ghosts would keep him
company, never quite visible, lurking always just beyond the
corner of his eye. But he would pin them down on paper
and when he had them there would inspect them with a
kind of literary credulity. For it was with him somewhat as
it was with Cotton Mather; useless to preach to the artist
against the existence of witches; the very breath of the artist
is witchery and magic.

CHAPTER XXII

"WE WALKED IN CLOUDS"

It was August 1706, and the sultry anniversary of a fast which Massachusetts had held in 1692 in behalf of the unforgotten witchcraft. Corn stood high in the field, and in the orchard where witches had grounded their sticks when Parris owned the place, the apples were already round in the tree. Goldenrod showed in the meadows and crickets chirped busily.

Within the dusk of the meeting-house on this bright day, the congregation sat in the dead hush of complete attention. Not the smallest child wriggled now, and all eyes turned to the woman who, clad in white cap, kerchief and long-gown of seemly sad-coloured stuff, had risen at her place. In the pulpit the Reverend Joseph Green prepared to read her "confession."

The woman was still young; though more than a decade ago she had been one of the most notorious figures in Massachusetts, she was not now more than six-and-twenty. But she looked older; life had been hard, and the younger Ann Putnam, daughter of a sickly, high-strung mother, had never been strong at best.

She stood here to-day a suppliant for the right hand of fellowship of her church. There were churches—the Brattle Church in Boston for instance—where the old Puritan custom of requiring an applicant to make public confession of his faith had fallen out of fashion. But Salem Village had never set store by fashion, nor did its pastor for all his comparative youth and cheerful ways. Indeed it was Green, who knew Ann's heart, who had expressly stipulated that before she sought communion in the church she should undertake a moral cleansing by publicly asking pardon of those who had grievous cause to contemn her.

Ann, standing solitary at her place, dared not lift her eyes to these. To the right, to the left, were kinsmen of Rebecca Nurse who had not forgotten, who could never forget how once in this meeting-house this suppliant had howled at their mother, and how the poor lady had cried, "Oh Lord help me!" Ann's howls had killed their mother as surely as if they had been so many stones, and Ann's confession could not raise her from the grave where the children of Rebecca had secretly laid her. Yet here Ann stood and asked them to forgive.

"I desire to be humbled before God." It was Parson Green's voice, but the words were Ann's. "It was a great delusion of Satan that deceived me in that sad time. . . . I did it not out of any anger, malice, or ill-will."

The kin of Rebecca would have been more than human if they had not stirred in their seats at that. Not malice or ill-will. What had the witchcraft been but a triumph of malice? Why this woman as a mere babe had sucked spite from her mother's breasts. Yet the malice came from the elder not the younger Ann, and the elder had gone to a higher judgment these half-dozen years back. They looked into the ashy face of the suppliant and felt pity. After all, it was not with Ann as with so many of her confederates; she had not turned from "affliction" to lewdness. She had lived in shamefaced decency, and frail as she was, an invalid at times, had managed to give her siblings a godly raising.

Parson Green read on. Until now Ann's plea had been little more than the accepted formula of the day; "the delusion of Satan" was a phrase that anyone might use. But now her confession came to something more personal.

"And particularly as I was a chief instrument of accusing Goodwife Nurse and her two sisters, I desire to lie in the dust and be humbled for it, in that I was a cause with others of so sad a calamity to them and their families. . . . I desire to lie in the dust and earnestly beg forgiveness of all those unto whom I have given just cause of sorrow and offence, whose relations were taken away and accused."

The phrases were still clichés out of the ritual; Parris had used them in "Meditations for Peace" and had found small grace thereby. Could Ann by her incoherent repetitions fare better? Yet what more could the poor girl say than what she had said? The inwardness of the dark time of her wrong-doing was dim and uncomprehended, almost as if it had happened to another person. How could she, a child at the time, explain the torments which had baffled the wisest, physicians, magistrates and ministers? What else to call it but "a delusion of Satan"?

Ann at her place, her hands clenched until the knuckles showed white, knew only that like Rebecca she could not die with a sin "still unrepented of." Now in 1706 her time was growing short. Would God forgive such a sin as hers? God was omnipotent, but there was one sin unpardonable even by Him; was it hers?

Kind Parson Green had said no. Christ who had died between thieves understood all sins, even the delusions of Satan. He would intercede for forgiveness if the repentance was true.

The reading was over. Gravely the minister looked up from the paper and into the eyes of his congregation. Was it their will that this sinner be forgiven, that this lost sheep be received into the fold?

It was. Not for nothing had Green worked among them all these years preaching charity. Ann sank back to her bench, the tears raining down her cheeks. God had given a sign, for surely what His children had done, what Rebecca's children had done, He would do also.

2

Ann was not the first to repent publicly for what had been done in the witchcraft; rather she was almost the last. It was nearly a decade since a wave of penitence had broken over Massachusetts, and this penitence had been an honourable thing. Say what you will of the Puritans, their narrowness, their intolerance, there was soundness in them too, and never more than at the moment when God humbled them by taking their power from them. For theocracy in the political sense had received its deathblow from the new charter; never again in their time would God rule directly on earth through these His chosen people. Yet in the act of surrendering temporal control, the Puritans had achieved a new moral eminence. It is only given to the strong and spiritually whole to say before the world, "I was wrong. Let God and man forgive me and guide me in a better way."

On Christmas Eve, some ten years before the confession of Ann, Samuel Sewall had sat by candlelight with a Latin testament in his hand, listening to the younger Sam recite. His heart was heavy; there was death in the house; in an upper chamber the women were laying out the body of his little Sarah. And although his eldest son was outwardly hale, all was not well with him. It was as if the lad belonged to a weaker, insecurer generation which lacked the heroic decision, the vein of iron of the elder. Young Sam did only middling well in his studies, was vague and vacillating about his vocation. That he would grow in grace and bring distinction to the family was now improbable. Yet one did what one could, and the elder Samuel sat testament in hand while his son struggled through Matthew xii, 6–12.

"If ye had known what this meaneth," laboured the lad, "'I will have mercy and not sacrifice,' ye would not have condemned the guiltless."

The boy plodded on, but the father sat blankly, not attending to a word, his mind wrenched from family cares to a darker matter. It was as if God had entered the room and spoken to him directly. To what could the text possibly apply if not to the "Salem Tragedie" and his own part therein? Had his strength of decision, the want of which he lamented in his son, been only a devil's delusion, leading him from mercy?

Yet he had not been an unmerciful man. His own diary could bear him witness that he had not—not to his personal friends. He had prayed with John Alden in time of sorrow and when the latter was vindicated had called on his family to express his regret "for their sorrow and temptation by reason of his imprisonment" and his joy at his rehabilitation. He had stood by the dissident Judge Saltonstall when the girls had accused him, had not for a moment believed or countenanced the outcry against his own pastor, Willard. Yes, he had been loyal to his friends, but even a wolf is loyal to other wolves. What mercy had he shown to the friendless, to the people outside his circle, who did not sup with governors or prepare their sons for Harvard? (Or at least try; he threw another look at young Sam.) If his hands and his conscience were clean, why was he sometimes haunted; why could he not bar from his mind the faces of Rebecca Nurse, John Procter, Mary Esty, George Burroughs, and even sometimes the pert, not ungallant figure of Susanna Martin? "If ye had known . . . ye would not have condemned the guiltless."

Thanks largely to the efforts of Willard, 15 January 1697 was set apart as a day of fast in Massachusetts, a day of repentance for wrongs committed in the witchcraft. After the revelation which Sewall had received on Christmas Eve from, of all people, his feckless son, he dared not let the opportunity pass. He too stood in church, like Ann after him, when his bill of confession was read; publicly, before men he acknowledged his misgiving of error, his desire to take on himself "the blame and shame of it," his repentance.

On that same day the jurors sought similar relief. "We ourselves were not capable to understand nor able to withstand the mysterious delusion of the power of darkness and prince of the air," they had written, "whereby we fear we have been instrumental with others, though ignorantly and unwillingly, to bring upon ourselves the guilt of innocent blood." To the survivors of their victims they expressed their "deep sense of sorrow" and humbly begged forgiveness.

Thomas Fisk was one of the signers, that same Thomas Fisk who as foreman of the jury had once looked helplessly up at William Stoughton on a day when the jury had been more merciful than the judge but could not find the will to abide by their decision.

Stoughton, man of granite, confessed no error, made no

personal suit for forgiveness. True, by his authorizing the general fast (Phips having died in 1695 Stoughton was now acting governor) he tacitly acknowledged that he too had sometimes been in error in the late trials. But in his eyes an honest error was not wrongdoing. He had done to the best of his ability what seemed just at the time. No more can be asked of any man, and no man who has done so need grovel in the dust. It was a hard view but self-respecting and it commanded respect. There was never to come on the inflexible judge the odium that had come on the repentant Parris. Even men outside the Covenant continued to vote for him, and when at last a Crown appointee was sent from England to fill the place left vacant by Phips, many of Stoughton's enemies would have preferred him to the new royal governor, who was, for the sins of Massachusetts, none other than Andros's creature, Joseph Dudley.

3

"We walked in clouds and could not see our way. And we have most cause to be humbled for error . . . which cannot be retrieved."

The confession of the Reverend John Hale of Beverly, late witness against Bridget Bishop, was the most thorough of any. He wrote out the entire story as he had experienced it and published it as *A Modest Inquiry into the Nature of Witchcraft*. Old John Higginson, venerable senior pastor of the First Church of Salem, indicated his sympathy with the viewpoint in a preface.

Even in the fall of 1692 Hale had not covered up the fact that his own wife had been accused. There was by then no real danger in being frank, and since Mrs Hale had the warm affection and entire respect of her fellow townsmen, the result was merely that these united in calling the accuser a liar. Hale himself was not so sure; the devil was a liar certainly, as certainly as his wife was innocent; nevertheless he found in the reported apparition of Mary Esty a deep symbolic truth which would not let him rest until he had re-examined the whole story and made public his reconsidered conviction.

Hale did not, however, use the ghost story to account for his change of heart; it would have been hardly appropriate since he like the judges had renounced spectral evidence; instead he applied himself to interpretation of less disputable fact.

He described how the multiplication of the confessors had first stilled doubts as to the veracity of the girls and then deepened them. "You are one that brings this man to death," he had once said to a confessor who accused George Burroughs. "If you have charged anything upon him that is not true, recall it before it be too late, while he is yet alive." Yet the confessor had stuck stubbornly to his story, and poor Burroughs went to the gallows unconfessed and unforgiven. Though this arrangement seemed just to Hale at the time, it had implications which presently gave him no rest. How could a man like Burroughs, trained in theology, how could so many witches, reared in the gospel, go unconfessing to their death though given every opportunity to repent? And what of the "confessor" who survived and whose tenure of life depended on his willingness not only to go on confessing but to accuse others as the need arose? His early misgivings on this subject were to be only too well justified when the "general jail delivery" began and every witch on the docket, barring a few mental defectives, renounced his confession, saying that he had been forced into it.

The unconscionable increase of the number of the "afflicted" had also troubled Hale. One would have supposed that such stringent efforts to stamp out witchcraft would have resulted in relief to the afflicted. On the contrary, not only did the fits punctually recur, but the ranks of the afflicted grew steadily. All over the county, girls, matrons, and sometimes boys fell into possession and "cried out"; in time the very number of these—at least fifty without counting "confessors"—raised doubts as to their moral responsibility. If they were really hag-ridden one might have predicted that the jail delivery would have produced chaos. Yet nothing of the sort had happened; "the Lord chained up Satan that the afflicted grew presently well." Nothing, said Hale in 1697, had been heard of them for five years now.

Samuel Sewall had been disturbed when he heard of this soul-searching on the part of Hale and his plans to publish the results. He feared that the pastor would "go too far the other way," possibly to the detriment of the reputation of the judges. But Hale treated the latter considerately. "I am abundantly satisfied that those who were most concerned to act and judge in these matters did not willingly depart from the rules of righteousness." It was "the darkness of that day, the tortures and lamentations of the afflicted and the power of former precedents" which misled them. Deny, however, that they had been misled he could not.

No one was wholly innocent in the tragedy; it was chargeable to a kind of collective guilt on the part of all Massachusetts in falling away from the high consecration of its founders. "We have much forgotten what our fathers came in the wilderness to see. The sealing ordinances of the covenant of grace and church communion have been much slighted and neglected; and the fury of the storm raised by Satan hath fallen very heavily upon many that lived under these neglects. The Lord sent Evil Angels to awaken and punish our negligence."

Thus in honourable retraction of grievous error, wrote Hale in 1697, which was a year of such retractions. Even Cotton Mather was affected by the general urge to such repentance. To his diary in January he confided that he was "afflicted last night with discouraging thoughts, as if unavoidable marks of the Divine displeasure might overtake my family for my not appearing with *Vigour* to stop the proceedings of the judges when the Inexplicable Storm from the Invisible World assaulted the country."

It was a pity from the point of view of his reputation that he found no opportunity to make such reflections public. For him to have sought relief like Sewall in public confession would have been presumption, for actually he had nothing to confess to; there were only his books, his "scientific" investigations, and Mather, currently smarting under the attacks of Robert Calef, had by no means the humility to make public a retraction of anything in these even if there had been anything tangible to retract, which in truth there was not.

What he did make public at this time was his life of William Phips (deceased in 1695) in which he had another opportunity to touch on the witchcraft. This time he took pains to deny the validity of spectral evidence and acknowledge the error of the judges in accepting it. But in spite of his rational intentions, enough of the old wonder-tale crept into the book to arouse Brattle and Calef to action. If Mather would not let the subject drop, neither would they. It must have been at this point that they decided on formal publication of *More Wonders of the Invisible World*, a blow, not wholly merited, from which Mather's reputation has not to this day recovered.

4

The aroused conscience of Massachusetts on behalf of the victims of the witchcraft did not stop at words only. Early in the eighteenth century there was a movement to give atonement more negotiable form. Calef's book may well have provided some of the impetus, and the movement also had the backing of more recognized leaders such as Michael Wigglesworth, who as author of *Day of Doom* may have felt that theocracy had presumed in taking on the prerogatives of God as Judge.

The movement originated in the complaint of surviving witches in Andover and Topsfield to the General Court that "their names were exposed to infamy and reproach while their trial and condemnation stand on the public record." An address from twelve ministers of Essex County in July 1702 reinforced their plea that their names be cleared. But though the General Court took action to the extent of declaring the witchcraft procedure of 1692, especially the use of spectral evidence, unlawful, nothing was specifically done to relieve the sufferers.

In 1709 some twenty-one witches and children of witches were encouraged by public opinion to join Philip English in a bold demand. They wanted not only restoration of their reputation but amends for financial losses they had sustained. Other survivors added their petition in the following years: Isaac Esty, who not only mourned his wife but the fact that her estate had been "damnified by reason of such hellish molestation"; Benjamin Procter, who as eldest son had "helped bring up all my father's children by all his wives, one after another"; the daughters of Elizabeth How; the son of Sarah Wild; and all five children of George Burroughs, who bitterly opposed the making of any award at all to their stepmother, who had turned them "to shift for themselves without anything for so much as a remembrance of their father."

By now so powerful was the sentiment that a public wrong had been committed in 1692 that these petitions were honoured. On the basis of the fiscal claims made therein, the sum of £598 12s was appropriated in 1711 to recompense the survivors. Distribution was made through a committee headed by Stephen Sewall, who doled out the funds with somewhat eccentric effect, though this was caused not by caprice of the committee but by the claims of the survivors which varied from modest estimates of the cost of prison fees and travel to, in the case of Philip English, exorbitant demands. John and Elizabeth Procter headed the list with £150; George Jacobs followed with £70 and Burroughs with £50. The life of Martha Carrier was estimated by her survivors at only £7 6s, though Abigail Hobbs, who in her role of confessor was more accuser than victim and had not been put to death, got £10. Giles and Martha Cory together brought only £21; but the survivors of the pipe-smoking Sarah Good got £30, a sum which might have been justly applied to the rehabilitation of her daughter Dorcas, who still, two decades after, suffered a psychological stunting as a result of spending so many months of her childhood in prison.

Philip English, who had demanded £1,500, got nothing. Though the sum was a plausible estimate of what he had lost by Sheriff Corwin's seizure of his property, it seemed excessive to a committee which had at its disposal little more than a third of that sum out of which to recompense all the sufferers; besides, his recent behaviour had not been endearing. He was not, however, a man to suffer such a slight in silence. He went on petitioning and suing, and though this action was in his lifetime fruitless, after his death the colony relented and awarded his heirs £200.

According to tradition the children of Rebecca Nurse had little interest in financial adjustment and made it plain that they would not accept a penny if the award were not accompanied by a clearing of their mother's good name. This satisfaction, however, had already been given them in October 1710, when the General Court reversed the attainders of those victims of the witchcraft whose survivors had so petitioned. Technically the reversal was imperfect, for Governor Dudley, for all his earlier interest in the witchcraft, somehow never got around to signing this act; also there was by no means a wholesale clearing of reputations since the attainder stood and stands to this day on such unfortunates, for instance, Bridget Bishop, as had no one to speak up for them.

Technicalities are, however, of more interest to historians than to contemporaries. Besides, the children of Rebecca had a deeper satisfaction. On 2 March 1712 the First Church of Salem revoked the excommunication of Sister Nurse "that it may no longer be a reproach to her memory and an occasion of grief to her children."

The children, themselves now far gone in years, wiped their eyes, remembering that dreadful occasion of twenty years ago when their mother like a true Puritan had submitted to "damnation for the glory of God." It had not after all been required of her, for God was merciful and men could repent.

The excommunication of Giles Cory, who had also belonged to this communion, was revoked as well, and this act cleared the accounts of the First Church of Salem with its witches.

5

Massachusetts had come out of its delusion not without honour. There had been misery, injustice, bloodshed, but at the worst nothing on such a scale as had in the recent past been suffered in witch-hunts in England, on the Continent, and in Sweden. In comparison with historical precedents, the panic in Massachusetts had been distinguished less by its violence than by the pertinacity with which sanity had struggled for domination from the first and by which it had finally prevailed.

A sick commonwealth had healed itself without outside intervention. It is true that royal authority had intervened in the person of Sir William Phips, but he himself was a New Englander and in any case had acted not under pressure from England (which at no point did more than approve his reports) but from Massachusetts. If the opinion of the Dutch ministers had precipitated his decision, that was only because it fortified points of view already outspokenly expressed in the Bay Colony.

It is not surprising that delusion comes among men, nor is it any enduring cause for terror so long as in men can be found the faith and courage to wring enlightenment from delusion. In Massachusetts, with all its bigotries, had been found the spiritual health to renounce its error without waiting for the dubious assistance of an army of occupation. Now as the new century began, that century which so many had awaited in fear, supposing it would usher in Doomsday, the keener minds in Massachusetts felt the stirring of a new moral and intellectual season. Perhaps the bitter intensities of the era just past had been but the equinoctials marking the transition from the late medievalism of the seventeenth century to what is called "the Enlightenment," "the Age of Reason."

Moral seasons come and go. Late in the nineteenth century, when it was much the fashion to memorialize the witchcraft delusion, honest men discussed it with wondering pity as something wholly gone from the world and no longer quite comprehensible. But such condescension is not for the twentieth century. Heaven forgive us, "demoniac possession" is with us still, even if the label is different, and mass mania, and bloodshed on a scale that the judges of old Salem would find incredible. Our age too is beset by ideological "heresies" in almost the medieval sense, and our scientists have taken over the office of Michael Wigglesworth in forcing on us the contemplation of Doomsday. What one feels now for deluded Salem Village is less pity than admiration and hope—admiration for men whose sanity in the end proved stronger than madness, hope that "enlightenment" too is a phenomenon that may recur.

NOTES

Code: The primary source most frequently mentioned in these notes, the Essex County Archives, *Salem Witchcraft,* is referred to for brevity's sake as ECA, SW.

CHAPTER I
THE EASIEST ROOM IN HELL

1

The description of Abigail Williams is deduced largely from her later behaviour in the witchcraft proceedings. Little Betty Parris was withdrawn from the public eye so early that very little is known of her except her age and the nature of her "affliction." This account of her is derived partly from the later testimony of Tituba (see Chapter IV), and by analogy, from descriptions in the diaries of Samuel Sewall and Cotton Mather of the spiritual crises of their own children.

The reference to "the easiest room in hell" is from a famous passage in Michael Wigglesworth's *Day of Doom* describing God's mercy to children dying unbaptized.

> A crime it is; therefore in bliss,
> You may not hope to dwell,
> But unto you I shall allow
> The easiest room in hell.

2

The story of the Reverend Samuel Parris and his early relations with Salem Village follows Charles W. Upham's *Salem Witchcraft,* I, pp. 286 ff. In reference to the character of Parris, it is only fair to add that one authority on the witchcraft, Winfield S. Nevins, takes the viewpoint that he was, though misguided, essentially sincere and honest.

CHAPTER II

YOUNG PEOPLE'S CIRCLE

1

The relation of the children's sport with Tituba is based on tradition rather than on recorded history. Evidence of the slave's real affection for Betty may be found in the court record of her examination as described in Chapter IV.

3

The girls described in this chapter have been identified from the part they later played in the witch prosecutions. Historians of the witchcraft often assume that at this early stage they were holding regular "circles," not unlike mediumistic séances, in Tituba's kitchen. (See Nevins, pp. 46 ff.) Allen Putnam, in *Witchcraft of New England*, points out that the distance these girls lived from each other made any regular "circle meetings" highly improbable.

4

The unhappy story of the elder Ann Putnam is recounted at length in Upham, II, pp. 253 ff.

CHAPTER III

THE POSSESSED

1

No detailed contemporary account of the early phases of the "affliction" exists, though nearly every historian of this witchcraft has undertaken to "reconstruct" the probabilities of the situation. My own reconstruction is based on the following sources: (1) the early course of the similar affliction of the Goodwin children in Boston as recorded in Cotton Mather's *Memorable Providences*; (2) an acute analysis made by Putnam of Corwin's report of Tituba's examination in his *Witchcraft of New England*, pp. 301 ff., in which he sets the earliest date of Betty's affliction as 20 January; (3) the general characteristics of early phases of hysteria as described in Sigmund Freud's *Selected Papers on Hysteria and Other Psychoneuroses*.

The "barking" phase is what I suppose would now be called "respiratory hysteria." Many historians assume that all the girls burst into "possession" simultaneously. Though there is no psychological reason why this could not have happened, aside from the improbability that the girls could have held séances with full attendance, contemporary sources definitely indicate that "possession" appeared first in the Parris and then the Walcott household.

An unusual theory of the origin of the affliction has been suggested to me by Donald Willard of the *Boston Globe*. Some years ago, while he was living in Marblehead, not far from Salem, two of his children, both then under four, were taken with convulsive seizures, falling fits, and spasms of pain. One symptom was a burning and twitching in the extremities which reminded him, even at the time, of the witches' "pin-pricking" described by the afflicted children of 1692.

His physician, baffled at first, eventually hit on the fact that both children had been handling dry stalks and burrs of Jimson weed, a poisonous member of the nightshade family. Mr Willard discovered through research that this weed had been brought into this country from the West Indies during the 1600's, and evolved the theory that Tituba, acquainted with the weed's properties in the Barbados, had been dosing the girls with concoctions made from it.

His hypothesis is ingenious, and since more than one factor may have been involved in the illness of the girls, it is worth mentioning. However, there is no historical evidence that Tituba had been dosing the children. The copious records of her examinations include no such accusation, barring the "witch cake" mentioned at the end of this chapter.

One other episode of the witchcraft, however, might be plausibly ascribed to Jimson weed—the story of the crazed oxen of Salisbury Beach mentioned in the evidence against Susanna Martin. (See Chapter XIV, Section 3.)

2

My description of Nicholas Noyes may be unfair to his general personality at such times as he was not coping with witchcraft. Sibley's *Harvard Graduates*, II, pp. 239 ff., reports him as fat, cheerful, and "all that's delightful in conversation."

Upham, II, pp. 257-9, in reporting Hale's earlier conduct in dealing with witch charges, regards his change of heart as indefensible. On the basis of Hale's own record in *A Modest Inquiry*, I see him as an essentially honest man, and far more merciful than Parris.

The exact date of the ministers' meeting in Salem Village is unspecified. See Nevins, p. 49.

3

The later appearance of insanity in the Parris family leads me to wonder if Parris himself may not have had psychotic tendencies.

An excellent analysis of medieval outbreaks is found in Arturo Castiglione's *Adventures of the Mind*.

4

The episode of the witch cake is mentioned by Robert Calef in George Lincoln Burr's *Narratives of the Witchcraft Cases*, p. 348. Joseph B. Felt's *Annals of Salem from Its First Settlements* gives the date as 25 February. On 25 March Mary Sibley was reprimanded before the congregation of the village church for her part in the affair; see Upham, II, pp. 95–8.

CHAPTER IV
TITUBA

1

Henry Herrick's testimony about Sarah Good's attempts to sleep in his barn is from ECA, SW, I, p. 9; Samuel Braybrook's deposition, ibid., pp. 17–19.

Sarah Osburne's earlier misadventures are recorded in Upham, II, pp. 17–19.

2

An exceptionally careful analysis of both the examinations and trials of the witches is found in Nevins, Chapter IV. In his opinion, the effects of the lack of formal legal training on the conduct of the magistrates have been exaggerated.

The books used by magistrates and judges are listed in John Hale's "Modest Inquiry," Burr, pp. 415–16. The principles on which convictions were to be obtained are described on pp. 411–12.

3

The arrival of the magistrates and the setting up of the court in church are described by Upham, II, pp. 11 ff.

4

For Sarah Good's examination see ECA, SW, I, p. 7; for Sarah Osburne's, ibid., pp. 6, 7.

5

Tituba's explanation of the circumstances of her confession is mentioned by Robert Calef in "More Wonders of the Invisible World," Burr, p. 343.

The account hereby presented of Tituba's examination is pieced together from the two separate court reports: Cheever's, in the ECA, SW, I, p. 6; and a much longer and more interesting report by Corwin which I first ran across in Putnam, pp. 271–89. The original of the latter is in the Moore Library Collection in the New York Public Library.

CHAPTER V
GOSPEL WITCH

1

According to Deodat Lawson's "Brief and True Narrative," Burr, p. 160, Betty Parris's fits continued even after her removal to Stephen Sewall's house as late as 25 March.

The quotation from Joseph Putnam (he was father of Israel Putnam of Revolutionary fame) is from Charles Sutherland Tapley's *Rebecca Nurse*, p. 78; John Procter's statement is included in a deposition by Samuel Sibley, ECA, SW, I, p. 15. For Martha Cory's remark, see the report of her examination in the Essex Institute, *Witchcraft Papers*. This document is defective, and all that can be deciphered of Martha's words are "he went for all . . ."

2

The date of the fast of 11 March is from W. D. Love's *Fast and Thanksgiving Days of New England*, p. 257.

3

The original of the report of the interview with Martha Cory is in the ECA, SW, I, p. 13. Another document of interest is found in the Bowditch Manuscripts of the Massachusetts Historical Society and included among the WPA transcript of witch papers on file in the courthouse in Salem. In an apparent effort to be fair to Martha Cory, Thomas Putnam sent for her on Monday, 14 March, to interview his daughter Ann and her companion, Mercy Lewis. The girls promptly went into possession and saw visions which were discussed in the later examination.

Martha Cory's warrant or mittimus is in the ECA, SW, I, p. 12.

4

Deodat Lawson's account of his visit to the village is available in Burr, pp. 152–64; much of the rest of this chapter is based on his narrative.

5

The opening words from Martha Cory's examination and everything that follows are blended from Lawson's account and the official record of the examination in the Essex Institute. The latter is far longer than Lawson's record, but though it is in substantial agreement, it omits some picturesque details such as the "gospel witch" episode. Martha was repeatedly asked to explain her query to Putnam and Cheever, "Did she tell you what clothes I had on." Towards the end of the examination the accused gave way to spasms of apparently hysterical laughter, and sometimes burst out, "Ye are all against me, and I cannot help it."

6

The arrest of little Dorcas Good is mentioned by Lawson, in Burr, p. 159.

CHAPTER VI

"WHAT SIN UNREPENTED OF?"

1

The full story of the Bishop farm, which became the Nurses' property, is found in Upham, I, pp. 69–97.

For Rebecca Nurse's early history see Tapley's *Rebecca Nurse,* and Nevins, pp. 110–30.

The "flying out" at the neighbour episode is embodied in a charge later made by Sarah Holton, ECA, SW, I, p. 22.

2

The authenticity of the lilacs growing about Rebecca's home is something I cannot swear to. They are there now, doubtless thanks to the ministrations of the society for the Preservation of New England Antiquities which keeps up the old homestead; old photographs show that they were not there in the last century. In the whole episode of the Porters' visit I have embodied observations made during my own visits to this landmark.

The Porters' account of their visit to Rebecca Nurse is in the Essex Institute Manuscript Collection. Daniel Andrews was later accused of witchcraft; see Nevins, p. 255.

3

The complete text of the charges against Rebecca Nurse is printed in W. Elliot Woodward's *Records of the Salem Witchcraft,* I, pp. 88 ff. The official report of the examination is in ECA, SW, I, p. 20.

The sensational disturbance caused by the girls is described by Lawson in Burr, p. 159. In relation to the statement about Rebecca Nurse's "dry eyes," it is interesting to note Nathaniel Cary's account of his wife's examination in Chapter XI for an inconsistency on the part of the magistrates on this point.

4

Lawson's sermon, printed in England in 1704, is quoted in Upham, II, pp. 75–87. John Procter's outburst is recorded in a deposition by Samuel Sibley in ECA, SW, I, p. 15.

CHAPTER VII

JOHN PROCTER'S JADE

1

Sarah Cloyce's departure from church is mentioned by Calef in Burr, p. 346. The accusations of the girls *apropos* of the witches' sabbath are from Lawson in Burr, p. 161.

The original record of the Procter-Cloyce examination has been lost; fortunately most of it was copied *verbatim* by Hutchinson. (See his *History of Massachusetts*, Mayo edition, II, pp. 21–3.) A mass of depositions concerning the Procters, including some informal notes of the examination by Parris, is found in ECA, SW, I, pp. 14–17, 24–7; and in the witchcraft papers in the Boston Public Library.

John Putnam's accusation against Rebecca Nurse and her sister is in ECA, SW, I, p. 22.

2

Sewall's *Diary* briefly mentions the examination of 11 April. Upham, II, pp. 107 ff., contains a complete transcript of the court records as derived from Hutchinson.

3

The outburst against Elizabeth Procter, as reported by eyewitness Daniel Elliot, is in ECA, SW, I, p. 27. A confirming deposition by William Raymond is in ibid., I, p. 25.

4

The story of the seizure of Procter's property is quoted from Calef's "More Wonders," Burr, p. 361. Just when it took place does not appear, but a statement made by Procter himself (see Chapter XVI) indicates that it was well before his trial and condemnation.

The depositions by Mary English, Edward and Sarah Bishop, and Mary Esty on the ambivalent conduct of Mary Warren are printed in Woodward, I, pp. 135 ff. (The originals are in ECA, SW, I, p. 32.)

5

The account of Mary Warren's examination is derived from ECA, SW, I, p. 29; the records of her private examinations in prison on 21 April, 2 May, and 12 May are from Woodward, I, pp. 124–33. (Originals: ECA, SW, I, pp. 29–31.)

6

Sarah Ingersoll's report on Sarah Churchill is in Woodward, I, p. 14.

CHAPTER VIII
THE WEIRD SISTERS

1

The hypothetical description of the frightened ploughman is suggested by the confession of Samuel Wardwell (Chapter XV). Conjectures that the devil had probably been "let in" by a similar burst of temper were common in the later "confessions."

2

The report of Giles Cory's examination follows the court records as summarized in Upham, II, pp. 122–4.

Upham describes Bridget Bishop's earlier years in I, pp. 192–7, and her examination in II, pp. 125–8.

The court record of Abigail Hobbs's examination is in ECA, SW, I, p. 50. The pity that the afflicted girls felt for her is mentioned in the Lynde Diaries, 1690–1790; a copy of this report is in the WPA transcript of witchcraft papers, Volume II.

Abigail Hobbs's confessions, dated 12 May, are in the ECA, SW, I, p. 50.

3

Edward Bishop's treatment of John Indian is described in Calef, Burr, p. 348.

The text of Deliverance Hobbs's examination is printed in Woodward, II, pp. 186 ff.; that of her husband William, ibid., pp. 182 ff.

Mary Black's story is in Upham, II, pp. 136–7. One other negro picked up in the witch-hunt, Candy, was clever enough to divert the attention of the judges by convincing them that it was her mistress who had made a witch of her. (See Hutchinson, II, p. 26.)

The exoneration of Nehemiah Abbott is from Hutchinson, II, p. 35.

4

For Mary Esty's examination, see Upham, II, pp. 137–9, and the ECA, SW, I, p. 117. The papers accounting for her release are in the ECA, SW, I, p. 121. Upham, describing this event in II, pp. 200–5, was in apparent ignorance of the reason for her discharge.

CHAPTER IX
SMALL BLACK MINISTER

1

Most of the details of the witch confessions are derived from a series of remarkable statements by William Barker of Andover; these are found in the Massachusetts Archives, CXXXV, p. 37, the Miscellaneous Papers of the Essex Institute, and the Suffolk County Files, XXXII. Hale also interviewed the man and recorded the item about the witches' picnicking on bread and cheese in Burr, p. 418.

2

Dorcas Hoar's examination is in the ECA, SW, I, p. 78.

Ann Putnam's testimony on Burroughs is in the ECA, SW, II, p. 10. Abigail Williams's "interview" with the minister is recorded in Benjamin Hutchinson's testimony, ibid., II, p. 16. The Stonington witch she mentions may be one of the Connecticut witches alluded to in Barker's confession (see Chapter XV).

3

Burroughs's appeal is in the Maine Historical Society *Collections*, Second Series, V, pp. 316–17. The best general account of Burroughs's career is in Sibley's *Harvard Graduates*. The circumstances of the minister's arrest are traditional in origin; he was taken by John Partridge, Field Marshal of New Hampshire and Maine. Mrs Burroughs's subsequent conduct

was described by her stepchildren in their appeal for redress
in 1712. (See Woodward, II, pp. 237–40.)

4

Keysar's testimony is from the Thomas F. Madigan photo-
stats as transcribed in the WPA verbatim report; the examination itself, disappointingly brief, is in the ECA, SW, II, p. 9.

The ghosts of Burroughs's wives are made much of in Cotton
Mather's "Wonders," Burr, p. 218. He also gives a full account
of the minister's deeds of supernatural strength, ibid., pp. 219–
20. Increase Mather's *Cases of Conscience* reveals that he was
no less profoundly impressed by this sort of testimony.

Mercy Lewis's contribution is in the ECA, SW, II, p. 12.

CHAPTER X
PURITAN KNIGHT

1

Increase Mather's own account of his mission to England,
on which this section is largely based, is in Charles M. Andrews's *Narratives of the Insurrections, 1675–1690*, pp. 276–97.

The authority for the scene in which Mather broke the news
to King William of the Boston revolution is K. B. Murdock's
Increase Mather, p. 219.

The phrase "no discharge in God's holy war," is paraphrased
from Perry Miller's *The New England Mind*, p. 57.

2

The account of the life of Sir William Phips is drawn from
Cotton Mather's *Magnalia Christi Americana* (Andrus edition),
I, pp. 165–230.

3

The quotations from Phips are from his letter to England
written 12 October 1692, and included in Burr, pp. 196–8.

CHAPTER XI
DEMOCRACY FOR WITCHES

2

The story of Mrs Cary's examination is based on the record her husband wrote for Calef's "More Wonders," Burr, pp. 350–2.

3

John Alden's story of his court appearance is from the same source, pp. 353–5. In following his narrative I have occasionally shifted the order and have twice translated indirect to direct quotation.

4

The portrait of Philip English is based on George Chever's "Philip English" in the Essex Institute *Historical Collections*. See also Upham, II, pp. 142–4.

Martha Carrier's brush with the selectmen is described by Sarah Loring Bailey in *Historical Sketches of Andover*, pp. 202–8. The examination is found in ECA, SW, II, p. 56. Gibbs's comment is from Felt's *Annals*, p. 305. Cotton Mather's "More Wonders," Burr, pp. 241–4, gives in full the evidence against Martha Carrier.

5

Copious accusations against John Willard are in the ECA, SW, I, pp. 97–107.

CHAPTER XII
VILLAGE CIRCE

1

Mercy Short's interview with Sarah Good is described in Cotton Mather's "A Brand Pluck'd out of the Burning," Burr, pp. 259–60.

2

Thomas Newton, King's Attorney, may have been free of prejudice, but a letter reporting his first visit to the examina-

tions on 31 May shows him as susceptible to fantasy as any.
The letter is in the Massachusetts Archives, CXXXV, p. 23.

The entire account of Bridget Bishop, the malefaction she
practised on the meeting-house, the testimony against her, is
based on Cotton Mather's "Wonders," Burr, pp. 223–9. In reference to this testimony Calef reports (Burr, p. 356) that at
least one accuser, Samuel Gray, later disavowed his story.

The midwives' statement is in ECA, SW, I, p. 35; that of
the Bishops in Woodward, I, p. 135.

3

The recommendations of the ministers are in Thomas Hutchinson's *History of the Colony and Province of Massachusetts
Bay*, II, pp. 38–9.

CHAPTER XIII
DAMNED FOR THE GLORY OF GOD

1

Sarah Nurse's testimony I have from Abbie Peterson Towne
and Marrietta Clark's "Topsfield in the Witchcraft Delusion,"
Topsfield Historical Collections, XIII, p. 57.

The general story of Rebecca Nurse's trial, including her own
explanation of her comment on her remark about Deliverance
Hobbs, is drawn from Calef's "More Wonders," Burr, pp. 358–
60.

2

The excommunication of Rebecca Nurse is described by
Upham, II, pp. 290–1. The testimonials of Rebecca Nurse's
character are in the Bowditch Manuscripts of the Massachusetts
Historical Society. The reprieve is described in Calef's "More
Wonders," Burr, p. 359.

CHAPTER XIV
BLOOD TO DRINK

1

Calef mentions the accusation against Willard, Burr, p. 360;
Sibley, in his life of Willard in *Harvard Graduates*, says that

the judges explained the accusation as meant for John Willard, the constable.

Increase Mather summarizes the Groton incident in "Remarkable Providences," Burr, pp. 22–3.

Upham, II, pp. 218–19, describes the ministers' interview with Goody How.

2

The Ipswich incident is from Cotton Mather's "Wonders," Burr, pp. 237–40. The incident of the knife blade at Sarah Good's trial is from Calef, ibid., pp. 357–8.

3

The story of Susanna Martin follows Cotton Mather's "Wonders," ibid., pp. 229–36.

4

Sarah Good's retort to Noyes is from Calef's "More Wonders," ibid., p. 358.

CHAPTER XV
THE DEVIL IN ANDOVER

1

The prayers for John Alden are mentioned in Sewall's *Diary*, 20 July 1692.

Cary's description of his wife's escape is from Calef's "More Wonders," Burr, p. 352; Sewall also mentions the flight.

The account of Philip and Mary English is drawn from Chever's narrative, a second-hand document of questionable authenticity. Few court records of the English case have survived.

Alden mentions his escape in the account he wrote for Calef. The quotation, probably traditional, is paraphrased from Upham, II, p. 246.

2

The Andover episode is summarized in Calef's "More Wonders," Burr, pp. 371–6. Brattle's "Letter," ibid., pp. 180 ff., gives much attention to this case.

3

Mary Osgood's report, one of those collected by Increase Mather, is from Upham, II, p. 406.

Wardwell's "confession" is in Woodward, II, pp. 148–53. William Barker's statement cited here (also the confessions of several women in his family) is from the Massachusetts Archives, CXXXV, p. 37. Hale also records a statement made by this odd philosopher.

For the Foster-Lacy confessions see Woodward, II, p. 136, and Hutchinson, II, pp. 27–8.

Mary Tyler's story is in the Massachusetts Historical Society *Collections,* Second Series, III, pp. 221–5.

For Abigail Faulkner's statement, see Woodward, II, pp. 130 ff.

4

The reference to the legal action against the Andover accusers is from Calef in Burr, p. 372.

CHAPTER XVI

ON GALLOWS HILL

2

Calef includes the text of John Procter's petition in his "More Wonders," Burr, pp. 362–4. The original is in the ECA, SW, I, p. 17.

Increase Mather describes the Cambridge conference in his *Cases of Conscience,* Fowler edition, p. 253. His opinion of Burroughs is given on p. 286.

3

The petitions in behalf of Procter are in the ECA, SW, I, pp. 17 and 28.

The story of John Willard is drawn from Upham, II, pp. 322–4. The story of Burroughs's trial is based on Cotton Mather's "Wonders," Burr, pp. 215–22. The exact date of this trial, usually given as 5 August, is open to question. Nevins points out that though this may have been the opening date of this series of trials they necessarily spread over several days.

4

The record of George Jacobs's examination is in the ECA, SW, I, p. 86. Margaret Jacobs's recantation is described in Upham, II, pp. 316–20.

5

Calef, who may have been an eyewitness to this hanging, has described it in Burr, pp. 360–1. Further details are found in Sewall's *Diary*.

CHAPTER XVII

EIGHT FIREBRANDS OF HELL

1

Though extensive testimony both for and against Mary Bradbury remains in the records (see Woodward, II, pp. 161–74), the circumstances of her trial are mysterious. First complained on 26 May, she was indicted 26 July. Her survivors claimed in 1710 that she had been imprisoned six months, but since a notation on the court records (ECA, SW, II, pp. 34–40) explicitly says that she escaped, their statement is obviously erroneous; maybe they meant six weeks.

2

The petition for Dorcas Hoar is in the papers of George H. Milne of New York; I have them from the WPA transcripts in Salem. Sewall's *Diary* of 21 September 1692 refers to it.

Hale's misgivings about the confessors are summarized in a statement in his "Modest Inquiry," Burr, pp. 416–24. The ECA, SW, I, p. 80, contains Hale's deposition on Goody Hoar's earlier misdeeds.

3

Wilmot Redd's trial is summarized by Upham, II, pp. 324 ff. Ann Pudeator's petition is in Woodward, II, p. 22. Parris's interview with Martha Cory is quoted in Upham, II, pp. 324–5.

Calef in Burr, pp. 368–9, quotes Mary Esty's petition in full. (The original is in ECA, SW, I, p. 127.)

4

Thomas Putnam's letter describing the visions his daughter saw while Giles Cory was being pressed to death is in Mather's "Wonders," Burr, p. 250.

5

Noyes's remark is from Calef's "More Wonders," ibid., p. 369.

CHAPTER XVIII
THE GHOST OF MARY ESTY

1

Joseph Gerrish's account of the ghost of Mary Esty is printed in Burr, p. 369, footnote 1. Calef mentions the effect on Hale.

2

Increase Mather's outburst is mentioned in Brattle's "Letter," ibid., p. 180.

3

The letter by "R.P." is printed and analysed in Upham, II, pp. 448 ff. and 538–44. The original manuscript is in the Essex Institute.

4

The text of Brattle's letter is in Burr, pp. 169–90.

5

Hale's amazement at the number of the witches is expressed in his "Modest Inquiry," Burr, p. 423.

Governor Phips's decision to discourage publicity about the witches is mentioned in his letter of 12 October 1692, ibid., p. 197.

The Andover petitions are in the Massachusetts Archives, CXXXV, pp. 56, 59.

Sewall's *Diary*, 26 October 1692, mentions the dissolution of the Court of Oyer and Terminer. Phips mentions arrangements for the welfare of the witches in his report of 21 February 1693, Burr, p. 200. The new law on witchcraft is in the Massachusetts Archives, CXXXV, p. 67.

The Gloucester legend, the subject of Whittier's "Garrison of Cape Ann," is elaborated in Samuel Niles's "History of the Indian and French Wars," Massachusetts Historical Society *Collections*, Series Three, Volume VI, pp. 231–2.

The Ipswich episode is described in Calef's "More Wonders," Burr, p. 373.

CHAPTER XIX

JAIL DELIVERY

1

The report of the Dutch and French ministers is found in the Massachusetts Historical Society *Proceedings*, Series Two, Volume I, pp. 353–8.

The judges' change of heart is reported in Phips's letter of 21 February 1693, Burr, p. 200.

2

The judges' answer to the jury on spectral evidence is from Calef, ibid., p. 382. The remark on Elizabeth Johnson, ibid., p. 382 and footnote 4. For Stoughton's outburst, see Calef, ibid., p. 383, and also Phips's report, p. 201. For Judge Danforth's admonition to Sarah Daston, ibid., p. 383. The character of the juries is described on p. 384.

3

The fate of Mary Watkins and Tituba is mentioned by Calef in Burr, p. 384 and footnote 1.

The story of Margaret Jacobs is from Upham, II, pp. 353–4.

CHAPTER XX

THE DEVIL AND COTTON MATHER

1

It is irritating not to know exactly which of the afflicted girls "went bad." Certainly they did not include Ann Putnam, Elizabeth Parris, and probably not Abigail Williams, Mary Walcott, or Elizabeth Booth. That they did include others is indicated by a statement in the reversal of the attainder in 1711 which speaks of "some of the principal accusers" as having "discovered themselves to be persons of profligate and vicious conversation." (*Historical Collections* of the Topsfield Historical Society, XIII, pp. 135–7.)

3

Cotton Mather's letter to Judge Richards is in Barrett Wendell's *Cotton Mather*, p. 110.

4

The text of Mather's "Hortatory Address" is printed in Samuel P. Fowler's *Salem Witchcraft*, pp. 394–414.

5

Cotton Mather's story of Mercy Short, "A Brand Pluck'd out of the Burning," is printed from the manuscript in the possession of the American Antiquarian Society in Burr, pp. 259–87.

6

The trip to Salem is described in Cotton Mather's *Diary*, September 1693. Mather's interviews with Margaret Rule are from "Another Brand Pluckt out of the Burning" as incorporated in Calef's "More Wonders," Burr, pp. 307–23.

The seaman is quoted by Calef, ibid., p. 327; Mather's injunction to Margaret, ibid., p. 311; Calef's story of Margaret's ways with men, ibid., pp. 325–7.

Calef's attack on Mather and the latter's reaction are described in ibid., pp. 305, 335; the correspondence between the two, pp. 339–41.

7

Mather's successful resolution of the Margaret Rule affair is described in Wendell's *Cotton Mather*, pp. 104 ff.

CHAPTER XXI
VILLAGE PURGE

2

The voiding of Parris's salary is mentioned in Felt's *Annals*, p. 314. For Herrick's complaint see Massachusetts Archives, CXXXV, p. 66.

The complaint against Parris is found in Upham, II, p. 497.
Upham has printed all of the parish records relating to this controversy in an appendix to *Salem Witchcraft*, II.

Parris's "Meditations for Peace" is in ibid., pp. 547–50.

The statement of Rebecca Nurse's sons on the loss of their
mother is from the Massachusetts State Archives, CXXXV, p.
141.

The description of Parris's sermons is quoted from the parish
records in Upham, II, pp. 497–8; for the fate of the Parris
family, see ibid., pp. 499 ff.

3

The account of Joseph Green is based on Sibley, IV, pp.
228–33, and Samuel P. Fowler's "Biographical Sketch and Diary
of the Reverend Joseph Green" in the Essex Institute *Historical
Collections*, VIII and X.

The new seating arrangement of the church is described in
Upham, II, pp. 506–9.

4

Philip English's "revenge" is described in Upham, II, p. 470.

Nathaniel Hawthorne gives the story of Philip English's
deathbed repentance and of his descendants in his *American
Notebooks*, p. 27.

CHAPTER XXII
"WE WALKED IN CLOUDS"

1

The text of Ann Putnam's confession is found in Nevins,
p. 250.

2

Samuel Sewall's interview with his son is from his *Diary*,
24 December 1696.

The proclamation of the fast is in Calef, Burr, pp. 385–6; the
juror's statement, ibid., pp. 387–8.

3

All quotations in this section are from Hale's "A Modest Inquiry" (Burr).

Cotton Mather's misgivings are mentioned in his *Diary*, 15 January 1697.

4

Hale may have been the first to have advocated the rehabilitation of the witches. In his "Modest Inquiry," Burr, p. 427, he urged that something "be publicly done for clearing the good name" of the sufferers. The records of the restitution are in the Massachusetts State Archives, CXXXV, p. 145.

SELECTED BIBLIOGRAPHY

I

PRIMARY SOURCES

(A) *Court Records of the Witchcraft* (*Manuscript and Copies*)

Essex County Archives: *Salem Witchcraft, 1692*. Two volumes.

These two enormous volumes contain in manuscript the
bulk of the court reports of the examinations conducted by
John Hathorne and Jonathan Corwin, warrants, and depositions of witnesses. Although some important documents have
strayed into other collections, this is the most indispensable
source of the witchcraft.

Essex County Archives: *Salem Witchcraft, 1692*. One volume.

This is a fair copy of the documents mentioned above,
made in 1859 under the direction of Ira T. Watch, clerk. Like
the manuscript collection, it is available in the Essex County
Court House in Salem, Massachusetts.

Essex Institute: *Witchcraft Papers*.

The Essex Institute, also in Salem, possesses a miscellaneous assortment of the court records, the most important of
which is the examination of Martha Cory. Included in this
collection is a copy in clear handwriting of the early trials
of 1693.

Massachusetts Archives: Volume CXXXV, *Witchcraft, 1656 to
1750*.

These documents include some valuable material about the
1692 outbreak in Andover, many of the witch confessions,
petitions made by relatives of the witches in 1692 and 1710,
and some correspondence by William Stoughton and Thomas
Newton. They are available in the State House in Boston.

Suffolk County Files: Volume XXXII.

This collection of manuscripts is in the Clerk's Office of
the Suffolk Superior Criminal Court in the Suffolk County
Court House, Boston. Witch papers here are mingled with
much miscellaneous material of 1692. It is of minor interest,

but does contain the examinations of Job Tukey, William Procter, one of William Barker's several confessions, and the judgment of *ignoramus* passed on Tituba on 9 May 1693.

Suffolk County: Superior Court of Judicature, 1692–95.

The documents here were copied by hand in 1892 from the originals which are said to have been since destroyed by fire. They cover chiefly the sittings of the Superior Court in Salem from 3 January to 13 January 1693.

Woodward, W. Elliot. *Records of the Salem Witchcraft.* Printed in Roxbury, 1864. Two volumes.

A valuable, and so far as I have ever discovered, completely accurate printing of many of the documents available in manuscript both in the Essex County Court House and the Massachusetts State House. It is not complete.

Works Progress Administration. *Salem Witchcraft, 1692.*

A verbatim transcription of the Salem Witchcraft papers compiled under the supervision of Archie N. Frost, Clerk of Courts, 1938. Three volumes.

These typescript copies of original manuscripts constitute the most complete source in existence of the Salem witchcraft. They are on file in the Court House in Salem. Material covered includes not only all documents available in Salem, but the witchcraft papers in the Massachusetts and Suffolk County Archives, the Massachusetts Historical Society, the Boston and New York Public Libraries, and the George H. Milne papers. This achievement is said to be due to the energies of John H. Fitzgibbons, who was in charge of the WPA project.

I found the collection invaluable, and relied on it wholly for the following material: the Bowditch Manuscripts in the Massachusetts Historical Society; the Lynde Diaries; the papers of George H. Milne of New York; the Moore Collection in the New York Public Library.

(B) *Personal Narratives of the Salem Witchcraft*

Brattle, Thomas. Letter, 1692. Reprinted from the Massachusetts Historical Society *Collections* in George Lincoln Burr's *Narratives of the Witchcraft,* pp. 169–90.

Brattle's letter, the appearance of which marked a turning point in the witchcraft, is discussed in Chapter XVIII of the text.

Burr, George Lincoln, editor. *Narratives of the Witchcraft Cases,
1648–1706.* Scribner's, New York, 1914.

The most valuable single source on the Salem witchcraft
apart from the court records in Salem. For convenience I have
made a separate listing of the narratives by the following eye-
witnesses to the episode: Thomas Brattle, Robert Calef, John
Hale, Deodat Lawson, Cotton and Increase Mather, Sir William Phips.

Calef, Robert. "More Wonders of the Invisible World." London, 1700. Reprinted in Burr, pp. 296–393.

Written largely as an attack on Cotton Mather's "Wonders," this lively document contains much material not ob-
tainable elsewhere, including Nathaniel Cary's and John
Alden's own stories of their participation in the court proceedings.

Fowler, Samuel P., editor. *Salem Witchcraft.* H. P. Ives and
A. A. Smith, Salem, 1861.

Another reprint of Calef's "More Wonders," and Mather's
"Wonders"; it also contains documents in the controversy of
the Salem Village Church with Samuel Parris, and some editorial notes.

Hale, John. "A Modest Inquiry into the Nature of Witchcraft."
Boston, 1702. Reprinted in Burr, pp. 399–432.

An analysis of both the onset and the outcome of the
Salem witchcraft by a participant who had two occasions to
change his mind. It is quoted and discussed in Chapter XXII
of this text.

Lawson, Deodat. "A Brief and True Narrative." Boston, 1692.
Reprinted in Burr, pp. 152–64.

Of great interest in that it is the earliest eyewitness report
of the witchcraft; much of Chapter V is based on this document.

Mather, Cotton. "A Brand Pluck'd out of the Burning." 1693.
Printed in Burr, pp. 259–87.

The story of Mercy Short, discussed in Chapter XX.

——*Magnalia Christi Americana* or *The Ecclesiastical History
of New England, 1629–98.* Silas Andrus and Sons, Hartford,
1853. Two volumes.

References to the witchcraft are found in Volume I, pp.
204–213; Volume II, pp. 446–79.

——"Memorable Providences Relating to Witchcraft and Possession." Boston, 1689. Reprinted in Burr, pp. 93–143.

Mather's report on the case of Martha Goodwin and the "Witch Glover." Though this witchcraft episode had no direct connection with the later outbreak in Salem, this book is believed to have played a part in making the general public "witch-conscious." The work is briefly discussed in Chapter III.

——"Wonders of the Invisible World." Boston, 1693. Reprinted in Burr, pp. 209–51.

The official report on the witchcraft trials of 1692; many chapters owe much to this document, whose genesis is discussed in Chapter XX.

Mather, Increase. *Cases of Conscience Concerning Evil Spirits Personating Men; Witchcrafts.* John Russell Smith, London, 1862.

No editor is named for this reprint, which contains a wildly inaccurate introduction, Cotton Mather's "Wonders," and sundry less important documents. Increase Mather's monograph, written before he had revised his view on the Salem episode and printed in London in 1693, contains some observations on George Burroughs.

Maule, Thomas. *The Truth Held Forth and Maintained.* 1695.

This volume, which I consulted in the Massachusetts Historical Society, contains in Chapter XXIX a very cogent study of the witchcraft. Maule, who was a Quaker, seems to have written that chapter in 1693.

Phips, Sir William. Letters to the Home Government, 1692–3. Printed in Burr, pp. 196–202.

Two brief, administrative reports on the course and the disposition of the witchcraft by the harried royal governor.

Sewall, Samuel. Diary. *Collections.* Massachusetts Historical Society, Fifth Series, Volumes V–VII.

Sewall's diary contains several disappointingly brief references to his participation as judge in the witchcraft trials.

——Letter Book. *Collections.* Massachusetts Historical Society, Sixth Series, Volumes I, II.

A few of these letters, notably the one to Nathaniel Saltonstall, deal with the witchcraft.

Willard, Samuel. *Some Miscellaneous Observations on Our Present Debates respecting Witchcraft; a Dialogue between S. and B.* Philadelphia. Printed by William Bradford for Hezekiah Usher, 1692.

Modern scholarship attributes this volume to Willard, in

spite of the inscription "By P. E. and J. A." (presumably Philip English and John Alden). It probably was not printed in Philadelphia. Quotations from this book, which I inspected in the Massachusetts Historical Society, may be found in Chapter XVIII.

(C) General Background Sources of the Witchcraft Period

Andrews, Charles M., editor. *Narratives of the Insurrections, 1675–1690.* Scribner's, New York, 1915.

Pages 165–299, which contain eyewitness accounts of the overthrow of Andros in 1689, throw much light on the general gloom and confusion of the Massachusetts public in this period. This volume also contains Increase Mather's "Brief Account of the Agents, 1691," which is quoted in Chapter X.

Essex Institute. *The Probate Records of Essex County, Massachusetts.* Volume III. Essex Institute, Salem, Massachusetts, 1920.

Valuable incidental material on the possessions in clothing, household and farm gear, and livestock in old Salem.

Fowler, Samuel P. "Biographical Sketch and Diary of the Reverend Joseph Green of Salem Village." Essex Institute *Historical Collections*, VIII, pp. 91–6; 165–75; 215–25; X, pp. 73–104.

Unfortunately the diary itself is very brief; it does, however, afford a glimpse into the pleasanter period in Salem Village that followed the grim ministry of Parris.

Maine Historical Society, *Collections*. Second Series, Volume V. Portland, Maine, 1897.

A letter by George Burroughs appealing to the governor and General Court for help against the Indians is found on pages 316–17.

Mather, Cotton, Diary, 1681–1708. Massachusetts Historical Society *Collections*, Seventh Series, Volumes VII, VIII.

Too subjective to have the historical value of Sewall's delightful companion-piece. Several entries record Mather's feelings about the witchcraft.

Mather, Increase, "An Essay for the Recording of Illustrious Providences." Boston, 1684. Reprinted in Burr, pp. 8–38.

This deals with early and more sporadic cases of witchcraft in New England generally.

Murdock, Kenneth B., editor. *Selections from Cotton Mather*. Harcourt, Brace, New York, 1926.

Of particular interest in understanding the background of this troubled period, Mather's "Political Fables" and "Christian Philosopher."

II

SECONDARY SOURCES

(A) *Histories of the Salem Witchcraft and of Its Actors*

Chever, George F. "Philip English," in the *Historical Collections* of the Essex Institute, Volumes I, II, 1859, 1860.

So far as this account deals with English's connection with early mercantile history, it is based on documentary evidence; the witchcraft episodes are largely traditional.

Hutchinson, Thomas. *History of the Colony and Province of Massachusetts*. Edited by Lawrence Shaw Mayo. Harvard University Press, Cambridge, 1936.

Chapter I of Volume II deals with the Salem witchcraft and contains several original records since lost.

Nevins, Winfield S. *Witchcraft in Salem Village in 1692*. Salem Press Company, Salem, Massachusetts, 1916. (Fifth edition.)

The virtues of this record are discussed in the preface. It contains an appendix offering a reasonably full list of persons taken in the witchcraft.

Perley, M. V. B. *Salem Village Witchcraft Trials*. Perley Publishing Company, Salem, Massachusetts, 1911.

A fairly unimportant souvenir volume, but it contains some interesting sketches and maps and the verbatim report of the trial of Elizabeth How.

Poole, William E. "Witchcraft in Boston." I, pp. 130–72 in *The Memorial History of Boston*. Justin Winsor, editor. Ticknor, Boston, 1881.

Largely a discussion of the Witch Glover affair.

Putnam, Allen. *Witchcraft of New England Explained by Modern Spiritualism*. Colby and Rich, Boston, 1888.

Since spiritualism is unquestionably very similar to what was going on during the witchcraft outbreak in 1692, this is an unexpectedly helpful book. Putnam did a thorough job of research and uncovered documents apparently unknown to the classic Upham.

Tapley, Charles Sutherland. *Rebecca Nurse*. Marshall Jones Company, Boston, 1930.

Interesting as a repository of certain family traditions. Frank A. Manny, a descendant of Rebecca Nurse, has provided a preface.

Topsfield Historical Society. "Witchcraft Records Relating to Topsfield." *Historical Collections*, XIII (1908), pp. 39–142.

Some miscellaneous material concerning the Hobbs family, Sarah Wild, Mary Esty, Elizabeth How.

Towne, Mrs Abbie Peterson and Miss Marrietta Clark. "Topsfield in the Witchcraft Delusion." Topsfield Historical Society, *Historical Collections*, XIII (1908), pp. 23–39.

This contains some traditional material of interest.

Upham, Charles W. *Salem Witchcraft*. Wiggins and Lunt. Boston, 1867. Two volumes.

This, the classic in the field, is discussed in the preface.

Wendell, Barrett. "Were the Salem Witches Guiltless?" *Historical Collections* of the Essex Institute, XXIX.

Famous, but not too interesting. Wendell wrote it after reading up on spiritualism.

(B) *General Historical Background*

Adams, Brooks. *Emancipation of Massachusetts, the Dream and the Reality*. Houghton Mifflin, Boston, 1919.

Adams, who intensely dislikes theocrats, has nevertheless written an able analysis of their political manœuvres.

Andrews, Charles M. *The Colonial Period of American History*. The Settlements, I. Yale University Press, New Haven, 1934.

The authority in its field.

Bailey, Sarah Loring. *Historical Sketches of Andover*. Houghton Mifflin, Boston, 1880.

Not very thorough so far as the interesting Andover witchcraft is concerned, but it does contain some interesting material about Martha Carrier.

Boas, Ralph and Louise. *Cotton Mather, Keeper of the Puritan Conscience*. Harper's, New York, 1928.

A modern and friendly approach to the controversial Puritan; the authors' views on Thomas Brattle are of particular interest and originality.

Bridenbaugh, Carl. *Cities in the Wilderness*. The First Century of Urban Life in America, 1625–1742. The Ronald Press, New York, 1938.

Of particular value in painting in the background of living conditions in the Colonial Period.

Chase, George Wingate. *History of Haverhill*. Published by the author in Haverhill, 1861.

Some material on Judge Nathaniel Saltonstall.

Felt, Joseph B. *The Annals of Salem from Its First Settlement*. W. and S. B. Ives, Salem, 1827.

A friendly catch-all which occasionally gives bits of local information not found elsewhere.

Fleming, Sandford. *Children and Puritanism*. Yale University Press, New Haven, 1933.

Chapter XIII, "Emotional Response of Children," contributed something to the background of the first three chapters in this work.

Hawthorne, Nathaniel. *The American Notebooks*. Edited by Randall Stewart. Yale University Press, New Haven, 1932.

The descendant of both John Hathorne and Philip English, Hawthorne has some irreverent anecdotes to contribute about the latter.

Love, W. De Lacy, Jr. *The Fast and Thanksgiving Days of New England*. Houghton Mifflin, Boston, 1895.

Certain useful material about the various fasts held in connection with the witchcraft.

Miller, Perry. *The New England Mind*. Macmillan, New York, 1939.

A searching analysis, based largely on a study of Puritan sermons, of the backgrounds that shaped Puritan thinking.

Morgan, Edmund S. *The Puritan Family*. Trustees of the Public Library, Boston, Massachusetts, 1944.

Particularly good in its discussion of the place of children in Puritan family life.

Murdock, Kenneth B. *Increase Mather: The Foremost American Puritan*. Harvard University Press, Cambridge, 1926.

The authoritative study of the elder Mather and his place in American history.

Parrington, Vernon Louis. *Main Currents in American Thought*. Harcourt, Brace, New York, 1927, 1930.

Volume I, "The Colonial Mind," throws a valuable perspective on this phase of history.

Phillips, James Duncan. *Salem in the Seventeenth Century*. Houghton Mifflin, Boston, 1937.

One of the pro-Puritans, who spends much of his time defending his subject against aspersion; an excellent map.

Schneider, Herbert Wallace. *The Puritan Mind*. Henry Holt, New York, 1930.

Schneider's interest seems rather with such later Puritans as Jonathan Edwards than with his predecessors, but his study does throw a backward light on the former.

Sibley, John Langdon. *Biographical Sketches of the Graduates of Harvard University*. Charles William Sever, Cambridge, 1881.

Volumes II, III, IV contain authoritative material on most of the members of the ministry involved in the Salem outbreak.

Stowe, Harriet Beecher. *Oldtown Folks*. Houghton Mifflin, Boston, 1889.

Though this is nominally fiction, it is also a repository of reminiscences going back to Puritan times that is taken seriously by social historians. I found especially helpful Mrs Stowe's analysis of the effects of Calvinistic doctrine on the young.

Tawney, R. H. *Religion and the Rise of Capitalism*. Harcourt, Brace, New York, 1926.

Mainly devoted to a warm, intelligent and critical analysis of the rise of Puritanism out of the medieval church.

Walker, Williston. *A History of the Congregational Churches in the United States*. The Christian Literature Company, New York, 1894.

A careful analysis of the evolution of dogma.

Waters, Thomas Franklin. *Ipswich in the Massachusetts Bay Colony*. Ipswich Historical Society, 1905.

A good local history which touches on the witchcraft.

Wendell, Barrett. *Cotton Mather, the Puritan Priest*. Harvard University Press, Cambridge, 1926.

A careful portrait of the younger Mather done by a not uncritical admirer.

(C) *Psychological and Anthropological Sources*

Beard, George M. *Psychology of the Salem Witchcraft Excitement of 1692*. G. P. Putnam's Sons, New York, 1882.

Slight, out-of-date, but of interest as the first serious attempt to diagnose the "afflicted girls" as hysterics.

Castiglioni, Arturo. *Adventures of the Mind.* Translated by V. Gianturco. Alfred A. Knopf, Inc., New York, 1946.
A vivid study of the psychological origins of magic in primitive man and their transformation into the mass suggestion potent in modern societies.

Ehrenwald, Jan. *Telepathy and Medical Psychology.* Norton, New York, 1948.
Dr Ehrenwald's book, based in part on the experiments in extrasensory perception at Duke University, might be used to build up a hypothesis that telepathy may have been involved in some of the manifestations of the "afflicted girls" of Salem.

Estabrooks, G. H. *Hypnotism.* E. P. Dutton, New York, 1943.
This "popular" but sound discussion of hypnoid states throws a revealing light on hysteria and mob psychology.

Freud, Sigmund. *Selected Papers on Hysteria and Other Psychoneuroses.* Nervous and Mental Diseases Publishing Company, New York and Washington, 1920.
My authority in describing the probable origin of hysteria among the afflicted girls.

Hole, Christina. *Witchcraft in England.* B. T. Batsford, Ltd, London, 1945.
It is Miss Hole's thesis that medieval witchcraft often had objective reality in that it originated in survivals of pre-Christian rites. The only possible bearing her theory has on the Salem episode is in the voodoo probably practised by Tituba.

Janet, Pierre. *The Major Symptoms of Hysteria.* Macmillan, New York, 1929.
The classic descriptive study of hysteria.

Kittredge, George Lyman. *Witchcraft in Old and New England.* Harvard University Press, Cambridge, Massachusetts, 1929.
Another classic in its field, and one possessed of literary charm. Though the bulk of the work is concerned with English witchcraft, Dr Kittredge gives some attention to the Salem outbreak.

INDEX

ANCHOR BOOKS

ANCHOR BOOKS

CLASSICS AND MYTHOLOGY

THE AENEID OF VIRGIL—C. Day Lewis, trans., A20

FIVE COMEDIES OF ARISTOPHANES—Benjamin Bickley Rogers, trans.; Andrew Chiappe, ed., A57

FIVE STAGES OF GREEK RELIGION—Gilbert Murray, A51

FROM RITUAL TO ROMANCE: An Account of the Holy Grail from Ancient Ritual to Christian Symbol—Jessie L. Weston, A125

A HISTORY OF ROME—Moses Hadas, ed., A78

MIDDLE ENGLISH ANTHOLOGY—Ann S. Haskell, AO10

MYTHOLOGIES OF THE ANCIENT WORLD—Samuel Noah Kramer, ed., A229

THE ODYSSEY—Homer; Robert Fitzgerald, trans., A333

SOCRATES—A. E. Taylor, A9

ANCHOR BOOKS

AMERICAN HISTORY AND STUDIES

ANCHOR BOOKS

LITERARY ESSAYS AND CRITICISM

THE ALICE B. TOKLAS COOK BOOK—Alice B. Toklas, A196

THE AMERICAN NOVEL AND ITS TRADITION—Richard Chase, A116

AN APPROACH TO SHAKESPEARE, in two volumes—D. A. Traversi, A74a, b

ART AND REALITY—Joyce Cary, A260

THE BIBLE FOR STUDENTS OF LITERATURE AND ART—G. B. Harrison, ed., A394

THE BIRTH OF TRAGEDY AND THE GENEALOGY OF MORALS—Friedrich Nietzsche; Francis Golffing, trans., A81

BLAKE: PROPHET AGAINST EMPIRE—David V. Erdman, AO12

THE BOOK OF THE COURTIER—Baldesar Castiglione; Charles S. Singleton, trans.; Edgar de N. Mayhew, ed. of illustrative material, A186

CLASSIC, ROMANTIC AND MODERN—Jacques Barzun, revised and expanded second edition of Romanticism and the Modern Ego, A255

A COLLECTION OF ESSAYS—George Orwell, A29

COMEDY, "Laughter"—Henri Bergson, and "Essay on Comedy"; George Meredith, intro. and supplementary essay by Wylie Sypher, A87

A COMPANION TO SHAKESPEARE STUDIES—H. Granville-Barker and G. B. Harrison, eds., A191

THE COMPLETE POEMS AND SELECTED LETTERS AND PROSE OF HART CRANE—Brom Weber, ed., A537

DR. BOWDLER'S LEGACY: A History of Expurgated Books in England and America—Noel Perrin, A786

FORM AND VALUE IN MODERN POETRY—R. P. Blackmur, A96

FOUR STAGES OF RENAISSANCE STYLE: Transformations in Art and Literature 1400–1700—Wylie Sypher, A44

FROM RITUAL TO ROMANCE—Jessie Weston, A125

FROM SHAKESPEARE TO EXISTENTIALISM—Walter Kaufmann, A213

GOOD-BYE TO ALL THAT—Robert Graves, second edition revised, A123

A GUIDE TO ENGLISH LITERATURE—F. W. Bateson, second edition revised, A418a

THE LIBERAL IMAGINATION: Essays on Literature and Society—Lionel Trilling, A13

MIDDLE ENGLISH ANTHOLOGY—Ann S. Haskell, AO10

ON NATIVE GROUNDS: An Interpretation of Modern American Prose Literature—Alfred Kazin, abridged, A69

THE POETRY AND PROSE OF WILLIAM BLAKE—David V. Erdman, ed., commentary by Harold Bloom, AO17

POETRY IN OUR TIME—Babette Deutsch, A344

THE PROSE OF JOHN MILTON—J. Max Patrick, ed., ACO10
10Ab

ANCHOR BOOKS

HISTORY

AFRICA AND THE VICTORIANS—Ronald Robinson and John Gallagher, with Alice Denny, AO4

AGAINST THE WORLD: Attitudes of White South Africa—Douglas Brown, A671

THE AGE OF COURTS AND KINGS: Manners and Morals 1588–1715—Philippe Erlanger, A691

THE AGE OF GEORGE III—R. J. White, A706

AGRARIAN PROBLEMS AND PEASANT MOVEMENTS IN LATIN AMERICA—Rodolfo Stavenhagen, ed., A718

THE ANCIENT CITY—Fustel de Coulanges, A76

ANTIWORLDS AND "THE FIFTH AGE"—Andrei Voznesensky; Patricia Blake and Max Hayward, eds., bilingual edition, A595

THE ARAB WORLD TODAY—Morroe Berger, A406

BACK OF HISTORY, The Story of Our Origins—William Howells, revised edition, N34

BASIC WRITINGS ON POLITICS AND PHILOSOPHY—Karl Marx and Friedrich Engels; Lewis S. Feuer, ed., A185

THE BIBLE FOR STUDENTS OF LITERATURE AND ART—G. B. Harrison, ed., A394

THE BIBLICAL ARCHAEOLOGIST READER, Volume III—Edward F. Campbell, Jr. and David Noel Freedman, eds., A250c

BIRTH OF CIVILIZATION IN THE NEAR EAST—Henri Frankfort, A89

THE BOOK OF THE COURTIER—Baldesar Castiglione; Charles S. Singleton, trans., Edgar de N. Mayhew, ill. ed., A186

BRATSK STATION AND OTHER NEW POEMS, Yevgeny Yevtushenko—Tina Tupikina Glaessner, Geoffrey Dutton and Igor Mezhakoff-Koriakin, trans., intro. by Rosh Ireland, A558

CHOU EN-LAI—Kai-Yu Hsu, A652

CRISIS IN EUROPE: 1580–1660—Trevor Aston, ed., intro. by Christopher Hill, A575

DARWIN, MARX, WAGNER: Critique of a Heritage—Jacques Barzun, revised second edition, A127

THE DEAD SEA SCRIPTURES—Theodore Gaster, trans., revised and enlarged, A378

DEMOCRACY VERSUS EMPIRE: The Jamaica Riots of 1865 and the Governor Eyre Controversy—Bernard Semmel, A703

DISCOVERIES AND OPINIONS OF GALILEO—Stillman Drake, trans., A94

THE DISCOVERY OF INDIA—Jawaharlal Nehru; Robert I. Crane, ed., abridged, A200

EAGLES IN COBWEBS: Nationalism and Communism in the Balkans—Paul Lendvai, A687

EARLY MAN IN THE NEW WORLD—Kenneth MacGowan and Joseph A. Hester, Jr., revised edition, N22

THE EASTERN ORTHODOX CHURCH—Ernest Benz, A332

1848: The Revolution of the Intellectuals—Lewis Namier, A385
9Ab

9Cb

THE RELIGIONS OF MANKIND—Hans-Joachim Schoeps; Richard and Clara Winston, trans., A621

REVOLUTIONARY RUSSIA—Richard Pipes, ed., A685

RETURN TO LAUGHTER—Elenore Smith Bowen, Foreword by David Riesman, N36

THE RUSSIAN REVOLUTION: The Overthrow of Tzarism and the Triumph of the Soviets—Leon Trotsky: F. W. Dupee, ed., selected from The History of the Russian Revolution, Max Eastman, trans., A170

SCIENCE AND CIVIC LIFE IN THE ITALIAN RENAISSANCE—Eugenio Garin; Peter Munz, trans., A647

THE SEVENTEENTH-CENTURY BACKGROUND—Basil Willey, A19

A SHORT HISTORY OF SCIENCE: Origins and Results of the Scientific Revolution—Herbert Butterfield and Others, A180

SOCIALIST THOUGHT—Albert Fried and Ronald Sanders, eds., A384

SOCIETY AND DEMOCRACY IN GERMANY—Ralf Dahrendorf, A684

SOCRATES—A. E. Taylor, A9

THE SOUTHEAST ASIAN WORLD—Keith Buchanan, A639

THE SPLENDID CENTURY: Life in the France of Louis XIV—W. H. Lewis, A122

STUDIES OF LATIN AMERICAN SOCIETIES—T. Lynn Smith, A702

THE THIRTY YEARS WAR—C. V. Wedgwood, A249

THREE SHORT NOVELS OF DOSTOEVSKY—Constance Garnett, trans.; Avrahm Yarmolinsky, ed. and revised, A193

THREE WAYS OF THOUGHT IN ANCIENT CHINA—Arthur Waley, A75

TODAY'S LATIN AMERICA—Robert J. Alexander, second edition, revised, A327

TO THE FINLAND STATION: A Study in the Writing and Acting of History—Edmund Wilson, A6

THE TOWN LABOURER: The New Civilization 1760–1832—J. L. and Barbara Hammond, Preface by Asa Briggs, A632

THE TRIUMPH OF THE MIDDLE CLASSES—Charles Morazé, A633

VIETNAM: THE ORIGINS OF REVOLUTION—John T. McAlister, Jr., A761

THE VILLAGE OF VIRIATINO: An Ethnographic Study of a Russian Village from Before the Revolution to the Present—Sula Benet, trans. and ed., A758

THE WANING OF THE MIDDLE AGES—J. Huizanga, A42

WHITE MAN, LISTEN!—Richard Wright, A414

WRITINGS OF THE YOUNG MARX ON PHILOSOPHY AND SOCIETY—Loyd D. Easton and Kurt H. Guddat, trans. and ed., A583

A YEAR IS EIGHT MONTHS: Czechoslovakia 1968—Journalist M, A750